THE EARTHLY PARADISE
AND THE RENAISSANCE EPIC

The Earthly Paradise and the Renaissance Epic

A. BARTLETT GIAMATTI

PRINCETON UNIVERSITY PRESS
PRINCETON, NEW JERSEY

First Princeton Paperback Printing, 1969

Publication of this book has been aided by
the Whitney Darrow Publication Reserve Fund
of Princeton University Press

Printed in the United States of America by
Princeton University Press, Princeton, New Jersey

To My Mother and Father

ACKNOWLEDGMENTS

In the bibliographies following each chapter I have tried to acknowledge my many debts to other scholars. Here I express my deep gratitude to my mentors René Wellek, Thomas Greene and Lowry Nelson, Jr., for their wisdom and guidance; to Lowry Nelson, Jr., who, as director of this study when it was a dissertation at Yale in 1964, was extraordinarily patient and helpful; and to those who read the manuscript at various stages and made corrections and valuable suggestions: Stewart Baker, Thomas Bergin, Alban Forcione, Claudio Guillén, Cyrus Hamlin, Geoffrey Hartman, Harry Levin, John Pope, Thomas Roche, Jr., Michael Simpson and Eugene Waith. They, of course, bear no responsibility for the lapses which remain.

Eve Hanle has been a resourceful editor. My father and Richard Young first taught me to love the literatures of Italy and England. Claudio Guillén has been a constant friend and benefactor. My wife, in spite of her disclaimers, is owed the greatest debt of all.

A. Bartlett Giamatti

Princeton, New Jersey
January, 1966.

CONTENTS

Contents

THE EARTHLY PARADISE
AND THE RENAISSANCE EPIC

LIST OF ABBREVIATIONS

AIPHOS	*Annuaire de l'Institut de Philologie et d'Histoire Orientales et Slaves*
ACABL	*Arquivo Camoniano da Academia Brasileira de Letras*
CJ	*Cambridge Journal*
Cl.J.	*The Classical Journal*
CL	*Comparative Literature*
CQ	*The Classical Quarterly*
CSEL	*Corpus Scriptorum Ecclesiasticorum Latinorum*
EA	*Études Anglaises*
EF	*Études Franciscaines*
EPP	*Encyclopedia of Poetry and Poetics, ed. Preminger, Warnke, Hardison*
ELH	*Journal of English Literary History*
GD	*Giornale Dantesco*
HLB	*Harvard Library Bulletin*
JEGP	*Journal of English and Germanic Philology*
JHI	*Journal of the History of Ideas*
MLN	*Modern Language Notes*
MLQ	*Modern Language Quarterly*
MP	*Modern Philology*
N&Q	*Notes & Queries*
PBA	*Proceedings of the British Academy*
PL	*Patrologia Latina, ed. J.-P. Migne*
PMLA	*Publications of the Modern Language Association*
PQ	*Philological Quarterly*
RES	*Review of English Studies*
RJ	*Romanistisches Jahrbuch*
RLA	*Revista de Letras da Faculdade de Filosofia Ciências e Letras de Assis*
SEL	*Studies in English Literature*
SP	*Studies in Philology*
ST	*Studi Tassiani*
UTSE	*University of Texas Studies in English*
UTQ	*University of Toronto Quarterly*
YCL	*Yale Classical Studies*

Introduction

THE DESIRE for a state of perfect repose and life eternal has always haunted mankind, and poets have forever been the spokesmen for the dream. For the Sumerians and Greeks, the place of this existence lay at the other side of the world. Hither was Utnapishtim taken to "the land of Dilmun, in the garden of the sun."[1] Hither was Menelaus translated to the Elysian Fields (*Odyssey*, IV). For the Greeks, the place had other names as well: the Fortunate Islands or Islands of the Blessed, and the Garden of the Hesperides. In terms of time, they referred to that period of human history when Cronos reigned and the world was young, the age of the Golden race, and said it still existed to the north in the land of the Scythians and Hyperboreans. And as poets sang of this happy place, ancient geographers and historians charted and described it—sight unseen, save with the mind's eye. Other classical writers portrayed a place of spiritual repose and bodily ease and never labeled it, except as a scene of shade, song, and love. Idylls, eclogues, odes, epithalamia, epics, satires, romances, and occasional verses all abound with descriptions of such an ideal life in an ideal landscape.

In the Judeo-Christian tradition, the garden in Eden, or the landscape of the Canticle, reminded men there had once existed perfect love and harmony in a beautiful place. Adam and Eve lived such an existence till their Fall; after them, legend said, the prophets Enoch and Elias, the Good Thief of Luke 23:43, and the souls of certain elect would inhabit the place until the day of Judgment.

[1] *The Epic of Gilgamesh*, tr. N. K. Sandars, Penguin Books (Baltimore, 1960), p. 94.

Throughout the Middle Ages, the Fathers and Doctors, saints, monks and martyrs argued endlessly about the location and nature of man's lost state of bliss. Where was it now? Who was there? What was it like and what did it mean? The answers were complex and various. But for richness, none of the arguments produced by medieval churchmen matched the legends and stories unceasingly repeated by medieval man. As Christianity had replaced the locus of the Golden Age with the place of the Fall, so the popular mind changed the name of the Fortunate Islands or land of the Hyperboreans to the Country of Prester John or land of Cocaigne. St. Brendan's voyage to an otherworld of delight was no less renowned than the vision of Tnugdal or the fabled travels of John Maundeville. Just as Pliny, Plutarch, and Strabo had said they knew where the place was located, so also the Middle Ages and Renaissance flourished with maps and treatises describing its position, now east, now west, now on an island, now behind or upon a mountain— but always remote, always inaccessible. Columbus thought he had found the blessed land across the wide waters, and he was certainly not the last man to search.

Obviously there are as many versions of the blessed place as people who have ever dreamed aloud about a life of peace and ease. No one can, nor should he, hope to examine all this material; such an effort would only produce acute boredom and profound frustration. However, some of this legend and literature does underlie the subject of my essay, an examination of the dominant traditions of the place of harmony and repose, particularly as they find their culmination in the gardens of the Renaissance epic. In the first chapter, I am concerned with the word "paradise" and its various meanings, with the classical concept of the Golden

Age and the beautiful sites associated with it, and with the *locus amoenus* or lovely place found throughout classical verse. This last line of inquiry leads me into a similar survey of medieval verse, and I look briefly at the gardens, bowers, and "paradises" found in troubadour lyrics, some romances, and the various kinds of long, "philosophical" allegories and narratives which the Middle Ages found so enjoyable and edifying. The chapter concludes with a consideration of the specifically Christian earthly paradise as it appears in both Latin and vernacular verse throughout the Middle Ages.

All this material is offered as background to the study of the Renaissance epics. I should say that I do not propose this first chapter as an exhaustive study of the beautiful or blessed landscape, nor do I wish to claim or imply "influence" for all of the poets studied on any or all of their successors. I realize that a series of examples drawn from European literature does not constitute "proof" of a specific tradition, and such incidents in chronological order do not necessarily stand as a "history" of a given literary type or convention. My aim has simply been to indicate the vast extent of man's preoccupation with the place of bliss and delight, and to single out, often arbitrarily, some of the forms in which his desires were expressed in literature.

After Dante, who is concerned with the "historical" Eden, there is a shift in attitude toward the place of bliss and repose, and a change in the kind of garden described. Now many, though not all, Renaissance poets begin to describe that particular kind of earthly paradise, the enchanted garden. The difference between the two can be expressed in various ways; essentially, one *is* what the other *seems to be*. A major difference is found in the character of the female inhabitant; in Dante's Eden, for instance, Matelda was descended from Eve. But in the enchanted gardens of Ariosto, Tasso and Spenser, Alcina, Armida and Acrasia are lineal descendants of Homer's Circe. They are sorceresses, and what is true of them is true of their gardens: the more attractive they appear, the more dangerous they are. Thus, the beautiful place, sought for centuries, becomes a trap to be avoided or, in the unique case of Camoens, allegorized. With Milton's garden, we return again to an image of the "true" Eden and the traditional Eve, though by now the situation is much more complex. Milton's earthly paradise, as he tells us repeatedly, ultimately includes all the gardens of the past; his Eve is ultimately related to all the previous women.

I contend that the ambiguous nature of the gardens represents the conflicting forces at the center of these Renaissance poems, the conflicts between classical heritage and Christian culture, between Love and Duty, woman and God, illusion and reality. And because I think that in a garden we are at the heart of a poem and the problems it poses, I have used the gardens as images of the epics, and as means for talking about the poems as wholes.

In the epics of the Renaissance, the garden was dealt with at length for perhaps the last time in Western literature. We would be mistaken, however, if we concluded that man ceased to search for the lost state of bliss and innocence. Indeed, the hope of finding it seemed to increase enormously with the discovery of the New World, and American literature itself is constantly read as a record of the quest for happiness and innocence in the great unspoiled garden. And though we no longer have any hope of finding Dilmun or

Elysium or Eden in the outer world, the search still goes on; for many, it seems to be the road of psychological therapy which may lead to the oasis of harmony across the awesome wastes of the mind. Man's need to find the place has in no way diminished; though, the more he turns in, the more his hope of arriving there has waned.

This bibliography, and those following each chapter, are not meant to be comprehensive, nor are they intended for the specialist. They are simply intended as introductions to each poet in general and to the topic of the garden in particular.

For the Sumerian paradise and related texts, see *Ancient Near Eastern Texts Relating to the Old Testament*, ed. J. B. Pritchard (Princeton, 1950), pp. 37ff. On the idea of paradise in general, a good place to begin is with M. Eliade, *The Myth of the Eternal Return*, tr. W. R. Trask (New York, 1954), and his article, "The Yearning for Paradise in Primitive Tradition," *Daedalus*, 88 (1959), pp. 255-267; also H. Petriconi, "Die Verlorenen Paradiese," *RJ*, 10 (1959), pp. 167-199. H. R. Patch, *The Otherworld according to Descriptions in Medieval Literature* (Cambridge, Mass., 1950) includes a great deal more than the title indicates and is an interesting work on many texts related to our investigations.

On the Christian concepts of paradise and related beliefs, one should consult the brilliant discussion by G. H. Williams, *Wilderness and Paradise in Christian Thought* (New York, 1962), as well as the more detailed discussions of J. Daniélou, S. J., "Terre et Paradis chez les Pères de l'Église," *Eranos-Jahrbuch*, 23 (1954), pp. 433-472, and I. Ayer de Vuippens, O. M. Cap., "Où plaça-t-on le paradis terrestre?" *ÉF*, 36 (1924), pp. 117-140, 371-398, 561-589; 37 (1925), pp. 21-44, 113-145; and A. Fiske, "Paradisus Homo Amicus," *Speculum*, 40 (1965), pp. 436-459. There is much to be learned on the religious backgrounds of the earthly paradise in Sister M. I. Corcoran's *Milton's Paradise with Reference to the Hexaemeral Background* (Washington, D.C., 1945), esp. Chapters ii-iii; there is a good summary of the earthly paradise beliefs of later medieval churchmen in C. S. Singleton's "Stars over Eden," *Seventy-Fifth Annual Report of the Dante Society* (Cambridge, Mass., 1957), pp. 1-18, reprinted in his *Journey to Beatrice, Dante Studies 2* (Cambridge, Mass., 1958), Chapter ix. An excellent book bearing on the Christian beliefs concerning paradise is G. Ladner's *The Idea of Reform* (Cambridge, Mass., 1959), esp. pp. 63-82. One should also consult the massively documented studies of A. Graf, *Miti, Leggende e Superstizioni del Medio Evo* (Torino, 1892), Vol. I, Chapters i-iv and Appendix I, and E. Coli, *Il Paradiso Terrestre Dantesco* (Firenze, 1897). Finally, the "paradise" approach seems particularly popular in the study of American literature and culture; for interesting material and insights, see H. N. Smith, *Virgin Land* (Cambridge, Mass., 1950), and more recently, among many others, C. L. Sanford, *The Quest for Paradise* (University of Illinois Press, 1961), H. M. Jones, *O Strange New World* (New York, 1964), and L. Marx, *The Machine in the Garden* (New York, 1964).

On the literature of voyages and visions, see G. Boas, *Essays in Primitivism and Related Ideas in the Middle Ages* (Baltimore, 1948), esp. pp. 154-174; also Patch, *Otherworld*, Chapter iv; for an account of maps and the geography of the earthly paradise, see L. Olschki, *Storia Lettèraria delle Scoperte Geografiche* (Firenze, 1937); Coli, *Paradiso Terrestre*, Chapter iv, and Graf, *Miti*, Chapters i-ii; and for a partial bibliography of accounts and treatises concerning the earthly paradise in the nineteenth century, see S. Baring-Gould, *Curious Myths of the Middle Ages* (London, 1869), pp. 264-265 and, in general, Graf, *Miti*, intro. xxii-xxiii, n. 5. For particular studies of legendary voyages, see K. Helleiner, "Prester John's Letter: A Medieval Utopia," *The Phoenix*, 13, 2 (Summer, 1959), pp. 47-57; A. H. Krappe, "The Subterranean Voyage," *PQ*, 20 (1941), pp. 119-130; and also M. V. Anastos, "Pletho, Strabo and Columbus," *AIPHOS*, 12 (1952), pp. 1-18.—Two recent and general treatments of the paradise myth are L.-I. Ringbom, *Paradisus Terrestris, Myt, Bild Och Verklighet* (Helsingforsiae, 1958) which traces paradise in Middle Eastern and Christian art and in the light of recent excavations in Persian Azerbaijan; and H. Baudet, *Paradise on Earth; Some Thoughts on European Images of Non-European Man*, tr. E. Wentholt (New Haven, 1965).

CHAPTER ONE

Gardens and Paradises

I · THE WORD

THE PLACE of perfect repose and inner harmony is always remembered as a garden. Or, as we shall refer to it in this essay, an earthly paradise, for the word "paradise" meant a garden surely as long as a garden designated some kind of perfect place. Thus, when "paradise" is finally used to refer to a specific site, such as the garden in Eden, a long tradition is only being continued, not broken.

The word "paradise" derives from the Old Persian word *pairidaēza*—formed on *pairi* (around) and *diz* (to mould, to form) which meant the royal park, enclosure, or orchard of the Persian king. Even at its origin, the word signified a specific natural place with a special (in this case, royal) character. The subsequent history of the word has two branches: it becomes Hebrew *pardēs*, and it is adapted by the Greek and, through Latin, French, and Middle English, becomes our word "paradise."

The Hebrew word, *pardēs*, meant a park or garden and was used only three times in the Old Testament.[1] There it meant specific, verdant enclosures, but had no connection with what we commonly call the earthly paradise or garden in Eden of Genesis 2:8. That specific identification was to come in later commentaries, apocalyptic and rabbinical, after *pardēs* had been influenced by its Greek cognate *para-*

---

[1] "I made me *gardens* and orchards" (Eccles. 2:5); "A *garden* enclosed is my sister, my spouse" (Cant. 4:12) "And a letter unto Asaph, the keeper of the king's *forest*" (Neh. 2:8).

deisos. In the apocalyptic tradition of the Jews, *pardēs* signified the garden in Eden or the opposite of Gehenna, and was the home of the blessed dead after their Resurrection (a concept introduced around 200 B.C.). In the rabbinical tradition, *pardēs* designated the blessed part of Sheol where the good souls awaited the Resurrection. In all cases, whether it meant the opposite of Gehenna or a blessed part of Sheol, the eternal home of the blessed dead or a temporary resting place, *pardēs* was used with specific reference to the garden in Eden. However, before the use of *paradeisos* colored subsequent usages of *pardēs*, the Hebrew word referred only to those gardens, forests, or parks in the Old Testament, and maintained the original meaning of *pairidaēza.*

The earliest link between the simple word and the specific place, between garden and the garden in Eden, paradise and the earthly paradise, occurs through the Greek adaptation of *pairidaēza* into *paradeisos*. The word first occurs in Xenophon and means a royal park;[2] but when it is used in a Biblical context, *paradeisos* exhibits the two other meanings it conferred on the interpretation of *pardēs* in later Jewish literature: the garden in Eden and Heaven or the Abode of the Blessed Dead.

It is in the Septuagint translation of the *Pentateuch*, completed at Alexandria by the middle of the third century B.C., that *paradeisos* is consistently used by the LXX to refer to the garden in Genesis. And, in the complete Septuagint

[2] There Cyrus had a palace and a large *park* full of wild animals . . . (*Anabasis*, I, ii, 7). See also *Anabasis*, II, iv, 14 and *Cyropaedia*, I, ii, 7. Texts in Loeb Library *Cyropaedia*, tr. W. Miller (London-New York, 1925), vol. I and *Hellenica, Books VI and VII, Anabasis, Books I-IV*, tr. C. I. Brownson (New York-London, 1932).

translation of the Old Testament, *paradeisos* is also used to render the three instances of *pardēs* noticed above—Nehemiah 2:8, Ecclesiastes 2:5, Canticle 4:12. Thus, through the Greek, all gardens designated as unique by *pardēs* are semantically linked to the garden in Eden; all "paradises" are somehow versions of the "earthly paradise."[3]

Gardens or orchards and the garden in Eden are not, however, the only concepts transmitted by *paradeisos*. Two New Testament authors also use the Greek word and give it a third meaning. We find it in Luke and in Paul where the references to *paradeisos* are understood to mean Heaven, the celestial paradise.[4] Thus, *paradeisos*, through Xenophon, New Testament writers, and the LXX, has three distinct meanings: a park or royal garden, the celestial paradise or Heaven, and—most important of all—the earthly paradise or garden in Eden. The intermingling in *paradeisos* of general garden-motifs with the particular spiritual attributes of the garden in Eden not only reflected ancient (Sumerian, Babylonian, and Greek) convictions about the garden as the place of bodily ease and inward harmony; it also provided a node of spiritual and aesthetic associations for generations of Christian writers who wanted to refer to the state of body and soul which once we possessed and then we lost.[5]

[3] For instance, John the Divine, writing probably under the reign of Domitian (A.D. 81-96) uses *paradeisos* to refer back to the garden in Eden: "To him that overcometh, to him will I give to eat of the tree of Life, which is in the Paradise of God" (Rev. 2:7).

[4] "Today thou shalt be with me in Paradise" (Luke 23:43); ". . . he was caught up into paradise, and heard unspeakable words . . ." (II Ep. Cor. 12:4).

[5] The meaning of *paradeisos* as a garden or park was perpetuated in the *paradeisoi*, set pieces of lush, natural description. These became

From the Greek the word was borrowed by Latin as *paradisus*. Here again we distinguish the three meanings observed in the Greek. *Paradisus* is present by implication when Aulus Gellius in his *Noctes Atticae* cites in Greek the word *paradeisos* and says it means what Varro called a *leporaria* and men now designate as a *vivaria*, that is, a natural enclosure for wild animals.[6] Tertullian, and the Vulgate translation of Luke 23:43, both use *paradisus* to refer to the celestial paradise,[7] and finally, St. Jerome uses the word in two letters to designate the garden in Eden.[8]

As we know, the discussion concerning the nature, location, and accessibility of the earthly paradise raged among men in the Christian church from its earliest times down to the fifteenth century. In the main, there were two schools of thought. Some, notably Ambrose and John Chrysostom, followed the allegorizing and spiritualist tendencies of Clement and Origen and considered the earthly paradise a

---

standard motifs in the Greek Romances, and in Longus' *Daphne and Chloe*, 4, 2 and Achilles Tatius' *Leucippe and Clitophon*, 1, 15 there are elaborate *paradeisoi*. Both works were well known in the Renaissance.

Another basic source for the radical meaning of *paradeisos* was the *Geoponica*, a Greek compilation of rustic scenes and agricultural lore from ancient authors made in the tenth century by Cassianus Bassus at the request of Constantine VII, Emperor of the East. It was in twenty books, and 3, 13; 10, 1; and 11, 23 were the set pieces or *paradeisoi*. (Book 3 is on agricultural duties suitable to each month; Books 10 and 11 on horticulture.) A Latin translation by Janus Cornarius appeared at Venice in 1538, and a Greek text was edited at Basil by Brassicanus in 1539.

[6] *Noctes Atticae*, II, xx, 4. Text in Loeb Library edition of J. C. Rolfe (New York-London, 1927), vol. I. Much later Saint Augustine uses *paradisus* to mean "garden" in *Sermone 343, n. 1, De Susanna*; see *PL*, XXXIX, 1,505.

[7] *Apologeticum*, XLVII. Text in *PL*, I, 520A; "Hodie mecum eris in Paradiso."

[8] Letters 52, para. 5, and 69, para. 6. Text in *PL*, XXII, 532 and 659.

symbol of the celestial home of the souls, the Kingdom of Heaven. Others in this tradition regarded the earthly paradise as simply an image of the Heavenly City, while still others located it in one, or a series, of the planetary spheres. The second school, comprising with enormous variations many of the Western church writers, thought of the earthly paradise as a truly "terrestrial" place, "in some normally inaccessible part of the earth, which might become the goal of man's search and, in a literal as well as metaphorical way, the object of his dreams."[9] However, before examining the Christian tradition of the earthly paradise, and its delightful and dangerous counterparts in the Renaissance epic, we must pause and go back to the beginnings of Western literature.

Here, previous and parallel to what Ladner has called the " 'geographical' and literal" Christian tradition of the garden, are the pagan traditions "of the Elysium, the Golden Age, the Millennium."[10] These pagan concepts, and the classical literature about gardens and landscapes as the proper site for love, harmony, and retirement, are immensely important for our considerations, because in these images from classical literature, medieval and Renaissance writers found whatever they wanted—"philosophic" analogues, models, or motifs—for their own gardens. Indeed, it would not be unfair to say that Christian poets plundered Elysium to decorate the earthly paradise.

II · THE GOLDEN AGE

The Golden Age has been described as "an imaginary existence different from the hardships of real life—an exist-

---

[9] G. Ladner, *The Idea of Reform* (Cambridge, Mass., 1959), p. 66.
[10] *Ibid.*

ence blessed with Nature's bounty, untroubled by strife or
want." It is a state of body and soul "always placed somewhere or sometime outside normal human experience,
whether 'off the map' in some remote quarter of the world,
or in Elysium after death, or in the dim future or distant
past."[11] In short, the term refers both to a (pseudo-) historical place and a way of life, and is man's earliest image
of "paradise lost."

It has been conjectured that the myth of the Golden Age
goes back to the description of the Elysian Fields which are
promised Menelaus in the fourth book of the *Odyssey*.[12]

> . . . the gods intend you for Elysion
> with golden Rhadamanthos at the world's end,
> where all existence is a dream of ease.
> Snowfall is never known there, nor long
> frost of winter, nor torrential rain,
> but only mild and lulling airs from Ocean
> bearing refreshment for the souls of men—
> the West Wind always blowing.   (561-568)[13]

Here where "all existence is a dream of ease," the characteristics of the Golden Age life are summed up most succinctly. And motifs which were to become standard in all
later descriptions of blessed places are introduced: no inclement weather but only Zephyr blowing, bringing com-

[11] H. C. Baldry, "Who Invented the Golden Age," *CQ*, New Series 2
(1951-1952), p. 81.

[12] A. O. Lovejoy and G. Boas, *Contributions to the History of Primitivism, Primitivism and Related Ideas in Antiquity* (Baltimore, 1935),
p. 291. One should see also *Odyssey*, VI, 41-69, for another influential
passage, the top of Olympus.

[13] *The Odyssey*, tr. R. Fitzgerald (Garden City, 1961), p. 81. All translations from the *Odyssey* are from this version.

fort for body and soul. Of course, Homer is referring to Elysium, that place at the ends of the earth beyond Ocean; there is no specific mention of the Golden Age, and, strictly speaking, we must distinguish between Elysium or any benign place and the Golden Age. But in fact the Golden Age, as specific place and as way of life, and all the blessed sites of antiquity, share the same characteristics. Indeed, later the Golden Age will be overtly identified with various blessed regions of the ancient world.[14]

The first mention of the Golden Age per se occurs, as is well known, in Hesiod's *Works and Days*. Hesiod delineates the five ages of man—golden, silver, bronze, age of Heroes, and present iron age, and associates the Golden Age with the reign of Cronos, father of Zeus. It is not an age of "gold" in the sense of great riches, but is "golden" because life was best at the beginning, simple, noble, comfortable.

> First of all the deathless gods who dwell on
> Olympus made a golden race of mortal men who
> lived in the time of Cronos when he was reigning
> in heaven. And they lived like gods without
> sorrow of heart, remote and free from toil and
> grief: miserable age rested not on them; but
> with legs and arms never failing they made merry
> with feasting beyond the reach of all evils.
> When they died, it was as though they were
> overcome with sleep, and they had all good things;
> for the fruitful earth unforced bore them

[14] Also, in encomiastic verse, some Latin writers will refer to an emperor's reign as a Golden Age (see n. 24 below), and Christian writers will allude to various phases of Christianity as the Golden Age.

fruit abundantly and without stint. They dwelt
in ease and peace upon their lands with many
good things, rich in flocks and loved by the
blessed gods.   (109-120)[15]

This is the first expression of the Golden Age as a state
of existence in the dim past. In the pleasures of body
(plenty of food and flocks, fine weather) and soul (no
grief or misery; being beloved of the gods), we note the
influence of Homer's account of Elysium. But this account
in Hesiod is not attached to any specific place; it is simply
a desirable way of life. It is only later in the poem that
Hesiod associates the Golden Age with a particular place.

But to the others father Zeus the son of Cronos
gave a living and an abode apart from men,
and made them dwell at the ends of the earth.
And they lived untouched by sorrow in the
islands of the blessed along the shore of
deep swirling Ocean, happy heroes for whom
the grain-giving earth bears honey-sweet
fruit flourishing thrice a year, far from
the deathless gods, and Cronos rules over them.

(167-169)[16]

---

[15] Text in Loeb Library *Hesiod, The Homeric Hymns and Homerica,*
tr. H. G. Evelyn-White (Cambridge, Mass.-London, 1936). All subsequent
references to Hesiod, or the Homeric Hymns, are to this edition by line
number. For anticipations of the description cited above, see ll. 42-46
and 90-92. I have used the term "Golden Age" throughout, though the
Greeks always referred to the "golden race."

[16] There has been some dispute surrounding the crucial line 169:
"far from the deathless gods, and Cronos rules over them." In a scholium,
Proclus (mid-first century A.D.) preserves the line by saying that others
reject it, and the subsequent four, because the lines do not make sense

Here Hesiod applies it to those inhabitants of the fourth age of men, the Heroes. We sense that this is a Golden Age existence because the description of the climate, earth, and way of life coincides with the Golden Age description at the beginning of time, and because the Golden Age is always associated with Cronos. The Golden Age exists wherever Cronos rules, and here Hesiod says Cronos rules over the Heroes. But the poet tells us something even more important: these Heroes live under Cronos in a specific place, the "islands of the blessed." We are further aware that this Golden Age place is in exactly the same location as Homer's Elysium—at the world's end. The seeds for the identification of the Golden Age existence with Elysium, or the Elysian Fields, so important for later Christian earthly paradises, are here planted.

So far, the Golden Age is not necessarily fixed to a specific time of the world, nor known by one particular place-name. It is a state of being whose happiness is symbolized by munificent and harmonious Nature under the reign of Cronos.[17] Hesiod hints at a third characteristic even later in

(for scholium, see A. Petrusi, *Scholia Veteri in Hesiodi Carmina* [Milano, 1955], pp. 64-65); thereafter, the best manuscripts preserve only the scholium, while inferior manuscripts adapt the line from the scholium. For discussions, which follow Rzach's definitive Teubner edition of *Hesiod* (Leipzig, 1902; ed. minor, 1913) in accepting the line, see H. M. Hayes, *Notes on the Works and Days of Hesiod* (Chicago, 1918) and H. G. Evelyn-White in *CQ*, 7 (1913), pp. 219-220. Thus I cite ll. 167-169, i.e. ll. 167, 168, 170, 171, 172, 173, 169, as they appear in the Loeb Library edition, tr. Evelyn-White, pp. 14-15.

[17] Hayes cites the *Odyssey*, IV, 561-569 and Hesiod, *Works and Days*, 167-173, and says, "The manner of life in both cases is that of the golden age and the location is the same, only in Homer it is the Elysian Plain, in Hesiod it is the Islands of the Blest" (*Notes*, p. 218). Hesiod also touches upon another place which later became the site of a Golden Age

his poem, a notion of morality (*Works,* 225-237). In the advice to his brother Perses, Hesiod tells of what accrues to those men "who do true justice." Their land is rich, their families and flocks are happy, and they are not visited by war, famine or disaster. Here a Golden Age type of existence is implied as a reward for virtue. No longer are we dealing with those virtuous men at the creation of the world, nor even the legendary Heroes of the previous age; now a kind of Golden Age is open to men who deserve it by their just and virtuous lives. This note of morality, sounded early in the literature of the Golden Age, reverberated throughout poetic treatments of the classical myth and rendered Golden Age places "safe" for Christian adaptation.

Though the Homeric Hymns occasionally mention people living what resembles a Golden Age existence,[18] Pindar has two poems which bear directly on the Golden Age and life in a blessed spot: *Pythian X* and *Olympian II. Pythian X,* composed about 498 B.C. when the poet was twenty years old, tells of the Hyperboreans, a people supposed to live far to the North. They were sacred to Apollo and their land was a blessed place.

> Never the Muse is absent

---

existence—the Hesperides. He tells of their creation "beyond glorious Ocean" in *Theogony,* 215-216, thus locating them in the same place as Homer's Elysium and his own Islands of the Blessed.

[18] III, *To Delian Apollo,* 145-161; XXX, *To Earth the Mother of All,* 5-16. The vigor of the Ionians, in III, and the fecund landscape, in XXX, recall the Hyperboreans and some of the bliss described by Hesiod. But no mention is made of the Golden Age or of Cronos, and a detail like the wealth of the happy ones in XXX, 11-12, is completely at variance with the traditional Golden Age state.

from their ways; lyres clash, and the flutes cry,
and everywhere maiden choruses whirling.
They bind their hair in golden laurel and take
their holiday.
Neither disease or bitter old age is mixed
in their sacred blood; far from labor and battle

.   .   .   .

they live. They escape scandal
and litigation.[19]

The Golden Age attributes of youth, harmony, and freedom from strife are here associated with the Hyperboreans. Farnell notes this Hyperborean myth as indicative of Pindar's interest in " 'Paradise-poetry', which he here attempts for the first time in a manner which foreshadows his triumph in the second Olympian."[20]

In *Olympian II*, written for Theron of Akragas in 476, Pindar identifies the blessed life after death with the Islands of the Blest, with Cronos who rules over the islands (his rule implying a Golden Age existence), and with morality. Only the just and good, who have passed through judgment and three earthly reincarnations without leaving the path of virtue, are rewarded with this eternal bliss. There they

have life without labor, disquieting not the earth
in strength of hand,
never the sea's water

[19] *The Odes of Pindar*, tr. R. Lattimore (Chicago, 1947), p. 88. Subsequent references to Pindar are to this translation by page number.

[20] L. R. Farnell, *The Works of Pindar, Translated with Literary and Critical Commentary* (London, 1930), I, 143. For comments on paradise in *Olympian II*, see Farnell, I, 15.

for emptiness of living. Beside the high gods
who had joy in keeping faith lead a life
without fears. (p. 7)

And where is this life? It is by

God's way to the tower of Kronos; there
winds sweep from the Ocean
across the Islands of the Blessed. (p. 7)

As Hesiod had placed the blissful life on the Islands of the
Blessed under Cronos, so Pindar. And as Homer (and
Hesiod) had placed their ideal spots at the same "end of
the earth" with Rhadamanthos, so Pindar. For the just
will find there

Rhadamanthys,
whom the husband of Rhea, high throned above all,
our great father, keeps in the chair of state
beside him. (p. 7)

Using elements from Homer and Hesiod, Pindar has
created his vision of the blessed life. By now, both Homer's
Elysium and Hesiod's Islands of the Blessed where Cronos
rules have become models for the site of the Golden Age
life. Pindar has firmly introduced the idea of this existence
as a reward for virtue—a concept first implied by Hesiod—
and that motif becomes as conventional as the phrases about
climate and social harmony. There will be variations on
the theme of the Golden Age, but its identification with
a remote part of the earth, a time not present, bountiful
nature, happy souls and the virtuous life under Cronos, are
now secure.[21]

[21] Plato tells of the harmony of life, fecundity of nature, and nobility

The Romans, however, do change certain things. Where the Greeks consistently referred to this existence as that of a "golden race" under Cronos, it is the Romans who actually introduce the term "Golden Age" and of course refer to the reign of Saturn. In the hands of Latin poets, the whole idea of the Golden Age became so hackneyed and commonplace that even before the close of the first century A.D. the theme was regarded as stale.[22]

Among the Roman poets, Virgil is foremost in his treatment of the Golden Age existence. The most famous instance is his celebrated Fourth Eclogue, probably written for Pollio's son, which offers a variant to the Greek Golden Age view by predicting the Golden Age in the near future.

> ✻ magnus ab integro saeclorum nascitur ordo.
> iam redit et Virgo, redeunt Saturnia regna;
> iam nova progenies caelo demittitur alto.
> tu modo nascenti puero, quo ferrea primum
> desinet ac toto surget gens aurea mundo,
> casta fave Lucina: tuus iam regnat Apollo.   (5-10)[23]

✻ the great line of the centuries begins anew. Now the Virgin returns, the reign of Saturn returns; now a new generation descends from heaven on high. Only do thou, pure Lucina, smile on the birth of the child, under whom the iron brood shall first cease, and a golden race spring up throughout the world! Thine own Apollo now is king!

---

of man under Cronos, though with no particular geographical designation, in *Politics*, 271d-272b; *Laws*, 712e-714b; and *Cratylus*, 397e. See also Theocritus, *Idyll*, XII, 15-16.

[22] In the pseudo-Virgilian *Aetna*, 9-16, the Golden Age is considered, then rejected, as a suitable topic for poetry. There were also those poets who, implicitly or explicitly, condemned the whole idea of an earlier Golden Age; see Aeschylus, *Prometheus Bound*, 440-468, where Prometheus tells of the early ignorance and misery of man; Lucretius, *De Rerum Natura*, V, 975ff., on the savagery of man at the creation, which was

Having forecast the return of the golden race, Virgil goes on to catalogue (18-46) the attributes of that existence. Earth will pour forth her bounty, animals will live in harmony with one another, and man (37ff.) will not feel the strain of toil. This is a thrilling prophecy, and the poem rolls to a climax at line 59 and then subsides, ending quietly with an address to the boy whose birth has signaled the commencement of a new cycle for mankind. Virgil has adapted the traditional Golden Age vision for prophetic purposes, and it is small wonder that Christians regarded this Eclogue as a forecast of Christ. Henceforth the Golden Age will be utilized for a time in the future as well as an image of the past.[24]

---

adopted by Horace, *Satires*, I, iii, 99-110. Juvenal, XIII, 30ff., is ambiguous in his attitude toward man's earliest existence; Statius, *Silvae*, I, vi, 39-42, is jovially certain things are better now than before; and Claudian, *In Rufinum*, I, 50ff., has an interesting variation whereby Alecto promises the other denizens of Hell a Golden Age when they overthrow Order.

[23] The Latin text and English translation throughout are from the Loeb Library *Virgil*, tr. H. R. Fairclough, rev. ed., 2 vols. (Cambridge, Mass.-London, 1935).

[24] For other statements on the Golden Age in Virgil, see *Georgic*, I, 125-128, for the happy earth under Saturn; *Georgic*, II, 140-176, where Italy is seen as the land of peace and plenty surpassing all others; II, 324-345, where springtime as the best season for planting leads to a splendid vision of the Earth's renewal, which is then associated with the Golden Age at 336-338; and 513-540, where the country life of the Old Italians (Sabines and Etruscans) before Jupiter was a golden time.

Virgil's *Eclogue* IV, with its Golden Age prophecy, was much imitated. In Calpurnius Siculus's *Eclogue* I, 41-88, Nero is said to initiate the Golden Age; also under Nero were written those two eclogues known by the name of their tenth century manuscripts, *Einsiedeln*. The first, line 23, imitates Virgil's *Eclogue* IV, 6, and again because Nero is Emperor, the Golden Age has arrived. Texts in Loeb Library *Minor Latin Poets*, tr. J. W. Duff and A. M. Duff (Cambridge, Mass.-London, 1934). Ausonius imitates *Eclogue* IV in the last poem in his series on the pro-

Virgil specifically treats the Golden Age twice in the *Aeneid*. In Book VI, Anchises in Elysium forecasts the future of Rome to Aeneas:

> ⁎ Hic vir, hic est, tibi quem promitti saepius audis,
> Augustus Caesar, Divi genus, aurea condet
> saecula qui rursus Latio regnata per arva
> Saturno quondam, super et Garamantas et Indos
> proferet imperium.   (791-795)

And then, as if to provide precedent for this Golden Age Evander, in Book VIII (314-329), describes to Aeneas how Saturn fled from Jove and set up the first Golden Age in Latium. Thus for patriotic and poetic purposes, Italy is identified as the land of both a previous and a future Golden Age. However, Virgil may have another motive for introducing the concept of the Golden Age in Book VI. We remember that Hesiod and Pindar identified the Golden Age with the Islands of the Blessed. Now, Virgil does not deal with these islands, but he does treat at length a place which after him was identified with the islands and which exhibits standard Golden Age characteristics. This is, of course, Elysium.

In Book VI, Elysium is inhabited by those who are blessed forever (like Anchises) and those (most of the rest) who

⁎ This, this is he, whom thou so oft hearest promised to thee, Augustus Caesar, son of a god, whom shall again set up the Golden Age in Latium amid the fields where Saturn once reigned, and shall spread his empire past Garamant and Indian. . . .

---

fessors of Bordeaux (XXVI), where he speaks of the return of the Golden Age; and in *Eclogue* V, 15, Ausonius alludes to the end and renewal of all the cycles of time, again with Virgil in mind. Text in Loeb Library *Ausonius*, tr. H. G. Evelyn-White (New York-London, 1919), I.

drink at Lethe and assume new bodies (VI, 739ff.). In Book
V, Anchises has appeared to Aeneas and told his son that
he dwells not in the sad shades of Tartarus,

> ✕ sed amoena piorum
> concilia Elysiumque colo. (734-735)[25]

Elysium is anticipated as a place of blessed spirits in Book
V and is the context in which the Golden Age prophecy
is made in Book VI. To my mind, these factors establish
an imaginative link between Virgil's Elysium in the *Aeneid*
and previous visions of the Islands of the Blessed, home of
the Golden Age. Furthermore, in Book VI, the opening view
of Elysium is that of a Golden Age scene, recalling the life
of the Hyperboreans in Pindar's *Pythian X. Aeneid*, VI
(637-644) describes how the inhabitants vie in sports, dance,
and song. Behind the activities in Elysium, scholars have
noted specific debts to Pindar and Lucretius, and behind the
landscape and its moral significance we sense the presence
of all the ancient places connected with a blessed and carefree
life in pleasant surroundings.[26]

We must not thrust the Elysium passages in the *Aeneid*
forward as positive instances of the Golden Age; Virgil is

✕ but I dwell in Elysium amid the sweet assemblies of the blest.

[25] Of line 735, Servius says that poets thought Elysium was in Hell, but
full of happiness; philosophers thought "Elysium est insulae fortunatae,"
and theologians put Elysium in the circle of the moon where the air is
purer. See *Commentarii in Virgilium Serviani*, ed. H. A. Lion (Göttingen,
1826), I, 343.

[26] For Pindar, see Hayes, *Notes*, p. 219, where Pindar's fragment 129 is
described; see also the commentary of J. Connington (*The Works of Virgil*

saving Italy as his avowed "golden" site, and Elysium is not specifically identified as the home of the Golden Age. But I think it is well to bear in mind the imaginative implications, hallowed by the fact that Homer's Elysium underlay Hesiod's concept of the Golden Age and by the identification of the Golden Age with the Islands of the Blessed, islands later identified with the Elysium of *Aeneid*, VI. The knot of associations, in poetry and the popular imagination, was tightening; all blessed places were becoming some kind of Golden Age site, all Golden Age sites were becoming blessed places. We might also conjecture that it was precisely because of the blessed quality of Elysium, buttressed by suggestions of the Golden Age, that Virgil's opening lines on Elysium became such a great source for later Christian Latin accounts of the earthly paradise.

The Golden Age is treated by two other Roman poets

[London, 1863], II, 499), to *Aeneid*, VI, 638-641, where Connington indicates how Homer's Elysium, through Hesiod and Pindar, was developed into the Islands of the Blessed, for which "Fortunatae insulae" is the Latin equivalent. Virgil may have been attempting to allude to the type of existence associated with "fortunatae insulae" with his "Fortunatorum nemorum"; in the first word we sense the presence of the ancient isles; in the second, "nemora"—groves—there is an allusion to the classical tradition of blessed mountain sites which was developed in later Latin and Christian-Latin literature. *Sedesque beatas* also echoes an earlier mountain top, for it resembles Lucretius' *sedesque quietae* (*De Rerum Natura*, III, 18) which appears in a passage closely adapting the Homeric description of the top of Olympus (*Odyssey*, VI, 44ff.).

Servius also says of line 638—"Alludit autem ad insulas fortunatas"— and of line 640—"Nam et supra (V, 735) diximus, campii Elysii aut apud inferos sunt, aut in insulis fortunatis, aut in Lunari circulo." *Commentarii*, ed. Lion, p. 392.

who did much to influence later literature and who, each in his own fashion, widened the scope of the Golden Age conception. They were Horace and Ovid.

Horace's Sixteenth Epode was written about the same time as Virgil's Fourth Eclogue (*ca*. 40 B.C.) and the similarities between them have often been noticed. The last forty lines of Horace's poem present a vision of refuge and peace from the carnage of the Civil War. The description of life beyond the "Etruscan shore" is long and includes what are now standard ingredients in the recipe for a happy life: beautiful nature, fecund earth, ideal weather, and harmony among all living creatures. What is noteworthy is that Horace also does what Hesiod and Pindar did—he identifies the Islands of the Blessed with the Golden Age. It is to these islands that he advises flight.

> ⁎ arva, beata
> petamus arva divites et insulas. (41-42)²⁷

And after the description of life on the islands, Horace ends with

> ⁎ Juppiter illa piae secrevit litora genti,
> ut inquinavit aere tempus aureum;
> aere, dehinc ferro duravit saecula, quorum
> piis secunda vate me datur fuga. (63-66)

⁎ Let us seek the Fields, the Happy Fields, and the Islands of the Blest.

⁎ Jupiter set apart these shores for a righteous folk, ever since with bronze he dimmed the lustre of the Golden Age. With bronze and then with iron did he harden the ages, from which a happy escape is offered to the righteous, if my prophecy be heeded.

²⁷ All Latin texts and English translations from the Loeb Library *Horace, The Odes and Epodes*, tr. C. E. Bennett (Cambridge, Mass.-London, 1946).

As Baldry points out, these lines obviously echo Hesiod, though Baldry's statement that Horace's linking of the Islands of the Blessed and the Golden Age "may be his own idea" is questionable in the light of similar associations already noted.[28] Horace has clearly indicated a locus for that second Golden Age, the one for those worthy people who live under Jupiter while the ages of man are running their course.[29]

Though he was by no means the last to write of the Golden Age in Latin, Ovid was the last ancient poet to make a statement which had any great influence. Indeed, he is probably second only to Hesiod in influence on this particular point. Ovid's most famous treatment of the Golden Age comes in the *Metamorphoses*, I, 89-112. He says it was a time when there were no wars, no laws; when

[28] Baldry, "Who Invented the Golden Age," *CQ*, p. 88.

[29] For mention of the "first" or original Golden Age, see *Odes*, IV, ii, 39-40, where Caesar is praised; for the Islands of the Blessed, see *Odes*, IV, viii, 27.

After Horace's strong affirmation of the Golden Age existing on the Islands of the Blessed, Strabo, in his *Geography*, I, i, 4-5, says that the Elysian Fields of Homer are really the Fortunate Islands, an idea we noted in Hesiod; about one hundred years later, Plutarch, in his *Life of Sertorius*, VIII-IX, 571-572 makes the same identification between Elysium and the islands, without reference to Homer, and in *De Facie in Orbe Lunae*, XXVI, 26, a-c, e, says Cronos lives on islands near Ogygia, and mentions the characteristic Golden Age climate and natural fecundity. Finally, Pliny, in his *Natural History*, VI [202-205], 32 [37], says the site of the good life is the Fortunate Islands, though all is far from perfect. Pliny, whose life spanned the middle of the first century A.D., represents the gradual decline in faith concerning the pristine grandeur and nobility of the Golden Age. By identifying, in one way or another, the Golden Age life with Elysium, these ancient men of science corroborate what we sensed in Virgil's Elysium. For texts of Strabo, Plutarch, and Pliny, see Lovejoy and Boas, *Primitivism in Antiquity*, pp. 294-299.

men lived in harmony with each other and the land. The earth produced goods spontaneously, springtime was eternal, Zephyr fanned the flowers. Streams of milk and nectar flowed, and honey came from the oak. This is a typical picture of that self-contained age before men sailed the sea or built walls around cities. It was then that Saturn ruled the fresh world (l. 113) and Astraea, the Virgin emblematic of universal justice, lived with man. Though he does not locate the Golden Age in any particular place, Ovid does give us the essence of the Golden Age as it evolved—social harmony, natural fecundity, political peace, economic security, personal happiness; a time noble and simple, rustic and blissful.[30]

Christian writers, as they would in so many things, simply appropriated the Golden Age to their own purposes. An interesting example is provided by the African Lactantius (*ca.* 260-330) who was one of the most elegant and educated, if not profound, of the early Latin Fathers. In his monumental *Divinae Institutiones*, V, v, he sets out to prove that God was truly, if unknowingly, worshipped in the reign of Saturn and that the Golden Age of fecund nature and peaceful society was really a time of true spiritual communion. Lactantius pieces together a wonderful version of the Golden Age by drawing on various pagan sources. The Greek Aratus' *Phaenomena*, a work on astronomical bodies which contains a well-known statement on the Golden Age, is cited by way of the Latin translations of Germanicus Caesar and Cicero in his *De Natura Deorum*, as are Virgil's *Georgic*, I and *Aeneid*, VIII and Ovid's *Metamorphoses*, I. Sometimes Lactantius admonishes us to understand the pagan

[30] See also *Metamorphoses*, III, 157-160; XV, 96-98 and 260-261; also *Ars Armatoria*, II, 277-278.

poets allegorically, other times he tells us they speak the literal truth. After describing the age under Saturn, he turns like any classical poet to the depravity of the world under Jupiter.

In its patchwork of citations and allusions, *Divinae Institutiones*, V, v, demonstrates how pagan learning and literature were means to Christian ends and how Christian doctrine could slowly emerge from the very world the early Fathers were so intent on renouncing. More than once in Lactantius the Golden Age is recalled in its pagan dress as a witness for Christianity.[31]

The ancient idea of the Golden Age is also used by secular Christian writers like Prudentius (348-405). Where Lactantius had looked back to the Golden Age as a time when God was truly adored, Prudentius, in the Second Book of *Contra Symmachum*, has the figure of Rome look forward to the reign of Christ as a new Golden Age. Rome says her gray hair will turn to gold as the age of Christ's reign and triumph commences. And as the description of the age under its new Emperor continues, the poet weaves in the standard Golden Age motifs of social harmony and plentiful crops.[32] The pagans had seen the Golden Age now in the past, now in the future; Christian writers also saw Christian harmony and peace in whatever period of the world best served their purposes. Christian writers closely resemble their pagan predecessors in using the Golden Age as a happy time and in shifting it about in human history. Only

[31] See also Book V, Chapter vi, and the *Epitome Divinarum Institutionum*, Chapter xxv. Text in S. Brandt's edition in *Opera Omnia*, CSEL, Vol. XIX.

[32] For text, see Loeb Library *Prudentius*, tr. H. J. Thomson (Cambridge, Mass.-London, 1949), II, 58ff.

now, the myth is used to denigrate the very classical culture whence it sprang.

An interesting variant on the Christian use of these classical ideas presents itself in Isidore of Seville (*ca.* 560-636). In his *Etymologiae*, XIV, vi, 8, he speaks of the "Fortunatae insulae." They are situated to the west in the stream of Ocean and are marked by fruit, precious trees, slopes covered with vines, crops, and garden vegetables. Because of the "fecundity of the soil," says Isidore, gentile and pagan poets have confused these islands with Paradise. The fact that Isidore is at pains to point out that this is *not* the case argues for an amalgamation of the traditional Fortunate Islands–Golden Age concept with the Christian idea of the garden in Eden or earthly paradise. Isidore's desire to maintain the proper distinction is wholly justified from the perspective of the Church, and offers a clue to what had been happening on a secular level: early Christian descriptions of the earthly paradise owed as much to ancient literature as to Christian Biblical literature, and finally the two strands became inseparable.[33]

The ancient image of an island, east or west, or of an Elysium; with perfect climate, perpetual springtime, a sweet west wind, fecund earth, shade and water; where under Cronos there was communal and personal harmony, bliss and ease—this image declined at times but never died. As Isidore feared, it had indeed infiltrated the Christian consciousness and helped to form the Christian image of the earthly paradise. Because in fundamental terms of climate, food, and shelter, it represented a dream of peace for mankind, it was not dropped from Christian literature. It

---

[33] For text, see Lovejoy and Boas, *Primitivism in Antiquity*, p. 297.

continued to appear in different guises for different purposes,[34] and never failed, or fails yet, to evoke that time when the world was fresh with dew and man was happy.

III · CLASSICAL GARDENS

There is a second great source for the Christian earthly paradise, though it defies precise classification. This is the wealth of literature which treats gardens and landscapes in a great variety of classical genres. Generally, we can discern three main types of description: gardens of all sorts, set pieces of natural description which correspond to the prose *paradeisoi* of the Greek Romances, and those landscapes found in pastoral poetry. All these types of description overlap as to motifs, and all imply the presence of inner harmony or ideal love or behavior. But these accounts do not include the same ethical conditions found in a Golden Age site or, later, a Christian earthly paradise; these *loci* are not the symbol or scene for a reward because of adherence to a moral scale of values. Thus Virgil's Elysium is not discussed under this section, though many landscapes whose descriptions were influenced by the Virgilian passage in *Aeneid*, VI are included.

[34] The myth of the Golden Age is treated by Dante, *Inferno*, XIV, 94-120, in the figure of the Old Man of Crete, and is mentioned in *Purgatorio*, XXVIII, 139-140, by Matelda. An influential statement on the Golden Age in the Renaissance occurs in Shakespeare's *The Tempest*, II, i, 147ff., in "the commonwealth" over which Gonzalo "would with such perfection govern, sir,/To excel the Golden Age" (167-168); one of the main sources for this passage is presumed to be John Florio's translation of Montaigne's "Of the Cannibals" where a similar ideal, "natural" state is described. Tasso's famous chorus, beginning "O bella età de l'oro," in *Aminta*, I, ii, was widely imitated, and the whole myth receives grand treatment in Cervantes' *Don Quixote*, I, Chapter xi, when the Knight lectures the friendly goatherds on the Golden Age.

What I hope to indicate is the various forms the idea of a garden or landscape took in classical poetry, and how there were certain main themes around which many types of description clustered. In this sketch I shall include more than Curtius includes in his chapter on the *Ideal Landscape* where the *topos* of the *locus amoenus* is rigidly expounded.[35] However, Curtius' concept does give my inquiry focus because he crystallizes one central theme in ancient garden and landscape poetry. That is, in a garden, meadow or field poets have always felt Nature most nearly approximates the ideals of harmony, beauty, and peace which men constantly seek in some form or other. Such places, simple or ornate, realistic or idealized, are always used to symbolize some kind of satisfying experience. What the nature of that experience is depends upon the poet's personal or aesthetic needs. However, due to man's sense of satisfaction in or with a garden or landscape, these passages became storehouses of motifs for succeeding poets of the Christian earthly paradise as well as for medieval and Renaissance writers of a less overtly religious bent.

The three types of description—landscape as garden, as conscious, set piece of description, and as pastoral landscape involving some sense of human love—are all found in Greek prototypes. The outstanding image of the garden in antiquity is, of course, the magnificent garden of Alcinous in the *Odyssey*, Book VII.[36]

[35] In his *European Literature and the Latin Middle Ages*, tr. W. R. Trask, Bollingen Series, XXXVI (New York, 1953), 192. Curtius cites *Aeneid*, VI, 638—Devenere locos laetos et amoena virecta—and shows how Servius connected *amoena* with *amor*; thus the topos of the "love-ly place."

[36] Curtius, *Literature*, pp. 185-186, also cites other passages from the *Iliad*

To left and right, outside, he saw an orchard
close by a pale—four spacious acres planted
with trees in bloom or weighted down for picking;
pear trees, pomegranates, brilliant apples,
luscious figs, and olives ripe and dark.
Fruit never failed upon these trees: winter
and summertime they bore, for through the year
the breathing Westwind ripened all in turn—
so one pear came to prime, and then another,
and so with apples, figs, and the vine's fruit
empurpled in the royal vineyard there.
Currants were dried at one end, on a platform
bare to the sun, beyond the vintage arbors
and vats the vintners trod; while near at hand
were new grapes barely formed as the green bloom fell,
or half-ripe clusters, faintly coloring.
After the vines came rows of vegetables
of all kinds that flourish in every season,
and though the garden plots and orchard ran
channels from one clear fountain, while another
gushed through a pipe under the courtyard entrance
to serve the house and all who came for water.
These were the gifts of heaven to Alkinöos.   (112-134)

This garden with its trees, fruit, water, Zephyr, and perpetual springtime reminds us, as so many of the ancient
landscapes will, of the various Golden Age sites. However,
the resemblances, numerous as they are, pertain only to
common details of physical Nature. None of the standard
Golden Age characteristics of social harmony or personal

---

and *Odyssey* where perpetual springtime, shade trees (notably the plane)
water, grass, and flowers are all prominent.

reward for merit finds its way into these passages. Nevertheless, this garden in the *Odyssey* does bring many descriptive elements together in a model which was to influence literary gardens for centuries to come.[37]

The Homeric Hymns provide us with the second grand type of natural description, the landscape, or wild garden, as a conventional set piece. In the *Hymn to Demeter*, we notice an important strain in this type of landscape description, a retelling of the myth of Proserpine. From the early Greek poets down to Claudian, the story of Proserpine would be told over and over, and every version would dwell

---

[37] A garden modeled on Alcinous' is that one inside the threshold of the palace of Aeetes in the *Argonautica* of Apollonius Rhodius, III, 218-227; besides vines, foliage, and blooms, one finds four fountains, of milk, wine, fragrant oil, and water, Text in the Loeb Library *Argonautica*, tr. R. C. Seaton (Cambridge, Mass.-London, 1955). This garden was one of the targets for Lucian's parody of the beautiful landscape which appears in his *True History*, II, 4-16, a hilarious treatment of the whole Fortunate Islands–Golden Age–Elysium tradition with every detail inflated to the point of absurdity. For text, see Lovejoy and Boas, *Primitivism in Antiquity*, pp. 299-303.

Traditional landscapes are found throughout Latin poetry; notable are the Elysium landscapes of Tibullus and Valerius Flaccus. That of Tibullus (I, iii, 57-67; text in the Loeb Library *Catullus, Tibullus and Pervigilium Veneris* [Cambridge, Mass.-London, 1962]) is a field where Love holds sway amid songs of birds, budding cassia, roses, and happy youths and maidens. Very different is the Elysium of Valerius Flaccus in his *Argonautica*, I, 843-846. Here the abode of the blessed is very close in language and sentiment to Virgil's Elysium. Text in Loeb Library *Valerius Flaccus*, tr. J. H. Mozley (Cambridge, Mass.-London, 1922).

The Garden of the Hesperides, important for Christian poets of the earthly paradise because here fruit was a traditional motif, is mentioned in Ovid, *Metamorphoses*, IV, 214-216, as the place where Apollo's horses feed on ambrosia; it also appears in Lucan, *De Bello Civili*, IX, 360-364, where the golden grove, its fruit, and a coiled serpent are all described. Milton, in *Paradise Lost*, IV, was to draw most obviously on this garden.

lovingly on the (by now traditional) field she walked in, flowers she picked, as well as the flora of Hades, and the renewal of Nature after the promise to Demeter. Landscape passages such as the following set the tone:

> . . . she was playing with the deep-bosomed daughters
> of Oceanus and gathering flowers over a soft
> meadow, roses and crocuses and beautiful violets,
> irises also and hyacinths and the narcissus,
> which Earth made to grow at the will of Zeus and
> to please the Host of Many, to be a snare for
> the bloom-like girl,—a marvelous radiant flower. (5-10)

This type of predictable landscape, strong in the Proserpine story but also appearing with minor changes to suit the theme in traditional descriptions of Elysian Fields and the Bower of Venus (in later Latin epithalamia), is simply a piece of lush description involving grass, flowers, and fertile earth and has no other function than to provide locale and ornament for the tale.[38]

The third general type of description is that found in pastoral poetry. The natural motifs of the garden and the wild landscape were picked up in part by Theocritus and other early pastoral poets and combined with an element implicit in the other types, but now overtly made part of the scene. Human love is linked to and set in the natural

---

[38] See also ll. 423-426 of this hymn for a similar set piece of landscape description; for other landscapes which make use of the conceit of the girl as a flower among flowers, see below, n. 49. See also for various descriptions of landscape in the Homeric Hymns: III, 244-245, 280-286, 300; IV, 227-232; V, 75ff., where the union of Aphrodite and Anchises, after elaborate preparations, is reminiscent of Zeus and Hera, *Iliad*, XIV, 347ff.

world.[39] Such an identification meant that Christians not only saw parallels to the Biblical metaphor of the Shepherd and the Flock in pastoral poetry, but also parallels to the Biblical tradition of perfect *eros* and *agape* in the garden in Eden. Though love in pastoral poetry was by no means the love of Adam and Eve, the love in the ancient poems was certainly "idealized" in a sense; and the remote analogies between the pagan and Christian visions were enough to justify, here as elsewhere, a newly converted Christian's adaptation of the classical material. In this way pastoral poetry became a great source of natural motifs for those later writers who wanted to create some kind of garden or landscape of Love. However, pastoral poetry will yield to no classification. It picked up elements from all kinds of preceding description and passed these elements on to all succeeding generations. Perhaps in the final scene in Theocritus' famous *Idyll VII* we can see how many of the strands of landscape and garden poetry are woven into one rich tapestry:

> Many an aspen, many an elm bowed and rustled overhead, and hard by, the hallowed water welled purling forth of a cave of the Nymphs, while the brown cricket chirped busily amid the shady leafage, and the tree frog murmured aloof in the dense thornbrake. Lark and goldfinch sang and turtle moaned, and about the spring the bees hummed and hovered to and fro. All nature smelt of the opulent summertime, smelt of the season of fruit. Pears

[39] E. R. Curtius, *Literature*, p. 187, considers the fact that "the shepherd's world is linked to nature and to love" as the most important reason for the pastoral's tremendous influence. Of course, love as communal harmony was already basic to the myth of the Golden Age.

lay at our feet, apples on either side, rolling
                    abundantly.
And the young branches lay splayed upon the
ground because of the weight of their damsons.
                    (135-146)[40]

These three passages represent what I have arbitrarily
chosen to regard as the three main types of garden and
landscape description: a garden proper, a wild landscape to
decorate the tale, and a pastoral vista to provide proper
setting for love-song and ease. What all these descriptions
have in common is a sense of satisfaction and completeness,
both for the poet who created the scene and whatever character is involved in the scene. And it is this sense of individual, personal harmony with a garden, this ideal of some kind
of fulfillment in a landscape, that is passed on to the poets
of Rome.

AFTER Virgil, whose most influential landscapes were discussed in connection with the Golden Age, we can discern
many variations upon the basic types of landscapes and
garden presented in earlier poetry. Horace, for instance,
is not a poet in whom we should seek conventional or lush
landscapes. He is at pains to eschew the type of existence
luxury implies, whether it take a rural or an urban setting
(*Odes*, III, xxix, 10ff.). Horace's inner ideals find fulfillment
in a simple, harmonious setting and not in the glitter of
Rome or among the riches of a Calabrian beehive or a
Gallic pasture. In *Epode II*, he explains,

[40] See also *Idyll*, I, 63-142, for Nature's mourning at the death of
Daphnis; *Idyll*, XVIII, 26-32, for the landscape in the love-song to Helen;
and *Inscription*, IV for a garden and shrine to Priapus. Text and translation from the Loeb Library *The Greek Bucolic Poets*, tr. J. E. Edmonds
(Cambridge, Mass.-London, 1938).

✕ Beatus ille qui procul negotiis,
ut prisca gens mortalium,
paterna rura bobus exercit suis. (1-3)

And the "ideal" landscape of such a man?

✕ Libet iacere modo sub antiqua ilice,
modo in tenaci gramine.
labuntur altis interim ripis aquae,
querentur in silvis aves,
fontesque lymphis obstrepunt manantibus,
somnos quod invitet levis. (23-28)

In general Horace prefers a stream of pure water, a plot of
good land and a decent crop (*Odes*, III, xvi, 29-30). Sometimes he can sing of a landscape like that by the river of
Galaesus:

✕ Ille terrarum mihi praeter omnes
angulus ridet, ubi non Hymetto
mella decedunt viridique certat
baca Venafro;
ver ubi longum tepidasque praebet
Juppiter brumas et amicus Aulon
fertili Baccho minimum Falernis
invidet uvis.

✕ Happy the man who, far away from business cares, like the pristine
race of mortals, works his ancestral acres with his steers

✕ 'Tis pleasant, now to lie beneath some ancient ilex-tree, now on
the matted turf. Meanwhile the rills glide between their high banks;
birds warble in the woods; the fountains plash with their flowing
waters, a sound to invite soft slumbers.

✕ That corner of the world smiles for me beyond all others, where
the honey yields not to Mymettus, and the olive vies with the green

Ille te mecum locus et beatae
postulant arces;   (*Odes*, II, vi, 13-22)

But it is only when a spot is, in his mind, "beata" that
Horace accords it such lavish praise, and his description
reads like many of the more conventional landscapes.
Usually his skeptical ideals are most at home in a simple
natural setting:

> ˣ ego laudo ruris amoeni
> rivos et musco circumlita saxa nemusque,
> (*Epistles*, I, x, 6-7)[41]

This "rus amoenum," with its Virgilian overtones of selective
simplicity, is what Hōrace most admires; for such a garden
or landscape reflects the ideals of the man.

> ˣ Hoc erat in votis: modus agri non ita magnus,
> hortus ubi et tecto vicinus iugis aquae fons
> et paulum silvae super his foret. (*Satires*, II, vi, 2-3)[42]

Venafrum, where Jupiter vouchsafes long springs and winters mild,
and where Aulon, dear to fertile Bacchus, envies not the clusters of
Falernum. That place and its blessed heights summon thee and
me.

ˣ I praise the lovely country's brooks, its grove and moss grown
rocks

ˣ This is what I prayed for!—a piece of land not so very large, where
there would be a garden, and near the house a spring of ever-flowing
water, and up above these a bit of forest.

[41] Text in Loeb Library *Horace, Satires, Epistles and Ars Poetica*, tr.
H. R. Fairclough (Cambridge, Mass.-London, 1955).

[42] Text in Loeb *Horace, Satires, Epistles*, tr. Fairclough. For the blessings
of retirement, see *Odes*, I, iv, 17; III, i. For text here and above, see Loeb
Horace, Odes and Epodes, tr. Bennett.

The gardens of Horace per se were never imitated by his successors in the way the forms of his poems were, but the landscapes provided subsequent generations with an image of the ideal natural setting according to one man's vision of the proper harmony between internal standards and external surroundings. Though it would be impossible for me to trace the transmission of this theme through Latin poetry, we can take examples from various poets and see how each one adapted the idea of the garden or wild or erotic landscape to his own personal and poetic uses.

Ovid's *Fasti*, for instance, are dotted with the landscape as little garden. In *Fasti II* (ll. 703-704) there is a garden near a house, full of plants and rushing water. We are afforded only a quick glimpse, but the point is made: what seems a conventional closed garden, implies ease, retirement, harmony. In *Fasti V* (ll. 315-324), the opposite impression is conveyed through a garden. The speaker is despondent and, to communicate the measure of his melancholy, he recounts how he let a garden go to ruin ("nec in pretio fertilis hortus erat"). Lilies, violets, bright saffron—all wither. Zephyr comes to chide the negligent gardener, but to no avail. Olive trees, crops, vines, all sicken and die. Here again, the symbolic weight of a garden is brought to bear by a poet for a specific (negative) purpose. To waste a garden is the proper external symbol for a man's interior disintegration and uneasiness.

A final example of the closed garden, which on the surface looks merely conventional, i.e., a description for its own sake, is found in *Fasti V* (ll. 195-210). Flora, the goddess of flowers, tells of her origins.

⚹ Chloris eram, nymphe campi felicis, ubi audis
  rem fortunatis ante fuisse viris. (197-198)[43]

This could only refer to some pristine state of bliss such as the Islands of the Blessed. She was raped by Zephyr, but he made an honest nymph of her and now she is happy, for where she is:

⚹ vere fruor semper; semper nitidissimus annus,
  arbor habet frondes, pabula semper humus.
  est mihi fecundus dotalibus hortus in agris:
  aura fovet, liquidae fonte rigatur aquae. (207-210)

What we have presented in this short passage is a spiritual saga told through two landscapes. Flora came from those happy fields of delight before there were men, and presumably she participated with all her being in that bliss. Then she was violated and her spirits sank. But when the union of flowers and the west wind was brought into some state of fruitful harmony, the renewed joy and satisfaction of the goddess is symbolized by a beautiful landscape. Wherever her delight is, there Nature reflects it with magnificence.

These charming, if facile, miniatures of Ovid are a narrative variation on the lyric theme of Horace—that a landscape

> ⚹ Chloris I was, a nymph of the happy fields where,
>   as you have heard, dwelt fortunate men of old.

> ⚹ I enjoy perpetual spring; most buxom is the year
>   ever; ever the tree is clothed with leaves, the
>   ground with pasture. In the fields that are my
>   dower, I have a fruitful garden, fanned by the
>   breeze and watered by a spring of running water.

[43] For text, here and below see Loeb Library *Fasti*, tr. Sir J. G. Frazer (New York-London, 1931).

reflects one's interior state of soul. And Ovid's delicate art stands in direct contrast, therefore, on two points to the poetry of Statius. First, Statius is much more in the tradition of the landscape for its own sake; his descriptive nature verse appears in occasional poems, and these passages are meant to adorn the poem and flatter the recipient. Second, Statius' technique is the opposite of Ovid's or Horace's. Statius is incapable of restraint; his tapestries are very large and loosely woven. His descriptions of the natural settings for the villas of Manlius Volpiscus (*Silvae*, I, iii, 15ff.) and Pollio Felix (*Silvae*, II, ii, 52ff.) are exclamatory and rambling set pieces which involve some of the usual landscape motifs[44] and in which Statius is constantly asking how to describe something and then passing over it. In this manner he manages to mention almost everything but say very little—all at great length. In the *Achilleid*, however, there is an arresting passage which strikes us far more than all of the self-conscious descriptive passages in the *Silvae*,

> ✻ lucus Agenorei sublimis ad orgia Bacchi
> stabat et admissum caelo nemus. (I, 593-594)[45]

To have a sacred grove so high that it almost reaches heaven is an interesting classical precursor of what was to become

✻ There stood a lofty grove, scene of the rites of Agenorean Bacchus, a grove that reached to heaven.

---

[44] For instance, the eternal quiet and lack of inclement weather in *Silvae*, I, iii, 29-30; also the Neapolitan countryside, whose characteristics are those usually reserved for a Golden Age landscape in *Silvae*, III, v. Statius' lack of precision is exemplified in *Silvae*, IV, v, a lyric ode after Horace praising retirement to Septimius Severus; the landscape is constantly alluded to but never really described. Text in the Loeb Library *Statius*, tr. J. H. Mozley (New York-London, 1928), I.

[45] Text in Loeb *Statius*, tr. Mozley, II.

Christian belief: that the earthly paradise was on a mountain top, often so high that it touched the moon.[46]

Statius' vague effusions are themselves in direct contrast to Juvenal's verse, which shares with Horace's a distrust of the luxurious and a respect, at least verbal, for the virtues of a small, private landscape whose rugged and noble simplicity reflects the ideals of the inhabitant or beholder. Against the sprawling vistas of Statius, it is a relief to set a touch like this from *Satire III*.

⁑ ianua Baiarum est et gratum litus amoeni
  secessus. ego vel Prochytam praepono Suburae. (4-5)[47]

Here the single word "amoenus," which we heard in Virgil and Horace, serves to conjure up level green vistas, water, shade and fragrance. Here the ideal of retirement—life in "secessus"—recovers the idea of bringing one's environment into harmony with one's standards and needs. Even the idea of an island (Prochyta) as opposed to a city street (Saburra) reminds us of the contrast between city and country life alluded to in Virgil's First Eclogue and throughout Horace. These longings are not plentiful or premeditated in the works of Juvenal, and indeed, when we think of his ambiguity toward the Golden Age, it occurs to us that Juvenal would not be the poet he is without the gnawing, depraved sights, smells, and sounds of the city. Occasional

⁑ That is the gate of Baiae, a sweet retreat upon a pleasant shore; I myself would prefer even Prochyta to the Subura.

[46] The Christian belief grew out of the Pauline passage in the Second Epistle to the Corinthians, and the Greek Father's tendency to identify paradise with the third (Lunar) sphere. For further material, see Bibliography to *Introduction*.

[47] Text here and below in the Loeb Library *Juvenal and Persius*, tr. G. G. Ramsey, rev. ed. (Cambridge, Mass.-London, 1961).

or brief as they may be, descriptions of landscapes do appear in Juvenal and the image of the garden does shimmer behind invective against the city. Again in *Satire III*, Juvenal points out that one can live cheaply yet well at Sora or Frusino:

* hortulus hic puteusque brevis nec reste movendus
    in tenuis plantas facili diffunditur haustu.
    vive bidentis amans et culti vilicus horti,
    unde epulum possis centum dare Pythagoreis.   (226-229)

There is a wry note at the end in the reference to the vegetarian Pythagoreans, yet such an image of the garden is necessary for a satirist of urban life. For in a garden, a man was self-sufficient and busy, out of strife's and vice's way.

There was a practical earthy streak in the Roman character to which this ideal was attractive. The great folk hero of Rome, Cincinnatus, had to be recalled from the plow, not the Bath or the Forum. A garden, be it of flowers or vegetables, reflected a man's industry and his taste. Propertius at one point (IV, ii, 39-46) speaks of roses, cucumbers, gourds, and cabbage all together; the point is that he can raise anything and honor himself with it. His garden proves his worth. In an eclogue of Calpurnius Siculus (II, 75ff.), the shepherd Astacus is competing for the love of a maiden and as his best gift he offers his garden. This was the most he could do, for the garden was most expressive of himself.

Of course, this simple, rugged landscape and garden is not the only natural spot idealized in Roman poetry. For there are different poets and different standards, and there

---

* And you will there have a little garden, with a shallow well from which you can easily draw water, without need of a rope, to bedew your weakly plants. There make your abode, a friend of the mattock, tending a trim garden fit to feast a hundred Pythagoreans.

is still a strong tendency to indulge in the type of tour de force we noticed in Statius and, to a certain extent, in Ovid.[48]

It is Claudian who caps this type of description with the grand landscape in Book II of *De Raptu Proserpinae*. There the whole conspiracy of Nature to lure the girl and her friends into the field is depicted in detail, and every standard motif of this conventionalized ideal landscape is included. Lines 71 to 87 show Henna begging Zephyr to make the valley enticing. Bring the breeze and scents and fruit, she pleads. Bring the odor of Panchaea's incense-bearing wood, of Hydaspes' streams, and of all the spices of the Phoenix. And from lines 88 to 100, Zephyr spreads his bounty over flowers of every kind. But at line 101 the poet says, "Forma loci superat flores"—the countryside itself is the more beautiful sight. There follows a five-line description of the plain and a stream, and four lines cataloguing seven types of trees as well as ivy and the ubiquitous vine and elm, and finally at line 112, the description of a lake which completes the passage. Into the lovely landscape comes the girl, only to be snatched and carried away by the King of the Underworld. This is a set piece of elaborate description in the same manner, and the same myth, as we noted in the Homeric *Hymn to Demeter*.[49]

[48] Curtius, *Literature*, pp. 195-197, notes that the earliest Latin example of this "bravura rhetorical description" (195) occurs in Petronius; he also cites the lush verse of Tiberianus as well as Libanius, a late Greek poet of the fourth century A.D., whose formula:

> Causes of delight are springs and plantations,
> and gardens and soft breezes and flowers and
> bird-voices.

is a neat summation of the elements involved in the set piece of landscape description.

[49] Text in Loeb *Claudian*, tr. Platnauer, I, 324ff. For the Homeric Hymn, see p. 36 above. The image of the girl as a flower among flowers is of

IV · MEDIEVAL GARDENS

We are now at a point where we may distinguish two great poetic traditions which develop the garden of love. One tradition, written in Latin and the vulgar tongues by ecclesiastics and laymen alike, includes everything from allegorical and didactic treatises to the lyrics and epics of courtly love to the narrative art of Chaucer. This is the poetry of love, physical or transcendent, actual or academic, which has as its site and symbol a bower or garden or grove. Often there is a Christian or moralistic message or inspiration behind this poetry; often Eden is the imagina-

---

great antiquity; Catullus derives it from Sappho and gives us a variation on its treatment in the Proserpine myth. In Catullus, the image expands; see his famous epithalamium, LXII, 39-47, where the maiden-flower is the central concern. The landscape radiates from her, and is more symbolic of her than simply a setting for her. Text in Loeb *Catullus, Tibullus,* tr. Cornish.

Ovid's account of the Proserpine story, *Metamorphoses,* V, 386-401, is reminiscent of the Homeric Hymn and the conventional, lush type of landscape description; the image of the girl as a flower is only tentatively evoked (398-401), never stated because it is the landscape *qua* setting for the scene that is most important. Text in Loeb Library *Ovid Metamorphoses,* tr. F. J. Miller (Cambridge, Mass.-London, 1936), I.

An interesting variation on this image is found in Claudian's epithalamium, *De Nuptiis Honorii Augusti,* 243ff. Here we move beyond what was implied in Ovid and stated by Catullus—the girl is like a flower—because metaphor begins to collapse into identification; the virtues of the girl become those of the landscape, while the attributes of the landscape reflect those of the girl. Claudian moves in the direction of having everything at once. Text in Loeb *Claudian,* tr. Platnauer, I.

Though other examples are cited below, we might note that what happens in Claudian is taken to its greatest extreme in Andrew Marvell's *Upon Appleton House,* where Mary Fairfax "Seems with the Flow'rs a Flow'r to be" (302) and becomes "*She* yet more Pure, Sweet, Streight, and Fair,/Than Gardens, Woods, Meads, Rivers are" (695-696); she goes from Nature's finest example to its prototype.

tive source for the garden; but it is *not* what can be called
Christian, i.e. religious, poetry. It is the secular quality of
this tradition of verse that distinguishes it from the second
tradition.

The second is poetry specifically concerned with that
garden of love which is the Christian earthly paradise. The
poets of this tradition look back spiritually, as well as
aesthetically, to the garden in Genesis, or some version of
it, and their theme is a religious one. With the poetry of
the garden in Eden, we have the emergence of the particular earthly paradise which we shall trace in all its
permutations down into the Renaissance. There the image of
the enchanted garden will assert itself, and change the meaning, and in subtle ways the look, of the landscape once again.

One specific source for that tradition of medieval "secular" gardens of love is the epithalamic tradition after Catullus. Beginning with Statius' *Epithalamion in Stellum et
Violentillam* (*Silvae*, I, ii, ll. 51-64), a new element is added
to the classical epithalamium—a scene between Venus and
Cupid in Venus' bower or garden where the beauty of the
bride-to-be is extolled and plans to inflame her with love
are made. It has been said that this "wooden convention"
had little effect upon later epithalamia.⁵⁰ This is undoubtedly
true, but I think it will be admitted that the convention
had much to do with associating a garden or natural enclosure with physical love, and therefore it underlies much
of "courtly" or garden love literature. In Statius' poem
there is little natural description, for the scene is laid in
Venus' dwelling place in the Milky Way, but the conven-

---

⁵⁰ T. M. Greene, "Spenser and the Epithalamic Tradition," *CL*, 9
(1957), p. 216.

tion of the goddess surrounded by her attendants for a specific purpose is established.[51]

The most florid example of this convention occurs in Claudian's *Epithalamium de Nuptiis Honorii Augusti* (ll. 49-96). Venus' retreat is a mountain top, high above the Ionian Sea. "Invius humano gressu," it is so high as to be safe from frost, wind, or clouds. Like the sacred grove in Statius' *Achilleid*, it is an interesting anticipation of the gardens and paradises of medieval literature which culminated in the earthly paradise of the *Divine Comedy* and like them, it is fanned forever by gentle breezes.[52]

Here on the plain below the mountain slope is the enclosure of Venus:

* hunc aurea saepes
circuit et fulvo defendit prata metallo. (56-57)

Here bright flowers are cultivated by Zephyr, and chosen

* that a golden hedge encircles, guarding its meadows with yellow metal.

[51] Venus' Bower is also treated by Florus, the poet-friend of Hadrian, in a witty, ten-line trifle where the goddess's garden, verdant and alluring, is loved by Venus and certain to inspire love in the beholder. Reposianus (third century A.D.), enlarges upon the convention in his *De Concubitu Martis et Veneris* (33-50). The old story is told with freshness, and the link between Nature and love is given concentrated meaning and specific form: a secluded, enclosed, luxurious place devoted entirely to the adornment and uses of Venus. Text of Florus and Reposianus in Loeb *Minor Latin Poets*, tr. Duff and Duff.

[52] This passage exerted great influence on succeeding generations of Christian paradise poets, for the fact that Claudian's description coincided with Christian versions of the earthly paradise behind or upon a mountain meant he could safely be read as a secular (and pleasurable) analogue to what was religiously acceptable. Text in Loeb *Claudian*, tr. Platnauer, I.

birds sing among the poplar, plane, and alder. Here also are two fountains,

> ※ hic dulcis, amarus
> alter, et infusis corrumpunt mella venenis,
> unde Cupidineas armari fama sagittas,   (69-71)

and nymphs and cupids and, as there will be in so many later medieval love gardens, hosts of allegorical figures:

> ※ hic habitat nullo constricta Licentia nodo
> et flecti faciles Irae vinoque madentes
> Excubiae Lacrimaeque rudes et gratus amantum
> Pallor et in primis titubans Audacia furtis
> iucundique Metus et non secura Voluptas;
> et lasciva volant levibus Periuria ventis.
> quos inter petulans alta Iuventas cervice
> excludit Senium loco.   (78-85)

In the distance is Venus' palace, built by Vulcan from jewels and gold of every kind (86-91). In the courtyard grow spikenard, cassia, Panchaean cinnamon, and other sweet-smelling plants (92-96). This riot of color, smell, and sound, this inaccessible mountain, enclosed plain and gleaming castle, the attendants and allegorical "numina" are all for one purpose:

※ one of sweet water, the other of bitter, honey is mingled with the first, poison with the second, and in these streams 'tis said that Cupid dips his arrows.

※ Other deities, too, are here: Licence bound by no fetters, easily moved Anger, Wakes dripping with wine, inexperienced Fears, Pallor that lovers ever prize, Boldness trembling at his first thefts, happy Fears, unstable Pleasure, and lovers' Oaths, the sport of every lightest breeze. Amid them all wanton Youth with haughty neck shuts out Age from the grove.

᙮ luxuriae Venerique vacat. (54)

All is dedicated to Venus and pleasure, and in the hands of this pagan (though possibly nominally Christian), a rich and satisfying, albeit clogged, effect is achieved. Claudian is the last of the classical poets who had the discipline, if not the originality, to handle such a passage. Though we sense that he included everything, and therefore too much, his eye is constantly on the object, and he produces a lush but clearly delineated effect. In some ways he resembles Statius, but in Claudian we do not sense the digressive quality of mind which makes so much of Statius windy and rambling. Claudian had a keen eye and gift for organization, even if the material was overripe and blemished from too much handling.[53]

His legacy to the Middle Ages was to fix firmly the convention of a natural bower or grove or enclosure dedicated to Venus and her pastimes. He sums up all the natural motifs—birds, flowers, springs, Zephyr, perfume, eternal springtime, grass, shade, trees—of the Golden Age spots and conventional ancient landscapes and gives the pastoral associations of love a new setting and direction. Claudian's spot is sanctified not by the presence of virtuous souls, but by the presence of Venus. The sports of the ancient islands and Elysiums are now replaced by the dallyings of Cupid and the games of love. Passions and characteristics of passionate love, standard since Ovid, become allegorizations,

᙮ It is consecrate to pleasure and to Venus.

[53] See also Claudian's *Epithalamium dictum Palladio V.C. tribune et notario et Celerinae* (1-25) for another treatment of the Venus theme, this time centered on a cave. In the Loeb *Claudian*, tr. Platnauer, II, this poem is among the *Carminum Minorum Corpusculum* and is numbered by the editor XXV (XXX, XXXI).

the household gods of Venus' bower. These allegorical figures, or their progeny, populate the gardens of medieval and Renaissance literature in droves—though there they struggle about haunted by Christianity. Claudian neither invents them nor manipulates them; he simply puts them in a particular context. They seem to fit, they do not clash with their surroundings, and they go on to become indispensable.

Claudian's legacy is not fully received for centuries; many poets whose gardens of love owe much to this late Latin poet undoubtedly did not know it. He has crystallized much ancient garden poetry, and he stands at the threshold of the Christian world with the riches of antiquity carefully collected and arranged. It was the task of his beneficiaries to adapt what they could.

THE GARDENS, bowers, meadows on mountains, and lovely landscapes of medieval secular poetry have been often studied in terms of their sources and symbolism, and the reader can consult the Bibliography for many studies of this sort. My immediate task is rather to show how these gardens resembled the Christian earthly paradise while calling themselves, for excellent reasons, something else (home of Nature, Venus' abode, Garden of Delight, and the like) and how through the allegorical and courtly love gardens there is a line of descent into the great enchanted gardens, or false paradises, of the Renaissance.

How were these gardens similar to the traditional earthly paradise? In many of the details of natural description; often in explicit references to that garden; and in the fact many of the lush medieval sites were found on mountain tops, in accordance with the mountain-top tradition of the

Christian garden. However, these gardens were also strongly influenced by the bowers of late Latin literature, notably those in the epithalamia of Claudian; and this accounts, in part, for the super-abundance of allegorical figures, and the heavy emphasis on crystal walls, jeweled palaces, and valuable metals.[54] The classical influence can also account for the mountain-top location, for we have arrived at the point where Christian and classical traditions have become almost inextricably mingled. Essentially, of course, these medieval gardens differed most from the "true" earthly paradise in the absence of overt religious preoccupations.

There are two well-known and influential allegorical poems from the twelfth century whose gardens owe something to classical traditions, something to the Christian tradition of the earthly paradise. Alain de Lille's *Anticlaudianus* is the first. This poem, written in 1183, was strongly influenced by the Platonic school of thought at Chartres and particularly the *De Mundi Universitate* of Bernardus Sylvestris, and like Bernardus, Alain's "subject is . . . the creation of man, presented under the form of an allegory."[55] What immediately concerns us is the long (over fifty lines) description of the "realm" of Nature, and the somewhat shorter portrait of the palace of Nature.[56] The realm of

[54] Though there is a strain of jewels and gold in the Christian paradise tradition. Genesis 2: 11-12 and the description of the City in Revelation 21: 18-21—with its twelve foundations of gems, its twelve gates of pearl, and streets of gold—undoubtedly had an influence on the castles and palaces in later medieval literary gardens.

[55] F. J. E. Raby, *A History of Secular Latin Poetry* (Oxford, 1934), II, 16.

[56] Text of Alain in *The Anglo-Latin Satirical Poets and Epigrammatists of the Twelfth Century*, ed. T. Wright, Roll Series (London, 1872), II; for the Realm of Nature, see pp. 275-277; for the Palace, pp. 277-278.

Nature is painted in elaborate detail: flowers, breeze, eternal springtime, all kinds of fruits and trees, singing birds and sweet water—all exist in harmony. And following the description of the landscape, we are told that the palace of Nature stood in the midst of a grove whose trees touched the sky "and gave the clouds a kiss."

This passage, beginning a new chapter, goes on to describe the palace, which is on tall columns, gleaming with gems, burning with gold, and shimmering with silver. As so many later palaces would be, this one is covered with works of art, and the rest of the chapter relates the mythological stories depicted in the paintings. Patch has best summarized the dual traditions contributing to this typical landscape and palace: "In the whole description of this region the first part is clearly indebted to the ideas of the Earthly Paradise as even the opening line suggests ("Est locus a nostro secretus climate tractu") and the mention of eternal spring. The mountain plateau may also come from this tradition or from that of Claudian and the classical writers, from which also the account of the palace would seem to derive."[57]

The influences of Claudian and the earthly paradise tradition also make themselves felt in the *Architrenius* of Jean de Hauteville. The twelfth-century satire, dealing with a young man, the Arch Mourner, who weeps as Raby says "for his useless and purposeless youth,"[58] has two passages

[57] H. R. Patch, *The Otherworld according to Descriptions in Medieval Literature* (Cambridge, Mass., 1950), p. 178. On page 180, Patch shows how Alain uses the same elements—mountain, garden, house—in the account of the Realm of Fortune; for text, see *Anglo-Latin Satirical Poets*, ed. Wright, I, 396ff.

[58] Raby, *Secular Latin Poetry*, II, 100. Text in *Anglo-Latin Satirical Poets*, ed. Wright, I, 252ff.

which owe much to these twin sources of medieval land-scape. One tells of the youth's visit to the "domus aurea" of Venus which sits on a mountain and is decorated with works of art. The other passage, dealing with the Mount of Ambition, also resembles the classical tradition, for there is a magnificent dwelling on top of the mountain and a river gleaming with gems and precious metals in the sur-rounding landscape.[59] But the description of the Mount of Ambition itself recalls accounts of the earthly paradise. The mountain rises high into the heavens, passing the moon and almost touching the stars. This is again reminiscent of the tradition, developed by the Church Fathers, of the earthly paradise on a mountain which reaches the sphere of the moon. The mountain of Claudian, though above the wind, frost and clouds, does not rise to such specific altitudes. Here, of course, both the classical and Christian mountain-garden tradition entwine. Other earthly paradise-motifs are the west wind, all kinds of trees and flowers, and fruits, in-cluding seven kinds of pears.[60]

THESE two poems suffice as examples of the kind of land-scape and garden one encounters in medieval allegorical poems of a moral or didactic purpose. Their landscapes are not false paradises, whose purpose is to lure and harm the visitor; they are pseudo-paradises, drawing upon similar yet distinct traditions in classical and Christian literature. There is, however, another broad type of allegorical poem whose purpose is also didactic but whose message is much less "philosophically" oriented. Such a work is Brunetto Latini's

[59] *Anglo-Latin Satirical Poets*, ed. Wright, I, 292ff. for the garden and mountain top; pp. 294ff. for the house.
[60] *Anglo-Latin Satirical Poets*, ed. Wright, I, 294.

Tesoretto, and a consideration of landscape in this encyclo-
pedic poem will direct us toward an even greater tradition
of vistas and gardens.

In Chapter xix, the narrator says that after having

> ˣ Passate valle, e monti,
> Boschi, selve e ponti,
> I' giunsi in un bel prato
> Fiorito d' ogni lato,
> Lo più ricco del mondo.   (19-23)[61]

The air is now dim, now clear, and he discerns "houses,
and towers" and people involved in all sorts of activities.
Some run, some recline; some hunt, some flee, some enjoy,
some go mad, some laugh, some weep. It has been conjectured that the paradoxical language is meant to be emblematic of the changeful nature of love,[62] and whether or not
this is true, the narrator certainly learns that

> ˣ qui sta monsignore,
> Ch' è capo, e Dio d'amore   (61-62)

and later our wanderer sees Piacere (92) and four "donne
valenti" (95)—Paura, Disianza, Amore and Speranza (101-

> ˣ Passed valleys and mountains,
> Woods, forests and bridges,
> I reached a beautiful meadow
> Flowering on every side,
> The richest in the world.

> ˣ here is my lord,
> Who is the chief, and God of love.

[61] Text from *Il Tesoretto e il Favoletto di Ser Brunetto Latini,* ed. G. B.
Zanoni (Firenze, 1824). Citations are by the line numbers of this text.
[62] Patch, *Otherworld,* p. 184.

102). The climax to the narrator's sojourn comes when he turns

> ＊E in un ricco manto
> Vidi Ovidio maggiore. . . . (178-179)

Ovid is naturally writing verses on love, and to all of the narrator's questions, "he answered me in Italian" ("volgare," 193).

Brunetto's landscape of love, densely populated with personifications, is nevertheless very different from the landscapes set down in Latin by Alain or Jean de Hauteville. Ovid is here, both as a character and an influence, and the description—much more in the tradition of the set landscapes of Ovid and Statius—seems to owe little to the Christian earthly paradise. However, the emphasis on Ovid and the pains and joys of love in a natural setting point us to a tradition which did draw from the earthly paradise—the medieval literature of courtly love.

The doctrine of courtly love embraces many different genres: the lyrics of the troubadours, the narrative "dream visions" like the *Roman de la Rose* or *Parlement of Foules*, innumerable romances in verse, and prose treatises like Andreas Capellanus' *De Arte Honesti Amandi*. In these works we move from a consideration of broad allegorical vistas or landscapes to enclosed, walled areas—gardens of love. A title like Guillaume de Machaut's *Dit dou Vergier* or Jean Froissart's *Paradys d'Amours* gives us an indication of the kind of walled landscape with which we are confronted. And the titles are good indices—both poems open in a beautiful garden or grove, full of flowers, water and

> ＊And in a rich mantle
> I saw great Ovid

singing birds. Both gardens obviously owe their natural features to the earthly paradise tradition.[63]

In the elegant literature of *fin amors*, we find the troubadours using gardens as settings or backdrops for their poems. For instance, there is the opening stanza to the *vers* of Marcabru:

> ✠ A la fontana del vergier,
> On l'erb' es vertz jost a 'l gravier,
> A l'ombra d'un fust domesgier,
> En aiziment de blancas flors
> E de novelh chant costumier,
> Trobey sola, ses companhier,
> Selha que non vol mon solatz.   (1-7)[64]

In a stanza unique in Marcabru but typical of Provençal poetry, we see the familiar elements of the closed garden, fountain, grass, trees, flowers, and bird-song. It is the same garden implied in "Quan lo rius de la fontana" of Jaufré

> ✠ By the fountain of the garden
> Where the grass is green near the gravel,
> In the shade of a planted tree,
> Adorned with white flowers
> And the usual new singing,
> I found alone, without companion,
> She who does not wish my happiness.

[63] Patch (*Otherworld*, p. 204), points out how often Machaut explicitly compares his gardens to the earthly paradise; this is not uncommon either in the Middle Ages or the Renaissance, for as Patch indicates (p. 203 and n. 97), it is done by Watriquet de Couvin in *Li Mirreoirs as Dames* and John Gower, *Balades*, XXXVI, lines 1-2, and VII, stanza iv. We might also add that Spenser compares the Bower of Bliss to the garden in Eden in *The Faerie Queene*, II, xii, 52.

[64] Text in *Anthology of the Provençal Troubadours*, ed. R. T. Hill and T. G. Bergin (New Haven, 1941), p. 16.

Rudel; the garden explicitly described as a "bels jardis" in a *canso* of Giraut de Bornelh where the lady appears to the lover as "la bela flors de lis" and continues that ancient tradition of the beautiful lady as a flower among flowers.[65] The garden of love is used throughout Provençal love poetry as the secluded, ordered, beautiful setting for the seizure by, or the loss of, love. In its simplicity of motif and consecration to a kind of adoration, it reminds one of the earthly paradise—though one is always baffled by the question of specific literary sources for this poetry. But regardless of its roots, the gardens of the troubadours stand as excellent examples of that type of medieval garden we are surveying, the garden which may somehow be modeled on the earthly paradise but is not specifically the earthly paradise; a secular spot where love may (though not necessarily) be refined and "spiritual" but is not in any way religiously or divinely oriented.[66]

A poem which participates in all the allegorical, philosophic, and courtly love traditions is the *Roman de la Rose*. This poem is so immense we can do no more than indicate the various possibilities contained within it. However, it does present us with two gardens which when taken to-

[65] *Ibid.*, pp. 24 and 56.

[66] There is a sumptuous courtly love garden in the *De Arte Honesti Amandi* of Andreas Capellanus where the King of Love metes out punishment to those guilty of rejecting suitors. It is typical of many "secular" love gardens where the Christian archetype is embroidered with classical and "courtly" trimmings. For Latin text, see *Andreas Capellani De Amore Libri Tres*, ed. E. Trojel (Hauniae, 1892), p. 99; for English translation, see *The Art of Courtly Love by Andreas Capellanus*, tr. J. J. Parry, Records of Civilization, Sources and Studies, XXXIII (New York, 1941), 78. For another garden landscape, see Trojel, pp. 298ff., and Parry, pp. 178ff.

gether—though they appear at opposite ends of the poem—forecast the kind of situation we will meet in some Renaissance poems. The first garden, of course, is the garden of the Rose. It is encountered by the Dreamer early in the poem:

> ✻ Quant j'oi ung poi avant alé,
> Si vi un vergier grant e lé,
> Tot clos de haut mur bataillié,
> Portrait dehors e entaillié,
> A maintes riches escritures. (129-133)[67]

The Dreamer then describes for roughly 330 lines the allegorical figures inscribed on the garden wall. These are qualities which will never enter. C. S. Lewis reminds us that this "is the same garden which we have met in Andreas and, before him, in Claudian," and says that in some writers it "means Love; in Guillaume it is changed slightly and made to mean the life of the court, considered as the necessary sphere or field for love's operations." Lewis adds that the classical and erotic models only account for part of the garden. "Deeper than these lies the world-wide dream of the happy garden—the islands of the Hesperides, the earthly paradise, Tirnanogue."[68] Lewis hints at what we have found thus far to be true—that behind the secular gardens lurks the image of the Christian earthly paradise as well as the

> ✻ When I had gone a little bit ahead
> I saw a grand, large garden
> All closed round by a high castelled wall,
> Whereon were portrayed and chiseled
> Many handsome characters.

[67] Old French text in *Le Roman de la Rose*, ed. E. Langlois, Société des Anciens Textes Français, 5 vols. (Paris, 1914-1924). References in the text are to the line numbers of this edition.

[68] C. S. Lewis, *The Allegory of Love* (New York, 1958), pp. 119-120.

inspiration of obvious classical models. But the poet does far more than hint; for when Idleness (Oyseuse) opens the gate to the "vergier," the Dreamer exclaims:

> ⚹ Je fui liez e bauz e joianz;
> Et sachiez que je cuidai estre
> Por voir en parevis terrestre;
> Tant estoit li leus delitables
> Qu'il sembloit estre esperitables;
> Car, si come lors m'iert avis,
> Il ne fait en nul parevis
> Si bon estre, come il faisoit
> Ou vergier qui tant me plasoit.   (634-642)

The elements which compose the garden—birds, trees, fruits, fountains and streams, the fountain of Narcissus with its bright sand, the crystal stones, the rosebud surrounded by the hedge, the castle built by Jealousy—all are familiar to the reader; they derive from various sources, among which one would number the earthly paradise tradition.

What is most interesting in this early passage is that we are confronted with various ideas of paradise in rapid succession.[69] In the garden of the Rose passage, we must be

> ⚹ Once entered, I was joyous and glad
> And believe me that I thought I was
> Looking at the earthly paradise;
> The vistas were so charming
> It seemed to be heavenly;
> For, as I have been told,
> It is not as good to be in
> Any paradise, as it was
> Where the garden pleased me so.

[69] The contrast between versions of paradise will be explicit when we consider the other garden—the Good Pasture in Jean de Meung's part of the poem. See below, pp. 64-66.

careful to see what exactly the Dreamer says. First he says he was happy ("joiens") to be admitted to the garden ("vergier"; 633). Then the next couplet (635-636) presents a new idea: "Believe me that I thought I was/in the earthly paradise." The narrator has gone from one plane to another: from "vergier" to a specific garden with many more associations—"parevis terrestre." But the Dreamer does not say, "I was in the earthly paradise"; he says, "I *thought* I was in the earthly paradise." Thus, though he does not identify the garden with the garden in Eden and risk the doctrinal or artistic consequences, the Dreamer does manage to endow the "vergier" with a higher mode of existence. This is simply a delicate variation on the technique of comparing any lovely garden with *that* garden. The Dreamer can have the earthly paradise for aesthetic purposes without entering it in a narrative or allegorical sense. However, he is not finished with his metaphorical elevation of the garden of the Rose. "The spot was so delightful/it seemed to be heavenly," and at this point we have come as high as possible. The garden is now implicitly compared to the celestial paradise. The next four lines are ambiguous, but the sense seems to be "Though according to what I am told/there is no place in Paradise as good to be in, as it was/ [to be] in the garden [vergier] which made me so happy."

The point is that between the two uses of "vergier" (at ll. 633 and 642) for the garden, the narrator also implies comparison with the earthly and celestial paradises. The result, although never stated, is that this garden surpasses any of the paradise spots of which one can think. The poet is here summoning the image of the earthly paradise, which must have been in his mind as an artistic model, without identifying the garden with it. This association lends the garden of the Rose a certain imaginative acceptability and elegance, regardless of what we believe the "meaning" of the garden actually to be.

This technique of associating the earthly paradise and its venerable tradition with a secular or allegorical garden is a favorite device of Renaissance poets. And what happens to those Renaissance bowers or gardens so treated is precisely what happens to Guillaume de Lorris' garden of Delight late in Jean de Meung's part of the poem: they are condemned as false in spite of (or perhaps partly because of) their metaphorical relationship with the earthly paradise. They are condemned, as the garden of the Rose is, by the laws of Christianity.

Late in the *Roman de la Rose*, Genius makes an oration in the presence of Venus upon the duties of all men to live according to natural law, and according to fecund and eternal Nature. And Genius says that if a man lives a virtuous life, loving according to Nature and God (for Nature is a reflection of the Divine—and that idea is the key) then nothing will hinder him

* D'entrer ou parc dou champ joli. (19,935)

This Good Pasture, which is now described directly and indirectly for almost a thousand lines, is the reward for those who deserve it, and is obviously the celestial paradise. It is seen as a green meadow, with the Lamb leading the flock amid the joys of eternal springtime and daylight in a glistening, flowery landscape. Later (20,299) we learn that the wall around this Garden also has carvings upon it, and in fact it has most of the features we saw in the garden of the Rose. The difference is that this later Garden is the *real*

* From entering the place of the happy field.

garden; the early garden was "not only a copy, but that misleading kind of copy which the philosophers call *Schein* rather than *Erscheinung.* . . ."[70] As Lewis points out, this is how Jean de Meung "takes care" of courtly love; he not only implies it is wrong, but, from his Christian-Platonic point of view, says it is "unreal." To love openly and virtuously according to Nature, which imitates God, is to approach the condition of that superior garden, much elevated above the constricting and frivolous rules of courtly love which are symbolized by the garden of the Rose. The poet strains to describe the beauty of this place, and at times he sounds like Dante in the *Paradiso*: human speech and mind are unable to impart that which transcends human experience (20,374ff.). But after trying through comparisons and allusions to say that the Good Pasture is eternal, real and true and the garden of the Rose is passing, false and a fable, the narrator finds a concise way to make his point: remember only, he says,

> ⋇ Que qui la fourme et la matire
> Dou parc verrait bien pourrait dire
> Qu'onques en si bel paradis
> Ne fu fourmez Adans jadis.   (20,593-20,596)

Here the earthly paradise is introduced again by implication. This Good Pasture is more beautiful than any paradise since Adam was made. It is better, or more beautiful, because it is —we assume—the real paradise, superior in every way to

⋇ That whoever sees the form
And substance of the place, can truly say
That Adam was not created at an earlier time
In such a lovely paradise.

[70] Lewis, *Allegory*, p. 151.

that garden of the Rose which was only *like* the earthly paradise. The fact that the garden of the Rose even resembled the earthly paradise only made it more misleading and ultimately more worthy of condemnation.

The earthly paradise is used as an aesthetic model for the two important gardens, and it is also used as a touchstone for their reliability and veracity. Whatever is said to resemble the earthly paradise gains in beauty and acceptability; and whatever is shown to be superior to the earthly paradise automatically establishes itself as an ideal state of existence. The notion of the earthly paradise in the poem also introduces us to the problem of the beautiful-appearing garden of love which may not be what it seems—the outstanding characteristic of the enchanted gardens in the Renaissance epics.

The image of the earthly paradise haunts the *Roman de la Rose*, and the *Roman* haunts the literature of the succeeding centuries. Its allegories, its landscapes, its visions of love earthly and divine, left an indelible mark upon the imagination of the West. The *Roman* is the supreme example of the medieval poem preoccupied with love in a "paradise" setting; it sums up the artistic images of the earthly paradise as they appeared in didactic and courtly love poems and offers us an abstract of the problem such gardens will present in the Renaissance.

It is in the medieval verse-romances that we can see how the beautiful garden will actually appear within the structure of the Renaissance epics. Having examined the gardens in four such poems—*Thèbes, Floire et Blancheflor, Phillis et Flora*, and *Erec*—Faral concludes that although real enclosed medieval gardens may have had some impact on these passages, the most obvious influences are oriental sources, and "l'influence d'un souvenir vivant de la *Genèse*."[71] Indeed, when we allow for the differences in genre, date and place of composition, and for the classical influences such as Claudian, what Faral says for the romances would apply to many secular gardens in many medieval poems: "Il est remarquable qu'à la base de ces descriptions se trouve le souvenir du paradis terrestre, décrit d'abord dans la *Genèse*, puis, traditionnellement, par toute une série d'ecrivains dont M. Graf a groupé les passages intéressants à ce point de vue."[72] Faral refers to Graf's Appendix I where he gives selections from Christian treatments of the earthly paradise. Faral is correct when he assumes that these writers kept the orthodox view of the garden alive and influenced the poets we have been considering. As literature, this earthly paradise poetry certainly was not as popular as the later poems like the *Anticlaudianus* or the *Roman de la Rose* or the romances; but this poetry did capture and transmit the image of that garden in Eden and was responsible for the influence of that image in medieval literature.

V · CHRISTIAN LATIN PARADISES

Many and varied are the Christian accounts of the garden in Eden, as we can see from simply glancing at the *Index de Paradiso Terrestri* in Migne's *Patrologia Latina*.[73] Yet those poetic accounts which concern us in Latin and the vernacular can be treated in an orderly fashion, for these

---

[71] E. Faral, *Recherches sur les Sources Latines des Contes et de Romans Courtois du Moyen Age* (Paris, 1913), p. 372.

[72] *Ibid*. For Graf, see below, n. 74.

[73] *PL*, CCXIX, 67-70. Here are references to treatments in verse and prose by Christian writers under the categories "Ante Lapsum," "Per Lapsum," and "Post Lapsum."

texts[74] are not concerned so much with doctrine or with the position or nature of the earthly paradise as they are with evoking the image of that delightful (and instructive) garden. What is most remarkable is the assimilation of classical culture into Christian, for very often, Christian accounts of the earthly paradise reflect the scene, and echo the sound, of those Virgilian lines describing Elysium:

⁂ devenere locos laetos et amoena virecta
Fortunatorum Nemorum sedesque beatas.
(Aeneid, VI, 638-639)

Indeed, the garden of the new religion was associated with pagan gardens by some of the earliest Christian writers. In Chapter 47 of his *Apology,* Tertullian is intent on establishing that in reality pagans worshipped Christianity, though they did not know it, and to prove this he says pagan poets took their descriptions of the Elysian Fields from the earthly paradise. Justin Martyr, or the *Exhortations to the Greeks* commonly ascribed to Justin Martyr, says that Homer took from Moses the portrait of the garden of Alcinous. These statements, as Tertullian makes clear regarding his own, were meant to show that Christianity was older than pagan culture and therefore more worthy of

⁂ they came to a land of joy, the green pleasaunces and happy seats of the Blissful Groves.

[74] A. Graf, in his *Miti, Leggende e Superstizioni del Medio Evo* (Torino, 1892), vol. I, Appendix I, pp. 197-217, reprints twenty earthly paradise excerpts ranging from pseudo-Tertullian to Federico Frezzi. Graf gives almost no indications of where the passages come from; I have supplied the bibliographical data in the notes below. The compendium is helpful, however, for establishing the main line of descent for Christian Latin treatments of the earthly paradise.

belief.[75] However, in speaking of (the celestial) paradise, Tertullian gives himself away by designating it as a "locum divinae amoenitatis." Thus, regardless of what he says about pagan poets copying Christian "mysteries," it is obvious from the Virgilian ring to this phrase that Tertullian himself had a pagan text in mind.

This influence of the ancient literature upon the Christian, which Tertullian overtly denies but unconsciously reflects, appears throughout the early Christian poetry of the earthly paradise. Lest we assume too easily that the Middle Ages lost sight of the pagan world and only concentrated on Christian texts, let us note a small poem written by Theodulf of Orleans (*ca.* 760-821). In it one of the chief poets of the Carolingian Empire recommends reading the Church Fathers, and also

> Sedulius, Rutilus, Paulinus, Arator, Avitus,
> Et Fortunatus, tuque Juvence tonans,

as well as Prudentius. But he also recommends, as those in whom truth can be found under falsity, Virgil and "Naso loquax."[76] The traditions maintained in the ninth century were vital elsewhere, too. What is equally striking is that most of the Christian poets named by Theodulf are among those to whom we look for the best examples of earthly paradise poetry.

Perhaps the earliest piece of poetry describing the Christian earthly paradise is that strange and beautiful poem now almost certainly ascribed to Lactantius—*De Ave Phoenice.* The description of the happy land in the "distant east" was

---

[75] Patch (*Otherworld*, p. 135) has collected these passages most conveniently, though his reference for Tertullian should be *PL*, I, 520A.

[76] "De Libris Quos Legere Solebam," text in *PL*, CV, 331.

understood by all to be a portrait of the earthly paradise, and this section of the *Phoenix* surely influenced such obviously Christian earthly paradises as those in *De Judicio Domini* (Chapter viii), ascribed to Tertullian but probably written in the sixth century, and the Old English *Phoenix* which is attributed to Cynewulf.[77] The earthly paradises in the Latin *Phoenix* and *De Judicio Domini* can be regarded as fair examples of the standard portrait of paradise in early Christian literature. The weather is fair, springtime is perpetual, there is no suffering or disease, water flows from a spring, trees bear fruit, the grass is green. The *De Judicio Domini* spells out in greater detail the usual motifs of the trees, water, air and climate and emphasizes three motifs typical of many Christian descriptions of paradise. One of them, the marvelous odor of the spot, is stressed in conjunction with "cynamma" (cinnamon) and "amomum" (probably the Indian brush plant, from which an expensive balsam was made). The fragrance of the earthly paradise, not overly stressed in classical gardens, is much mentioned in Christian accounts. The other two conventional motifs found in the *De Judicio Domini* derive from the Bible.

According to the Vulgate, four rivers watered the garden in Eden: Phison, Gehon, Tigris and Euphrates. (In most modern translations the Tigris is rendered as the Hiddekel.) The pseudo-Tertullian poem says that a fountain in the

[77] There is a complete Latin text of the *Phoenice* in the Loeb Library *Minor Latin Poets*, tr. Duff and Duff, pp. 643-665; the section on the earthly paradise is in Graf, Appendix I, p. 205; also a Latin text with an English translation, an Old English text, and a lengthy introduction to Lactantius' poem in A. S. Cook, *The Old English Elene, Phoenix and Physiologus* (New Haven, 1919). A translation of the Old English poem can be found in C. W. Kennedy, *Early English Christian Poetry* (London, 1952). For the pseudo-Tertullian, see *PL*, II, 1,094-1,095.

garden divides into four streams ("Quattuor inde rigant partitas flumina terras"), and most descriptions of the earthly paradise make mention of the four rivers—usually around the trees or groves which have their prototypes in the Biblical Tree of Life and Tree of the Knowledge of Good and Evil.

The other motif in the *De Judicio Domini* which is always mentioned in Christian descriptions is the jewels of the earthly paradise. Phison flows round the land of Havilath, the land of gold, says the Vulgate:

⚹ Et aurum terrae illius optimum est; ibi
    invenitur bdellium, et lapis onychinus. (Genesis 2:12)

The pseudo-Tertullian poem says:

⚹ Inde nitet prasinus, illinc carbunculus ardet,
    Herbosaque viret praegrandis luce smaragdus;

The emerald and the carbuncle were to have a long career. All those medieval gardens and landscapes containing palaces and homes of gold and jewels had some authority in this Biblically inspired account (and others like it), as well as in Claudian's portrait of the castle of Venus.

Thus Genesis, in whatever account it was read, was the source for various standard motifs in the earthly paradise tradition. But the Bible was not the only model for the Christian accounts. In her *Cento*, Proba Falconia (fourth century) best reflects the classical influence on the earthly

⚹ And the gold of that land is the best; there is found bdellium and onyx stone.

⚹ there shines the *prasinus*, in that place burns the carbuncle, and the huge grassy green emerald glows with light. (The *prasinus* is a stone of a leek-green color.)

paradise, for her patchwork of Virgilian phrases in commentary on Biblical subjects aptly illustrates the great influence of the old literature on the new Christians. One example must suffice: when Proba comments on Genesis 2:15 ("And the Lord God took the man, and put him into the garden of Eden to dress it and to keep it") with *Aeneid*, VI, 639 ("fortunatorum nemorum sedesque beatas"), she diagrams for us the method of later Christian Latin poets.[78]

The most obvious classical influences appear in the works of that poet whom Theodulf called "desertissimus atque Christianissimus poetae"—the Spaniard Prudentius.[79] Virgil's Elysium is readily discernible behind his description of the earthly paradise (*Cathemerinon*, III, 101-110) which opens:

> ✕ tunc per amoena virecta jubet
> frondicomis habitare locis,

and closes with God's injunction not to touch the fruit,

> ✕ qui medio viret in nemore.[80]

The scene contains the standard elements of perpetual

> ✕ Then He bade man dwell in a leafy place,
> ranging over pleasant lawns.

> ✕ that grows in the midst of the wood.

[78] For a complete text of the *Cento Probae*, see Schenkl's edition in *CSEL*, XVI; for the earthly paradise excerpt, see Graf, Appendix I, p. 199.

[79] Theodulf, "De Ordine Baptismi," in *PL*, CV, 231.

[80] For a complete text of the *Cathemerinon*, see the Loeb Library *Prudentius*, tr. H. J. Thomson (Cambridge, Mass.-London, 1949), I, from which this translation is also taken. The earthly paradise in *Cath.*, III is also conveniently found in Graf, Appendix I, p. 199 and *PL*, LIX, 803-804; the garden in *Cath.*, V, in *PL*, LIX, 826-827. For texts of *Hamartigenia*, see Loeb edition above and, for good notes, the edition of J. Stam (Amsterdam, 1940).

spring, odors and beautiful meadows, and the specifically Christian motifs of the stream in four channels and the forbidden fruit. The whole description is ultimately modeled on Genesis, and there is no doubt as to its religious character. But there is also no doubt about the framing, Virgilian phrases; the "amoena virecta" and the "nemore" (from the *Fortunatorum Nemorum*) enclose the portrait of the Christian earthly paradise as effectively as they opened the description of the pagan Elysium in the *Aeneid*. Prudentius blends the best of both the worlds.[81]

These comments illustrate the fact that there were essentially conflicting strains running through even the most "orthodox" Christian accounts of the earthly (or its aesthetic relative, the celestial) paradise, strains which became more and more mixed as time went on. The inheritance of the classical legacies, or burdens, becomes clearer when we look at the earthly paradises of Christian-Latin poets of the fifth and sixth centuries. The poets and the earthly paradise passages in question are the following: there were three poets of Gaul, Claudius Marius Victor, rhetor at Marseilles who commented on Genesis 2:8 in the *Genesis* and the *Alethia*; Alcimus Ecdicius Avitus, Bishop of Vienne around 490 and author of a description of the garden in Eden in

---

[81] *Cathemerinon* (V, 113-124) and *Hamartigenia* (856ff.) portray the "land of the righteous" and the celestial paradise respectively. (For the purposes of literary study, I do not make a distinction between an earthly and a celestial paradise when descriptions of the latter are obviously modeled on accounts of the former.) What strikes us most about these passages is their pagan quality, and Stam glosses *Hamartigenia* (856) in part by stating that the pagans before Prudentius had shifted Elysium from under the ground to the heavens. That is the impression we receive—as if we were reading an account of the Elysium of Tibullus transferred to the upper spheres.

the beginning of the First Book (*De Initio Mundi*) of the five-book poem *De Mosaicae Historiae Gestis*; and Sollius Sidonius Apollinaris, Bishop of Clermont who wrote a sketch, pagan in tone but perhaps Christian in inspiration, of the garden of the sun in *Panegyric on Anthemius*. There is one African poet, perhaps the best Christian poet from Africa, Blossius Aemilius Dracontius, who has descriptions of the earthly paradise scattered through his *De Laudibus Dei*; and one Italian poet, Caelius Sedulius, of whom we know only that he was born in the early fifth century and in whose *Carmen Paschale* there is a sketch of the earthly paradise and of the paradise offered to the thief by Christ. Finally, there are two sixth-century poets who carry on elements of this earthly paradise tradition: Magnus Felix Ennodius, born in Arles, a relative of Boethius and author of an interesting poem with pagan overtones, *In Ingressu Horti*; and Arator, an Italian, who has left us an earthly paradise partially modeled on Sedulius in the *De Actibus Apostolorum*.[82]

The quality and spirit of these passages vary greatly. For instance, the pagan elements in Apollinaris, Ennodius

[82] For text of Victor, see excerpt in Graf, Appendix I, pp. 200-202 and *PL*, LXI, 943B; complete *Genesis* and *Alethia* in Schenkl's edition, *CSEL*, XVI.—For text of Avitus, see Graf, Appendix I, pp. 202-204 and *PL*, LIX, 328-329A.—For text of Sidonius, see Graf, Appendix I, pp. 205-206 and *PL*, LVIII, 654; also the Loeb Library *Sidonius Apollinaris*, tr. W. B. Anderson (Cambridge, Mass.-London, 1936), I, 42.—For text of Dracontius, *De Laudibus Dei*, I, 178ff., see Graf, Appendix I, pp. 199-200 and *PL*, LX, 704-706; also *De Laudibus Dei* I, Liber I, ed. J. F. Irwin (Philadelphia, 1942), p. 42; for *De Laudibus Dei*, I, 348ff., see *PL*, LX, 725 and Irwin, p. 40.—For text of Sedulius, see edition of J. Heumer, *CSEL*, X, 19-20, 130-131.—For text of Ennodius, see edition of W. Hartel, *CSEL*, VI, 571.—For text of Arator, see edition of A. P. McKinlay, *CSEL*, LXXII, 81.

and Arator stand out. These poets seem closer to Apollinaris' contemporary in Gaul, Ausonius (who was a nominal Christian), than to a poet like Prudentius; and it has been demonstrated how Apollinaris and Ennodius continued the epithalamic tradition, and all it implied, of Claudian.[83] Both Ennodius and Arator imitated the Christian poems of Sedulius, but they concentrated on the classical qualities rather than the religious ones.

The earthly paradises fall into several groups; for instance, the passages in the most "orthodox" poets, Victor, Avitus, and Dracontius (*De Laudibus*, I, 178ff.), all share certain characteristics. In their gardens, besides fruit, grass, flowers, trees, and perpetual springtime, we find the four rivers as well as the gems. For the most part, the descriptions are traditional and contain the motifs we noticed in the pseudo-Tertullian poem. The style of these passages is generally ornate and rich, with lists of flowers and descriptions of the fine climate swelling the verse. Also, the repetitiveness of the passages creates a sense of an overripe richness which mirrors the essence of the garden itself. Of course, it is not simply the traditional and Biblical motifs which create this lushness. In Victor, and to a lesser extent in Avitus, there is a great deal of enjambment. Line spills over into line, creating the image of fecundity and excess. The richness of these passages also comes from the resonance achieved by classical tags as well as from the traditional diction and serpentine syntax. As Raby remarks of Victor, "the *Georgics* provided him with flowers to gather,"[84] but phrases like

[83] Lewis, *Allegory*, pp. 76-77.
[84] F. J. E. Raby, *History of Christian Latin Poetry* (Oxford, 1927), p. 77.

"nemoris Paradisus amoeni" show us he knew more Virgil than the *Georgics*.

The Virgilian echoes lend a depth of tone to most of the Christian earthly paradises. And in some of the descriptions, the classical background becomes the whole scene. In Sedulius' passage on the earthly paradise (*Carmen Paschale*, I, 53-59) we hear nothing of gems or four rivers or Tree of Life or fruit; instead there is a

> ⁑ amoena virecta
> Florentum semper nemorum sedesque beatas.   (53-54)

and in *Carmen*, V, Christ describes paradise to the Good Thief as a place

> ⁑ ubi flore perenni
> Gramineus blanditur ager, nemorumque voluptas
> Inrigius nitritur aquis.   (222-224)

The last phrase of line 223 is almost an emblem of the amalgamation process, for it looks like a combination of the Virgilian "Nemorum sedesque beatas" and the Vulgate's "paradisum voluptatis" (Genesis 2:8).[85]

> ⁑ lovely plain
> of ever flowering groves and blessed seats.

> ⁑ where the grassy field
> is caressed with ever blooming flowers, and the delightful groves are nourished by plentiful waters.

[85] Even Dracontius, whose earthly paradise in *De Laudibus Dei*, I, 178ff., was "orthodox" as to motifs and spare in style compared to Avitus and Victor can, in *De Laudibus Dei*, III, describe the Celestial paradise in purely Virgilian terms:

> Judicio, Deus alme, tuo detur inde triumphus,
> Inter odoratos flores et amoena virecta
> Ad nemus aethereum veniam, sedesque beatas. (678-780)

The garden of Sedulius, in *Carmen*, I, 53ff., inspired Arator and Ennodius, and both imitated his Virgilian terminology—Arator most evidently in an avowedly Christian poem. In Ennodius we have a strange situation: here, Sedulius' Christian earthly paradise (modeled on Virgil) is the inspiration for the non-Christian "paradise" (composed by a Christian)—a garden which obviously anticipates the "secular" paradises of later medieval literature.

However Sidonius Apollinaris, a year before he was made Bishop, wrote a *Panegyric on Anthemius* whose First Book contains the most puzzling passage of all (ll. 407-419). As in the poems of Lactantius, the pseudo-Tertullian, Dracontius, and Avitus, this description of the garden of the sun starts with the formula "Est locus. . . ." Here is perpetual springtime, flowers of many sorts, and marvelous odors (myrrh and frankincense among others). There is also a reference to cinnamon and the phoenix, clearly recalling the poem ascribed to Lactantius. Finally, the home of Aurora, gold plated and covered with pearls, is touched upon. The opening formula, the odors (especially the Biblically hallowed myrrh and frankincense) and the phoenix reference, are all—if not here, at least elsewhere—connected with the Christian earthly paradise. Yet the classical setting and mood, and the jeweled house (though jewels and gold themselves are found in Revelation 21:18-21) all suggest poets from Ovid to Claudian. This is not a Christian poem, nor was it addressed to a Christian; but

[Then at your Final Judgment, blessed Lord, may the sign of victory be given, so that I may come through the fragrant flowers and the pleasant lawns to the heavenly groves and the blessed seats.] The text is in *PL*, LX, 899-900; I have amended "vireta" to "virecta." This is indeed the Elysium of Virgil transferred from under the ground to the heavens.

it was written by a man who would be a bishop soon and be canonized after his death.[86] The garden offers us an example of the strength of the pagan culture in the early Middle Ages among Christians and non-Christians alike, but the description must also owe something, as later nonreligious medieval gardens did, to the Christian earthly paradise tradition.

The paradise described by a Christian need not be a Christian paradise; like the gardens of Apollinaris or Ennodius, it might be a lovely landscape after Virgil or Tibullus. Most often, however, the Christian earthly paradise was the stated theme with strong classical overtones, as in Prudentius, Sedulius, Arator, and even Dracontius. And where overt classical echoes were not heard, the lush, fragrant and bejeweled gardens of the "orthodox" descriptions mingled motifs from the Bible with the embellishments from the imagination.

The descriptions of those poets most influenced by antiquity were the most "classical" in that they were stylistically the least elaborate. Like Virgil's description of Elysium, these passages tended to sum up the earthly paradise in a few evocative lines. Those who modeled themselves on the Bible (or previous "orthodox" accounts) had no such august literary check imposed upon them. They were free to expand, and they did. As time went on, what we have termed the "orthodox" type of description tended to dominate. The classical echoes become less noticeable, and when they occur

[86] See Loeb *Sidonius*, tr. Anderson, introduction, lii; Erich Auerbach, in his *Literary Language and Its Public in Late Latin Antiquity and in the Middle Ages*, tr. R. Manheim, Bollingen Series, LXXIV (New York, 1965), 195, is willing to consider Sidonius (and Claudian) as "certain Christians."

in later centuries, it seems a poet is echoing only a classically inspired early Christian poet and not the ancient source itself.

Toward the height of the Middle Ages, the descriptions of the earthly paradise become more numerous and more conventional. In the twelfth century Bernardus Silvestris, in *De Mundi Universitate*, and Godfrey of Viterbo, in *Pantheon*, and Alexander Neckham, a century later in *De Laudibus Divinae Sapientiae*, all present us with traditional portraits of the earthly paradise.[87] According to Bernardus and Godfrey, the garden is in the east and full of many flowers, fine odors, and water. Godfrey specifically refers to the Tree of Life, gems and gold, the four rivers, fruit, and the fact the inhabitants of the earthly paradise cannot die— a point not much stressed in previous poetic accounts. Godfrey's description is very Biblically oriented and compares with Bernardus' as the pseudo-Tertullian poem compared with the *Phoenix*: traditional detail as opposed to suggestive generalities.

Alexander Neckham gives a conventional account stressing the fruit, water, and clear air of the earthly paradise. He adds a touch which echoes much classical and Christian garden poetry of the past (and anticipates accounts of the future) when he says the "apex paradisi" reaches to the sphere of the moon. Neckham reports that paradise escaped the Flood and was the home of the prophets Enoch and Elias. These are ancient corollaries to the proposition that

---

[87] For Bernardus' paradise in *De Mundi Universitate*, I, iii, 16-17, see edition of C. S. Barach and J. Wrobel (Innsbruck, 1876), I, 24-25; for text of Godfrey, *Pantheon*, I, see edition of J. Pistorius, 3rd. ed., B. G. Struve (Ratisbon, 1726), II, 24, 58; for text in Neckham, *De Laudibus Divinae Sapientiae*, V, 35ff., see edition of T. Wright, Roll Series, XXXIV (London, 1863), 441. All these texts are cited and commented on in Patch, *Otherworld*, p. 151.

the earthly paradise was above harm and terrestrial and mortal imperfection. Neckham is also interesting because he maintains some of the classical echoes we have noticed throughout the Christian descriptions:

> ✻ Hunc spaciosa locum generosaque vitis amoenat,
> Et nitidi fontes fontiferumque nemus.

In his comment on the Flood, he includes a reference to Deucalion, perhaps the first time a classical allusion, as opposed to an "echo" or tag from classical literature, is used in a Christian description of the earthly paradise. We are approaching the Renaissance and its overt integration, or attempts at integration, of classical and Christian material.[88]

There are also vernacular accounts in various tongues which parallel in date of composition many of the secular medieval gardens discussed above. Though some of these vernacular accounts of the earthly paradise draw inspiration from Latin works, they all have common traits which set them apart from the Latin versions. Most important is the impression that the earthly paradise is absolutely unobtainable, that it is irrevocably lost. Hitherto we have noticed that Christian Latin poets saw the earthly paradise as high on a mountain and/or remote in the east. But there was always a sense of the garden's approximate position, always an awareness, perhaps because one was writing in Latin, that

> ✻ The broad and abundant vine, and the sparkling
> fountains, and the grove full of fountains,
> make this place pleasant.

[88] For earthly paradise descriptions of a distinctly classical flavor, see the *De Ornatu Mundi*, *PL*, CLXXI, 1,235-1,238, and the *Passio Sanctae Agnetis*, *PL*, CLXXI, 1,309D-1,310A, printed among the works of Hildebert of Lavardin; for a more "orthodox" account, see the *Hymnus de Gloria Paradisi* of Peter Damian, *PL*, CXLV, 861 *et seq.*

one was somehow in a tradition which maintained contact with the blessed spot. But in the vernacular accounts of the earthly paradise, we receive a very different impression and that is why I say we sense the garden is "irrevocably" lost. One feels that in the decline from the tongue of Church, learning and tradition, to the language of the people, there is a corresponding dip in mankind's hopes of seeing or (actually) attaining this happy place. We are slowly submerged in the undercurrent of despair that ran through so much of popular medieval piety.

In certain gardens and landscapes in Roman poetry, we asserted that the external world was an emblem for a man's inner being, and something of the same process is noticeable in the medieval vernacular accounts of the earthly paradise. Because the spot is *so* remote, it has more than ever become a landscape of the mind, a place in the topography of the soul. Of course Church writers long held "mystical" or allegorical interpretations of the earthly paradise, but those were the views and disputes of learned doctors and saints, and their attitudes rarely found their way into Christian Latin poetic accounts of the garden. Now a simpler, more ancient strain of emotion shows through the Christian vernacular descriptions—a longing for the earthly paradise made more poignant by a radical sense of spiritual alienation.

Graf has collected some relevant vernacular passages: a selection from *L'Image du Monde*, a work composed around 1247 in couplets by Gautier de Metz; a passage from the enormous, and at 33,472 lines, unfinished *Weltkronik* of Rudolf von Ems (d. *ca.* 1254); and the earthly paradises from two Dutch poems, the *Spieghel Historiael*, written 1282-1283 or 1289-1290 by Jacob van Maerlant, and

Der leken Spieghel, composed between 1325-1330 by Maerlant's follower, Jan van Boendale.[89] All the accounts place the earthly paradise in the east and all follow tradition in speaking of the four rivers. All but the *Weltkronik* speak of a fountain in the garden; the *Image du Monde* mentions the Tree of Life and fruit; while the Dutch poems stress the lack of wind or rain, heat or cold, hunger or thirst, and the characteristic of fine, clear air. *Der leken Spieghel* also speaks of precious stones and names the sapphire, while the *Spieghel Historiael* perpetuates the legend of Enoch and Elias as inhabitants of the earthly paradise. An important detail all of the poems stress is that animals inhabit the garden:

     * "bestes creuses et fieres" . . .
        "dar in sô vil gewürmes lît/und tiere" . . .
        "elken cruden diere."

These animals have no precedent in the Christian earthly paradise tradition as handed down by poets, and their presence seems to symbolize the exotic and awesome character of the place. The "gewürmes" in the *Weltkronik* is obviously a reference to the serpent found in gardens of

* cruel and wild beasts . . . wherein lay such evil snakes and animals . . . every wild animal.

[89] Graf, Appendix I, pp. 211-216, gives the passages on the earthly paradise and, in this case, the appropriate bibliographical references. He also includes an excerpt from the mid-fourteenth-century verse narrative *Beaudoin de Sebourg.*

    L'Image du Monde was taken from the *Imago Mundi* of Honorius d'Autun; the *Spieghel Historiael* from the encyclopedic *Speculum Historiale* of Vincent of Beauvais. Graf gives Jan Deckers as the author of *Der leken Spieghel;* on this point, see J. Te Winkel, *Geschiedenis der Nederlandsche Letterkunde van Middeleewen Rederijkerstyd* (Haarlem, 1922), II, p. 3, n. 2.

delight since *Gilgamesh,* most notably of course in the Bible account of the Fall; but the word can easily be generalized to include the spectre of a dragon. The animals and monsters in these accounts are the phantoms of the popular imagination; they serve to measure the extent of the Fall into fear and loneliness, and man's sense of distance from the place of that Fall. And when in the *Image du Monde,* Gautier de Metz says, "No man can find this place," he sums up simply the general mood of wonder and despair.

HERE for the first time, we notice how things are beginning to turn inward; how the earthly paradise, no longer securely anchored by faith and a rigid literary tradition to a place in the "real" world, will become increasingly a general symbol in the mind of man for the soul of man. We can note, in short, the origins of that process whereby Milton's traditional Eden will become finally "A paradise within thee, happier far." It is also interesting to note that those other Renaissance paradises, the enchanted gardens, will continue to reflect the dual qualities of magnificence and malevolence found in these medieval vernacular accounts. I am not claiming that these gardens in any way "influenced" those later ones. Where the image of Circe has been imposed on Eve, much greater, and more obvious, forces are at work. But in these melancholic accounts of Eden, we begin to see how the garden could be a place of bliss, perhaps, but not necessarily of blessedness.

VI · SUMMARY

Apart from the tremendous store of common descriptive motifs, what have our investigations of special or blessed gardens revealed? It seems that common to all the accounts

—whether Greek versions of the Golden Age, Horace's writings on retirement, Virgil's description of Elysium, or Claudian's of Venus' bower; whether medieval passages on a Court of Love, or Nature's realm, or Christian poets' versions of the earthly paradise—are two basic ideas. The place is remote in space or time (or both), and it involves some ideal of love or harmony. These twin themes, the first "external" and concerned with the place's "geography," the second "internal" and related to its way of life, are found in every account. It is a beautiful place because that is the best symbol for man's inner need and desire for peace and harmony; it is lost or far away or fortified or, as we shall see, false, because that is the only way to convey man's daily awareness of the impossibility of attaining his ideal.

These complementary themes of yearning and nonpossession, desire and inaccessibility, are imaged in a stylistic trait common to most of the garden descriptions. Patch has labeled this trait the "negative formula":[90] "there is no cold or heat," "nor can the fruit die nor the trees wither," "neither frost nor hail touch this place." It is the same kind of stylistic technique used by a great tradition of Western mystics, most remarkably Dionysius the pseudo-Areopagite, to "describe" the essence of God. Here is a sample passage from Dionysius' treatise *The Mystical Theology*:

> . . . nor is It kingship or wisdom; nor is It
> one, nor is It unity, nor is It Godhead or
> Goodness; nor is It a Spirit, as we understand
> the term, since It is not Sonship or Fatherhood[91]

---

[90] Patch, *Otherworld*, p. 12. Though he notes this technique fairly often, he never inquires into its significance.

[91] This is an example picked at random from Chapter v. See *Dionysius The Areopagite on the Divine Names and The Mystical Theology*, tr. C.

I am not trying to interpret the earthly paradise "mystically" at all. I only want to claim that Dionysius and the poets of the gardens use a common stylistic technique to a similar, though not identical, end. Both are trying to express the inexpressible: Dionysius is attempting to convey the nature of God; our poets are groping for a verbal image of the perfect life. And in order to reflect in limited, recalcitrant words what they see directly with the mind's eye, the poets must resort to a technique which says what the site and nature of the good life are *not*, as well as to descriptions of what it is. And this very spectacle, of words striving through traditional images and the negative formula to encompass an inner ideal, stylistically mirrors those central themes of earthly paradise literature—the place's desirability and inaccessibility.

The situation reflected in earthly paradise accounts is simply another version of the human predicament of being torn between what one wants and what one can have. Perhaps this is why that form of the earthly paradise, the false paradise or enchanted garden, appealed to some poets of the Renaissance. As symbol and setting, the false paradise embodies the split between what seems and what is; it looks like the true earthly paradise, but in the end it is not. It looks like the image of all a man thinks he has sought in his spiritual wanderings, but in the end it is the scene wherein he learns he was wrong; where he learns that his inner wishes were only the illusions a man creates for himself, and through which he must pass in his quest for true inner harmony, for a true earthly paradise existence.

E. Rolt, *Translations of Christian Literature,* Series I. Greek Texts (New York-London, 1920), p. 200.

BEFORE examining the false paradises, however, we shall concern ourselves with Dante's true earthly paradise. Dante, like Milton, is a poet of that "historical" Eden, which was "real" until Adam and Eve fell. In the *Divina Commedia* and *Paradise Lost*, we are offered versions of the "true" paradise in its pristine state; versions which frame the enchanted gardens of the Renaissance, and provide the standard by which those gardens are ultimately judged.

BIBLIOGRAPHY · CHAPTER ONE

I. THE WORD

For extended discussions of the word "paradise" and its changing meanings, see the articles under "Ciel" by Bernard in *Dictionnaire de Théologie Catholique*, II, 2, 247ff.; and Leclerq in *Dictionnaire d'Archeologie Chrétienne et de Liturgie*, XIII, 2, 1587ff.; and under "paradeisos" by Jeremias in *Theologisches Wörterbuch zum Neuen Testament*, V, 763-771. See also under the heading "Paradise" in *A Dictionary of the Bible*, ed. J. Hastings, 5 vols. (New York, 1900); *Encyclopedia Biblica*, ed. T. K. Cheyne and J. S. Black, 4 vols. (London, 1899); *Catholic Biblical Encyclopedia*, ed. J. Heinmuller and K. Sullivan (New York, 1956); and *The Interpreter's Bible*, ed. G. A. Buttrick *et al.*, 4 vols. (New York, 1962) under Genesis 2:8 *et seq.* And for instances of the word "Paradisus" in Latin, see *Totius Latinitatis Lexicon*, ed. Aegidius Forcellini *et al.* (Prati, 1868), Vol. IV.

II. THE GOLDEN AGE

On the Golden Age and related ideas, see A. O. Lovejoy and G. Boas, *Contributions to the History of Primitivism, Primitivism and Related Ideas in Antiquity* (Baltimore, 1935), pp. 291-303. There is also relevant material in P. H. Epps, "The Golden Age," *Cl.J.*, 29 (1933-1934), pp. 292-296; H. C. Baldry, "Who Invented the Golden Age," *CQ*, New Series 2 (1951-1952), pp. 81-92; see also his "Hesiod's Five Ages," *JHI*, 17 (1956), pp. 553-554, in answer to J. G. Griffiths, "Archaeology and Hesiod's Five Ages" in the same volume, pp. 108-119; and Griffiths' reply, "Did Hesiod Invent the 'Golden Ages,' " *JHI*, 19 (1958), pp. 91-93. H. M. Hayes, *Notes on the Works and Days of Hesiod* (Chicago, 1918), particularly pp. 91-92 on the Golden Age and references in later literature, and pp. 212-213, Appendix V, on the Golden Age and Cronos; also Petriconi, "Die Verlorenen Paradiese," pp. 172ff., and Ladner, *Reform*, p. 13 and Addenda, p. 491, for bibliography.

For the survival of the Golden Age motif into the Renaissance, see P. Meissner, "Das Goldene Zeitalter in der Englischen Renaissance," *Anglia*, 59 (1935), pp. 351-367; E. Lipsker, *Der Mythos vom goldenen Zeitalter in den Schäferdichtungen Italiens, Spaniens und*

Frankreichs zur zeit der Renaissance, Inaugural-Dissertation (Berlin, 1933), though this is mainly a collection of relevant texts. There is a wonderful essay by Johan Huizinga in *Men and Ideas: History, the Middle Ages, the Renaissance*, tr. by J. S. Holmes and H. van Marle, intro. by B. F. Hoselitz (Eyre and Spottiswoode, London, 1960), pp. 77-96, "Historical Ideals of Life," which treats the influence of the pastoral and Golden Age ideals on the Renaissance. Finally, the reader must consult Harry Levin's fine essay, "The Golden Age and the Renaissance," in *Literary Views: Critical and Historical Essays*, ed. Carroll Camden, Published for the William Marsh Rice University by the University of Chicago Press (1964), pp. 1-14. This is perhaps the best succinct treatment of the subject.

There is also valuable material in F. Cumont's *Afterlife in Roman Paganism* (New Haven, 1922), esp. Chapter viii which, like the Golden Age, bears on the classical antecedents of the Christian earthly paradise; on the Millennium, which provides mythic and philosophical background for the "paradise" literature later on, see Eliade, *Myth of Eternal Return*, pp. 120ff., and in Ladner, *Reform*, pp. 10-16 and his extensive bibliography.

III. CLASSICAL GARDENS

There is an enormous literature concerned with gardens, landscapes, and paradises (not to speak of Nature); all one can do is indicate what seem to be some of the best critical and scholarly works on the subject. Certainly the most important recent investigation of the garden in literature is Chapter x of E. R. Curtius' *European Literature and the Latin Middle Ages*, tr. W. R. Trask, Bollingen Series, XXXVI (New York, 1953), for in tracing the *topos* of the *locus amoenus*, Curtius ranges from the earliest classical texts down through the Renaissance. On Greek literature, with a framework including poets of the nineteenth century, there is an interesting essay by A. Parry, "Landscape in Greek Poetry," in *YCS*, 15 (1957), pp. 3-29. The recent study by J. J. Wilhelm, *The Cruelest Month: Spring, Nature and Love in Classical and Medieval Lyrics* (New Haven, 1965) provides acute analyses of texts from the *Vigil of Venus* down through the lyrics of the *stil novisti*; also a very helpful bibliography. On particular topics the following are useful: P.

Demetz's "The Elm and the Vine: Notes Toward the History of a Marriage Topos," *PMLA*, 73 (1958), pp. 521-532; T. M. Greene's "Spenser and the Epithalamic Tradition," *CL*, 9 (1957), pp. 215-228; A. S. Cook's "The House of Sleep: A Study in Comparative Literature," *MLN*, 5 (1890), pp. 5-11.

Though more specific references are given below, A. D. Scaglione's *Nature and Love in the late Middle Ages* (Berkeley, 1963), and the articles of E. G. Kern, "The Gardens in the *Decameron* Cornice," *PMLA*, 66 (1951), pp. 505-523, and I. Silver, "Ronsard's Reflections on Cosmogony and Nature," *PMLA*, 79 (1964), pp. 219-233, esp. n. 49, include much information on the Renaissance use of gardens and view of Nature.

For the use of landscape in English Renaissance literature, see K. W. Scoular's *Natural Magic: Studies in the presentation of Nature in English poetry from Spenser to Marvell* (Oxford, 1965); and particularly the incisive essay by M. Mack, "A Poet in His Landscape: Pope at Twickenham" in *From Sensibility to Romanticism: Essays Presented to Frederick A. Pottle*, ed. F. W. Hilles and H. Bloom (New York, 1965), pp. 3-29. See particularly pp. 9ff., and the studies cited there, especially M.-S. Røstvig, *The Happy Man: Studies in the Metamorphoses of a Classical Ideal*, 2 vols. (Oslo, 1954, 1958).

The pastoral, in all its variations, has been one of the most important vehicles for the transmission of landscapes and "ideal" natural settings throughout European literature. For an adequate account of pastoral literature, with excellent bibliographies, see the article by J. E. Congleton in *EPP*, pp. 603-606. For the pastoral in classical literature, see Curtius, *Literature*, esp. pp. 190ff., and Wilhelm, *Cruelest Month*, *passim*. For medieval and Renaissance pastoral poetry, see M. I. Gerhardt, *La Pastorale: Essai d'Analyse Littéraire* (Assen, 1950); the study covers France, Italy and Spain. For English literature, there is the anthology, with a fine introduction, *English Pastoral Poetry: From the Beginnings to Marvell*, ed. F. Kermode (London, 1952); also the broad and stimulating work of W. Empson, *Some Versions of Pastoral* (London, 1936). Shorter studies include the scattered articles of R. Poggioli, "The Oaten Flute," *HLB*, 11 (1957), pp. 147-184; "The Pastoral of the Self," *Daedalus*, 88 (1959), pp. 687-699; "Naboth's Vineyard or the Pastoral View of the Social

Order," *JHI*, 24 (1963), pp. 3-24. For a review of theories of the pastoral, citing these works and others, see the perceptive article of R. Magowan, "Fromentin and Jewett: Pastoral Narrative in the Nineteenth Century," *CL*, 16 (1964), pp. 331-337; also H. M. Richmond's " 'Rural Lyricism': A Renaissance Mutation of the Pastoral," *CL*, 16 (1964), pp. 193-210. And for insights into the role of the pastoral in Renaissance culture, see Huizinga's "Historical Ideals of Life" in *Men and Ideas*, esp. pp. 83ff. Finally, see *The Pastoral Elegy*, ed. T. P. Harrison, Jr. (Austin, Texas, 1939), an anthology of the elegy, with good notes and an introduction, from Theocritus to Matthew Arnold.

IV. MEDIEVAL GARDENS

Among the many studies of medieval poetry and prose, I have found the following to be most helpful (specific references on particular writers will be given below): F. J. E. Raby's monumental study *A History of Secular Latin Poetry*, 2 vols. (Oxford, 1934), particularly Volume II; C. S. Lewis' *The Allegory of Love* (first pub., 1936; rev. 1938). (I have used the Galaxy Book edition [New York, 1958]), and for the style and language of medieval literature, Curtius', *Literature* and Erich Auerbach's *Literary Language & Its Public in Late Latin Antiquity and in The Middle Ages*, tr. R. Mannheim, Bollingen Series, LXXIV (New York, 1965).

On the topic of gardens, Wilhelm, *Cruelest Month*, is valuable, as is the work of H. R. Patch; his valuable *The Otherworld according to Descriptions in Medieval Literature*, esp. Chapters vi on "Allegory" and vii on "The Romances" can be supplemented with his study of recurrent motifs and dominant themes and genres in "Some Elements in Mediaeval Descriptions of the Otherworld," *PMLA*, 33 (1918), pp. 601-643, and his *The Goddess Fortuna in Mediaeval Literature* (Cambridge, Mass., 1927). There is a potentially misleading but stimulating article by D. W. Robertson, Jr., "The Doctrine of Charity in Mediaeval Literary Gardens: A Topical Approach through Symbolism and Allegory," *Speculum*, 26 (1951), pp. 24-29, whose extremes have been modified somewhat by Robertson in his *A Preface to Chaucer: Studies in Medieval Perspectives* (Princeton, 1962), p. 92, n. 67. Robertson and B. F. Huppé have applied the exegetical methods of medieval Churchmen to the gardens in the *Parliament of Fowles* and the *Book of the Duchess* in *Fruyt and Chaf, Studies in Chaucer's Allegory* (Princeton, 1963). For a book on the assimilation of classical culture by medieval monastic culture, see the fine study by J. Leclerq, O.S.B., *The Love of Learning and the Desire for God*, tr. C. Misrahi, Mentor Omega Book (New York, 1961); as Leclerq shows (pp. 136ff.), the treatment of the earthly paradise affords an excellent occasion to observe this process.

On the subject of courtly love, one should consult, in addition to some of the works cited above, the succinct article by T. A. Kirby in the *EPP*, pp. 156-158, which has a good bibliography (and which may be supplemented by A. H. Schutz' article on *Provençal Poetry*, pp. 677-680, in the same volume). As guides to the use of the garden and landscape in courtly love and Romance literature in general, older accounts by W. A. Neilson, *The Origin and Sources of the Court of Love* (Boston, 1899), E. Faral, *Recherches sur les Sources Latines des Contes et Romans Courtois du Moyen Age* (Paris, 1913), and E. B. Fowler, *Spenser and the Courts of Love* (Menasha, 1921) are still helpful. See also Patch, *Otherworld*, pp. 195ff. and Wilhelm, *Cruelest Month*, esp. pp. 203-230 on the troubadours.

On Alain de Lille, see Raby, *Secular Latin Poetry*, II, 15-18, and Lewis, *Allegory*, 98ff.

On Jean de Hautville, see Raby, *Secular Latin Poetry*, II, 100ff., Patch, *Otherworld*, 181, and Lewis, Allegory, 109-111.

On the *Roman de la Rose*, see Patch, *Otherworld*, pp. 99-100 for motifs and sources, with a standard bibliography; one should consult the good chapter by Lewis, *Allegory* (iii) for sound critical comment; and for a full, if wooden, discussion of literary antecedents, E. Langlois' *Origines et Sources du Roman de La Rose* (Paris, 1890), Chapters ii-iv.

On courtly love, with reference to Chaucer particularly, see Robertson, *Preface to Chaucer*, Chapter v, "Some Medieval Doctrines of Love," pp. 391-503.

V. CHRISTIAN-LATIN PARADISES

On the subject of medieval Christian-Latin poetry, I have found Curtius, *Literature*, Chapter x; Patch, *Otherworld*, Chapter v, and

Corcoran, *Milton's Paradise*, Chapter iii most helpful. In English the standard history of this subject, to which I am most indebted, is F. J. E. Raby's *History of Christian Latin Poetry* (Oxford, 1927). See also E. S. Duckett, *Latin Writers of the Fifth Century* (New York, 1930), and F. A. Wright and T. A. Sinclair, *A History of Later Latin Literature* (London, 1931).

On the *Phoenix*, see the Introduction by A. S. Cook to his *The Old English Elene, Phoenix and Physiologus* (New Haven, 1919), and for a comparison of the Latin and Old English poems, O. F. Emerson's study in *RES*, II (1926), 18-31. On the Latin poem, see Patch, *Otherworld*, pp. 137-138, and Raby, *Christian Latin Poetry*, p. 15 and n. 2. For the eleventh-century manuscripts of a late Old English version containing an earthly paradise, see Cook, *Old English*, pp. 128-132. For a detailed study of ancient *Phoenix* literature, see the study by J. Hubaux and M. Leroy, *Le Mythe du Phénix dans les littératures Grecque et Latine* (Paris, 1939). For references to the Phoenix in Renaissance literature (Tasso, Du Bartas, Marino, Vondel, Milton) as well as its role in antiquity, see T. M. Greene's study, *The Descent from Heaven: A Study in Epic Continuity* (New Haven and London, 1963), pp. 397-399.

For a brief discussion of motifs in the *De Judicio Domini*, see Patch, *Otherworld*, p. 137.

On Proba and the Cento tradition, see Raby, *Christian Latin Poetry*, p. 16, and Patch, *Otherworld*, p. 138, for garden motifs.

On Prudentius, see Wilhelm, *Cruelest Month*, pp. 63-73, esp. pp. 70ff. on landscapes; also, in general, see Raby, *Christian Latin Poetry*, pp. 44-71. For a general survey and select bibliography on Prudentius, see B. Peebles, *The Poet Prudentius* (New York, 1951).

For commentary and general bibliography on Victor, see Raby, *Christian Latin Poetry*, p. 77, and Coli, *Paradiso Dantesco*, p. 173.

For Avitus, see Raby, *Christian Latin Poetry*, pp. 77-79, and Coli, *Paradiso Dantesco*, p. 175.

For Sidonius, see Raby, *Christian Latin Poetry*, pp. 79-82; and the stylistic comments by Auerbach, *Literary Language*, pp. 195ff. and 255ff.

For commentary on Dracontius, see Raby, *Christian Latin Poetry*, pp. 96-99.

For Sedulius, Raby, *Christian Latin Poetry*, pp. 108-110.

Ennodius is treated by Raby, *Christian Latin Poetry*, pp. 115-117, and Arator on pages 117-120.

On all of these poets, see Patch, *Otherworld*, pp. 138-140, for a brief discussion of landscape and garden motifs.

On Bernardus Silvestris, see for commentary Coli, *Paradiso Dantesco*, pp. 177ff., and Raby, *Christian Latin Poetry*, p. 297.

On Godfrey of Viterbo, see Raby, *Christian Latin Poetry*, pp. 291-292.

On Neckham, see commentary in Raby, *Christian Latin Poetry*, pp. 379-385, esp. 381ff.; and Coli, *Paradiso Dantesco*, pp. 177ff.

CHAPTER TWO

Dante

THAT a landscape or garden has been traditionally used to image the ideals, or condition, of a soul is an assertion substantiated by many of our observations. If this statement were true of no other work, it could be amply demonstrated with reference to the greatest poem devoted to chronicling the soul—the *Divina Commedia*. For again and again, Dante gives us a landscape or prospect whose physical characteristics provide an index to the spiritual or moral level of life. Setting constantly implies significance.

The movement of the poem is the movement of Christianity itself, from a wilderness to a City. The wilderness is the first of those significant landscapes—the very opening scene of the poem (*Inf.* I). Here the "selva oscura" (2), the "selva selvaggia e aspra e forte" (5), is a landscape wherein the soul is lost and confused. It is the thicket of the mind out of which there is no clear path. Though this scene is as well known as any in literature, we must note it once again; for, to paraphrase Yeats, it is where all the ladders start, those which lead up as well as down.

However, the tangled wood is not the only feature of this opening landscape; there is also the "colle" (13) which the pilgrim tries to climb. This hill, later referred to by Virgil as the "dilettoso monte" (77), is bathed in the light of the Good Friday morning and rears itself above the dark woods and empty plain (29). It is the mount of virtuous joy which man must ascend and obviously prefigures the mountain of Purgatory. Yet this hill is denied the pilgrim by the three beasts, and Dante begins now to learn that the way up is the way down; that to overcome sin the sinner must pass through and understand sin. These lessons are, of course, all in the future and, indeed, form the matter of the *Inferno* and *Purgatorio*. But the topography of the first half of Canto I projects symbolically the whole inner drama of the poem. It even projects prototypes of the dominant landscape motifs—wooded darkness and soaring light.

The next landscape description is brief, but it affords us another prototype—the castle in Limbo's green field (IV, 106-120). The castle, citadel of reason and creative human endeavor, is surrounded by a little river. Although their exact meaning has long been debated, what is interesting to us is that the castle of Limbo is the first of so many walled and buttressed edifices, the first of so many symbols, whether dedicated to good or evil, of the City. The setting is a

[*] prato di fresca verdura (111)

which the old commentator Benvenuto rightly noted was similar to scenes in the *Aeneid* and *Odyssey*.[1] Here Dante gives the pagan poets a dwelling place which approximates the best they portrayed in their poems. They live in an Elysium because Elysium was the highest state they could conceive. However, the pagan poets were virtuous men and this benign landscape blends, for the first time, the twin

[*] a meadow of fresh verdure

[1] On this scene (*Aeneid*, VI and *Odyssey*, XI), see Benevenuti De Rambaldis De Imola, *Comentum super Dantis Aldigherij Comoediam*, ed. G. F. Lacaita, 5 vols. (Florence, 1887), I, 159. All Italian citations are from *La Divina Commedia*, ed. G. Vandelli in *Le Opere Di Dante*, Testo Critico Della Società Dantesca Italiana, 2nd ed. (Firenze, 1960). All English translations are from Carlyle-Wicksteed versions in the Dent Temple Classics (*Inferno-Purgatorio*, 1941; *Paradiso*, 1932, London).

notions of City and Garden, later tentatively reconciled in Eden (*Purg.* XXXII) and finally luminously integrated in the rose of the City of God (*Par.* XXX).

In Canto IX, we have a vision of a very different city, the "città dolente" (22), the City of Dis. Drawing on Arles and Pola, the poet describes the vista inside the walls as a land of open tombs. The stifling smoke, the incessant sound, the enormous walls and battlements, the stench, the sepulchers— all contribute to the sense of miserable, unrelenting confinement. This is the self-imposed confinement of those who stopped up their ears, eyes, noses—minds—in a willful self-exile from the word of God. The pilgrim is free to pass among the prisoners, and pass he does; but the images of their spiritual isolation remain. The last words of the canto, "alti spaldi," remind us we have entered the City of Hell proper.

As we go deeper, landscapes still appear in the darkness, and Canto XIII presents one of the most striking of the infernal vistas. Here is not another city, but another wood— a ghastly variation on the opening theme. Entering a

✼bosco

che da nessun sentiero era segnato   (2-3)

the travelers find themselves in the tangled, desolate, arid wood of the suicides. The "alberi strani" (15), inhabited by harpies, are the suicides themselves who, having rejected their humanity, have become subhuman; the harpies are the dehumanized, torturing remnants of the suicides' conscience, haunting the lost souls until they regain their flesh and hang themselves for all eternity. Again, a wood

✼ a wood,
which by no path was marked.

without exit is the richly suggestive landscape for a soul in pain.

A further landscape variation is found in Cantos XIV and XV, the cantos of the blasphemers, sodomites and usurers. In a plain surrounded by a "dolorosa selva" (XIV, 10), these sinners suffer under an eternal rain of fire (29). Beyond is a dike upon which the travelers walk, and below them (in Canto XV) appears Brunetto Latini. The old teacher can never rest; he is constantly driven in a parody of the torment of Paolo and Francesca, just as his sin is a perversion of their impulse. Across the dry, burning desert the pilgrim surveys those who have misused natural goods and rendered themselves physically and spiritually sterile. There is melancholy in this canto, and pity for the pain, but there is no ambiguity to the landscape. It is sharply etched, the proper background for such powerful torments.

In the last two circles of Hell, landscape description of any kind is rare. As we go farther from God, Hell narrows. The soul is cramped in what it deserves. Light fails, space contracts. However, the poet does not forsake setting as a technical device. As the wood of suicides measured the distance from that tangled wood at the outset, so the vistas of the Malebolge and Cocytus indicate how much farther still into the world of evil we have come.

In Canto XVIII, the opening view of the Malebolge, with the references to "castelli" and "fortezze" (11, 14), reinforces the image of a city. If Dis was the City of Hell proper, Malebolge is its grimmest suburb. But it is in the last Canto, XXXIV, that all the landscapes of Hell are epitomized in Cocytus. Here, the flapping of Satan's wings, which freezes the lake (52), is a satanic parody of the "Spiritus Sanctus," just as Satan, with his busy jaws and wings, frozen in the ice, is the total inversion and parody of the unmoved mover. The ice is the final constriction, the last dungeon in a narrowing prison of souls. Opposite of the sun, it is also the final image of all the hellish vegetation, all the sad and tangled woods, because it is the ultimate negation of vegetation. And the ice is finally the greatest fortress of all the cities of Hell, for it is directly opposed to the City of God. It holds the worst sinners in unalterable isolation and the most degrading communion.

As THE journey away from God could be traced in terms of landscape, so may the journey back. And in the ascent of Mount Purgatory, the journey back means reaching the glorious garden of Eden at the very top. However, before gaining the earthly paradise, we like everyone else must pause in a landscape at the top of the ante-Purgatory. Here, in Cantos VII and VIII is the Valley of Princes, and it anticipates Eden in various interesting ways.

The Valley is truly a paradise in the most ancient sense of a "royal park," for here dwell those princes and rulers whose preoccupation with earthly things impeded them from attending to their spiritual salvation. The technique Dante uses in Canto VII to describe the Valley is to conjure up a splendid vision, and then say it is dull in comparison with what he actually saw. Thus the poet says that gold, silver, red and white pigment, indigo, clear wood, fresh cracked emeralds—all would be outshone by the flowers and grass within that place (71-78). All these objects are, among other things, artists' materials, and Dante continues the implied image and caps the description by saying:

✶ Non avea pur natura ivi dipinto,
ma di soavità di mille odori
vi facea uno incognito e indistinto. (79-81)

The Valley resembles Eden not only in the lushness of color, the mingling of odors, and the implied comfort, but in another way too. For the artistry Dante expends on the verse, coupled with the pigments and plastic materials enumerated above (73-74) and the extended metaphor of Nature as painter (79), give the Valley the aura of an "artifact"—that is, a thing consciously created by Nature (and the poet) as Eden was created by God. And finally, this very "artificiality," the sense that the Valley is *too* overtly made, that too much care is expended on its visible aspects, provides the proper setting for those who tended the external and secular world to the detriment of higher concerns.

The Valley of Princes prepares us, as it prepares the pilgrim, for Eden in even greater ways. These are evident in Canto VIII which opens with the fall of evening and the hymn of the inhabitants of the Valley. Without light, there is no will to travel and the pilgrims pause for the night. Lines 19-21 present us with the poet's warning to sharpen our sight and see the meaning under the veil. This admonition is strongly reminiscent of a similar tercet (61-63) in *Inferno*, IX, and what happens in this Valley recalls what happened outside the walls of Dis. Two angels, whose gowns were "Verdi, come fogliette pur mo nate" (VIII, 28), suddenly appear brandishing flaming swords and take up positions on either side of the Valley. Sordello explains that

---

✶ Not only had Nature painted there, but of the sweetness of a thousand scents made there one, unknown and indefinable.

they watch for the "serpente che verrà vie via" (39). Just as the angels' arrival recalls a place which is past, so it forecasts a place which is to come. As Miss Sayers remarks, the angels and their swords remind us of the angels placed at Eden after the Fall (Genesis 3: 24).[2] The green of their robes properly symbolizes Hope and recalls the color and state of mind of the earthly paradise. Dante's language itself (l. 28) suggests the innocence and freshness we associate with the garden.

Then, at line 95, Sordello catches sight of the snake.

> ✻ Da quella parte onde non ha riparo
> la picciola vallea, era una biscia,
> forse qual diede ad Eva il cibo amaro.   (97-99)

That "forse" sets the tone: perhaps it is the same snake that tempted Eve, perhaps not. The point is that the snake slithers into view and Eden comes to the poet's lips. The snake is pursued by the angels, and we feel that it came as if in a ritual and that the angels with their blunted swords were simply performing their part of the play. The effect is that in the simulacrum of Eden the old dream is enacted for the new souls to remind them not to procrastinate in those spiritual things but to be alert to the needs of the spirit; to remind them that beyond the Valley, whose similarity to Eden has been stressed for two cantos, lies the real garden. As if to make the lesson of the snake clear and to clarify the need to stiffen the will and keep the image of Eden in mind, Dante has Currado Malaspina say:

✻ On that side where the little vale hath no rampart, was a snake, perchance such as gave to Eve the bitter fruit.

[2] *The Divine Comedy II: Purgatory*, tr. D. Sayers, Penguin Classics (Baltimore, 1955), p. 130, under comments entitled *The Images*.

✕ "Se la lucerna che ti mena in alto
    truovi nel tuo arbitrio tanta cera
    quant'è mestiere infino al sommo smalto,"[3]
    cominciò ella. . . . (112-115)

This is said as a preface to a request for news from the world, but it makes its own point. Currado's words weave an image of light (the pilgrim's taper) through an injunction to exercise the will in pursuit of the earthly paradise.

There is one last oblique forecast of Eden, and that occurs in the pilgrim's dream in Canto IX. He dreams that an Eagle swoops down, seizes him like Ganymede, and carries him to the sphere of fire (30). There they are both consumed by flame. The meaning of the dream is clearly that the pilgrim, who will achieve the celestial paradise, is not yet ready for it; that he must first undergo the rigors of the mountain at whose summit lies the terrestrial paradise. When the pilgrim awakens, he is at the gates of Purgatory in a position to commence his climb. The forecast of the celestial paradise in the dream of the Eagle follows naturally and logically upon the anticipations of Eden scattered through the Valley of Princes. But the dream clearly under-

✕ "So may that light which guideth thee on high, find in thy will as much wax as is needful to reach the enamelled summit," he began . . .

    [3] It is interesting that "sommo smalto" which is a reference to the earthly paradise echoes "'l verde smalto" (the enamelled green) of the Limbo of the poets, *Inferno* IV, 118. Thus that Elysium is at once linked to, and distanced from, the true earthly paradise. Again we see how Dante's landscapes constantly anticipate Eden while serving to establish the physical, and moral, hierarchy of the universe. After Dante, "enamelled" elements become standard features in garden descriptions; see below Ch. III, n. 10.

lines the necessity for passage through the Garden as a prelude for acceptance in the Heavenly City.

· II ·

This brief survey of the landscapes and vistas of the *Inferno* and *Purgatorio* is meant to clarify the statement that Dante's landscapes imply a condition of the soul, and to assert further that all the vistas, whether of a city or garden or wood, reflect upon the garden of Eden. In terms of physical characteristics and spiritual significance, the earthly paradise is the norm and all other places in the sublunar universe are defective or incomplete according to its standards. Yet it is only the standard here below, for the earthly paradise is simply a prefiguration of the celestial paradise. In the *Divina Commedia*, Eden is a culmination and a commencement; it represents the end of self-purification in this life and the beginning of a state of blessedness. It is the end of Virgil's guidance and the beginning of Beatrice's. It is an image of man himself, with all his dignity and innocence, as he was before the Fall.

Outside the poem, Dante is most explicit about the significance of the earthly paradise. In the *Monarchia*, III, xvi, he tells us that Man, like the line on the horizon, is the middle term between two opposites, his corruptible body and incorruptible soul. Because every middle term participates in the two natures it unites, man participates in both natures; and because every nature has a final goal, man's goal is therefore twofold. The first goal is "happiness in this life, which consists in the exercise of his own powers and is typified by the earthly paradise; the second is the happiness of eternal life, which consists in the enjoyment of the divine countenance (which man cannot attain to of his own power but only by the aid of divine illumination) and is typified by the heavenly paradise."[4] Dante says we attain the first goal "by means of philosophical teaching, being faithful to it by exercising our moral and intellectual virtues. We arrive at the second by means of spiritual teaching (which transcends human reason) insofar as we exercise the theological virtues of faith, hope and charity." Human reason lights the first way, the Holy Spirit the second. In the framework of the *Monarchia*, Dante sees the two guides who "have been appointed for man to lead him to his twofold goal" as the Church (Pope) and Empire (Emperor). The Church (or Beatrice in the *Commedia*) will lead man "to eternal life in accordance with revelation"; the Empire (or Virgil) "in accordance with philosophical teaching is to lead man to temporal happiness." Though in the *Commedia* Virgil and Beatrice are both much more (though never less) than Reason and Revelation, their functions are clearly anticipated, their goals concisely outlined, in the *Monarchia*.

We can see the seeds of the earthly paradise planted even more subtly in the imagery of the *Monarchia* than in its precise prose statements. For in discussing the task of the Emperor, of philosophy and reason, humanity and art— Virgil—Dante says that no one would reach this "harbor" (temporal happiness or Eden) unless "the waves of alluring cupidity were assuaged" and man were freed from

[4] This and subsequent English translations from the *Monarchia* are taken from *Dante Monarchy and Three Political Letters*, tr. and ed. D. Nicholl and C. Hardie (New York, 1954), pp. 92-93; the Latin text is in *Monarchia*, ed. E. Rostagno, in Società Dantesca Italiana, *Opere*, p. 380.

them to rest in tranquility.[5] The imagery is interesting, for
we recall the *Purgatorio*:

> ✄ "Quant'è che tu venisti
> al piè del monte per le lontane acque?"
>   (VIII, 56-57)

asks Nino Visconti of the pilgrim in the Valley of Princes.
Thus, whenever Dante thinks of earthly happiness and the
earthly paradise, he sees it as the ancients saw it—as a safe
place across the water. This is at least how it appears in
its simplest form in the *Monarchia*. In the *Commedia,* in
the most elaborate symbol for the place of the earthly paradise, Dante sums up pagan and Christian concepts. He
sees not only island safety across a "mar si crudele," but also
a mountain with a sacred grove on top.

With the previous landscapes of the poem and Dante's
philosophic and symbolic considerations behind us, we now
approach that garden toward which the *Purgatorio*, and
the whole poem *so far*, has pointed. At the end of Canto
XXVII, in words whose stress on the pilgrim's will echo
Currado's (VIII, 112-114), Virgil says to Dante:

> ✄ "libero, dritto e sano è tuo arbitrio,
> e fallo fora non fare a suo senno: (140-141)

and then, in recognition of Dante's twofold nature and his

✄ "How long is it since thou camest to the foot of the mountain
over the far waters?"

✄ "Free, upright, and whole, is thy will, and 'twere a fault not to
act according to its prompting";

5 The Latin reads: "Et cum ad hunc portum vel nulli vel pauci, et
hii cum difficultate nimia, pervenire possint, nisi sedatis fluctibus blande
cupiditatis genus humanum liberum in pacis tranquillitate quiescat. . . ."

twofold goal which soon will find its end and its beginning, Virgil adds the magnificent

✗ "per ch'io te sovra te corono e te mitrio." (142)

The pilgrim then enters the garden of Eden.

· III ·

The differences between the garden in *Purg.* XXVIII and the opening of the poem, between the "divina foresta spessa e viva" (*Purg.* XXVIII, 2) and the grim "selva selvaggia e aspra e forte" (*Inf.* I, 5) have often been noted. Suffice it to say that when at the beginning of the poem the pilgrim lost his way in the wood, it was an occasion of terror. Now, in Canto XXVIII, when he walks in the "selva antica" of Eden and cannot see where he entered (24), it is not a cause for alarm at all. The difference in the physical settings, symbolic and expressive of the difference in the pilgrim's state of mind, shows us how far we have come. Confusion has been submitted to discipline and order; terror has become tranquility.

The physical characteristics of the garden are those of the earthly paradises of the past. Lines 6-36 describe the birds, foliage and soft breeze that we associate with such a place. The fountain is mentioned (124), the old motif of the four rivers is found in the twin rivers of Lethe and Eunoe (128-131) and extraordinary or spontaneous fertility is even implied at lines 118-120 when it is said that fruits grow here which do not grow on earth. Perpetual spring is, of course, an attribute of the place (143).

Near the end of the canto the whole notion of the pagan Golden Age is introduced.

✗ "wherefore I do crown and mitre thee over thyself."

✻ Quelli ch'anticamente poetaro
l'età de l'oro e suo stato felice,
forse in Parnaso esto loco sognaro.   (139-141)

It seems that here Dante, like Tertullian and others, is flatly claiming the primacy of the Faith and its garden. But the point is, I think, that again Dante compliments Virgil while at the same time showing his guide's limitations. The classical poets, the best men of the ancient world, had a dim perception of the Truth and could, with their vision of the Golden Age, approximate something of that place where

✻ fu innocente l'umana radice.   (142)

To this extent, they were wise and good men. But they lacked true sight, and their best was not the best there was. In this critique of ancient gardens and poets, by including them to show how they fall short, Dante is preparing the way for the path through Eden to bliss, a journey no pagan can make. In his awareness of what can surpass even this place, the pilgrim has outstripped his guide. It is necessary and just, therefore, that at the beginning of Canto XXIX we see the pilgrim walking ahead of Virgil who has said his last words (XXIX, 7-8).[6]

All the traditional paradise motifs provide the necessary background. The foreground, which now commands the pilgrim's attention and ours, is occupied by another variation on an old motif—the inhabitant of the garden now that Adam and Eve are gone.[7] We know that the Middle

✻ They who in olden times sang of the golden age and its happy place, perchance dreamed in Parnassus of this place.

✻ the root of man's race was innocent.

[6] XXVIII, 82, is the first indication that the pilgrim is ahead of Virgil.
[7] This is not to imply that Matelda is necessarily the permanent resident

Ages abounded in arguments and legends attesting to the presence of saints or martyrs or the prophets Enoch and Elias in the garden. In Canto XXVII, 100-108, Dante had a dream wherein he saw Leah gathering flowers, and she has been understood as a symbol of the active life. When he arrives in the garden, the pilgrim walks by the river Lethe and on the other side he sees a maiden. She is gathering flowers and singing and, as we casually discover in XXXIII, 119, her name is Matelda.[8] She is Dante's guide to Beatrice—a type of that active life which must necessarily precede the life of contemplation. Matelda is to Beatrice as Leah is to Rachel, or Martha was said to be to Mary, or the terrestrial paradise where man worships through the purity of his deeds is to the celestial paradise where the soul adores by reflecting the Divine Light. Matelda is the guide to that new life of joy and innocence wherein Dante will rediscover the "old flame" and find Beatrice and, through her, God. Matelda and the garden are inseparable; both are important for precisely the same reason: they represent a way of life, a level of awareness, a state of soul that one must attain in order to proceed to what is higher.

As Dante the pilgrim is admiring the green May branches,

---

of Eden; but she is certainly the resident when Dante the pilgrim arrives in the garden.

[8] The question of Matelda's identity has been debated for many years; and mystics, saints, a Countess, and girls from Dante's youth have all been nominated by various commentators. For reasons which will be evident in my discussion, I would identify Matelda, if at all, with the early friend of Beatrice who is mourned in section VIII of the *Vita Nuova*. Charles Grandgent, in his edition of *Dante's Divina Commedia* (Boston, 1933), p. 502, is also of this opinion: for the other candidates, see Vernon, *Readings*, pp. 441-442; Carroll, *Prisoners of Hope*, pp. 377-379, and Moore, *Third Series*, pp. 210-216. Complete references in Bibliography, pp. 121ff.

suddenly, like an emanation from them, she appears, and all else is thrust out of the beholder's mind. He hails her and asks her to come closer so he can hear her song. His address, "Deh, bella donna" (43), and his language, especially in describing her eyes (57, 63), has reminded many commentators of the language of the youthful love-poet of Florence. Indeed, his desire to be near her has led to wide speculation. Recent critics have particularly noted that the imagery Dante applies to their meeting has distinctly sensual, indeed sexual, implications.[9] The somewhat puzzling situation arises because, first, Dante tells Matelda that she reminds him of Proserpine

> ⚹ "nel tempo che perdette
> la madre lei, ed ella primavera." (50-51)

Then, at 64-66, Dante says that Matelda's eyes shone with a light not even Venus' burned with when she was accidentally wounded by Cupid. The reference is, of course, to the birth of the goddess' passion for Adonis. Finally, because he is on one side of the stream, she on the other, the poet says Leander hated not the Hellespont more because it would not open than he hates the river Lethe (71-75). I do not believe we are to regard the pilgrim still susceptible to some kind of sin. Granted, he has not drunk of Lethe and Eunoë, nor passed before Beatrice, but he has passed through all the terraces of Purgatory, been crowned and mitred, and admitted to the garden. Rather the appearance

⚹ "in the time her mother lost her, and she lost the spring flowers."

[9] Bernard Stambler, *Dante's Other World* (New York, 1957), p. 244, says "Dante's first view, then, of Matelda is described in a context of passionate, even violent desire." See also the discussion by C. S. Singleton, *Dante Studies 2* (Cambridge, Mass., 1958), pp. 211-218.

of Matelda, and the imagery used to present her, serve other purposes which are central to the garden.

In his progress upward through the poem, the pilgrim has been moving backward, in a sense, toward that state of radical purity and innocence which Adam and Eve possessed before the Fall. And the pilgrim's progress through the garden will be a perfecting of his own personal purification, culminating in his vision of Beatrice and in his contrition, confession and satisfaction in her presence. Dante will be there enacting on an individual level the process all souls, in their own way, must undergo; and on the individual level he will be reenacting, *in parvo*, the whole movement of the *Commedia*. Dante goes from a state of happiness, in the beginning, to extreme grief under the accusations of Beatrice (Cantos XXX, XXXI), to an even deeper insight, or higher state, at the end. The pilgrim learns that there are spiritual thorns in the earthly paradise; he learns that all is not joy in the garden of delight. This he must undergo to regain his sight of the true Beatrice, and thus regain his own radical sense of love. He must, in short, reexperience the New Life he left behind in order to gain eternal life.

Matelda plays a central role in this drama of Dante the pilgrim, for she leads him into the garden, into an examination of himself. What is important is that the classical imagery Dante applies to Matelda illustrates those precise moments when love was awakening, and so it is in the pilgrim. Matelda, on this level, is an image of the young Beatrice, the first love. On a more general level, Matelda is an image of Eve, man's first love. For those same classical images also associate Matelda with those two classical figures most like Eve: Proserpine, the virgin among flowers, and Venus, the embodiment of satisfied and satisfying love in a garden. And their fields and bowers most often paralleled the paradise of Eve. Here Matelda is the first of the female inhabitants of a modern earthly paradise, except she differs from her successors in that she will not lead one astray; she is an Eve who will not fall, a young Beatrice who will not die. Indeed, the process of old is now reversed. Dante is an Adam who will be raised, not degraded, by this Eve. It is Dante who has lapsed, as a lover, as a man. It is he who must be elevated to his previous state. As a lover, it first means finding the Beatrice of the *Vita Nuova*; as a man representing Man, it means finding the Beatrice who is God's emissary. Matelda has, by her loveliness and charm, awakened the lover. "Voi siete nuovi" (76) are her first words to the travelers. Therefore, she will—in this place of light and clarity—"disnebbiar vostro intelletto" (81). And to Dante the pilgrim she says, "purgherò la nebbia che ti fiede" (90). To him, to man and to lover, the process of enlightenment, of clarifying the "intelletto d'amore" which can lead to the *vita nuova*, has begun.

As the history of Dante as a "fedele d'amore," a faithful lover of Beatrice, is recalled by Matelda, so the history of the Church, through which man loves God, is recalled in its entirety in Canto XXIX. Matelda has been the guide to both the (yet unrecognized) personal and general revelations. And now it is time for the revelation which will fuse both the personal and general levels—the revelation of Beatrice. She appears in Canto XXX, and as she comes, Dante says

⋇ d'antico amor sentì la gran potenza (39)

⋇ [I] felt the mighty power of ancient love.

and he turns to Virgil to say

⋇ conosco i segni dell'antica fiamma.   (48)

But Virgil is gone. He is no longer needed. In seeing Beatrice, Dante, as a man representing mankind, has surpassed
the need for Virgil. He needs none of the guidance Virgil
can offer, for Dante is, as it were, his own man. And it is at
this moment of loss, when the pilgrim feels most abandoned,
that he is most "complete." Beatrice emphasizes the pilgrim's
maturation with her very first word: "Dante" (XXX, 55).
This is the only time in the poem that the poet-pilgrim's
name is uttered and it is altogether proper that this should
be the time and place. For in the loss of Virgil, Dante has
gained—himself. He is now a total human being, using
his own powers; and his entirety as a man is sealed by the
revelation of his identity.

Now commences the pilgrim's lesson in himself. Beatrice
reveals her name to him and commands his gaze (73-75).
He is ashamed (96) and this is the beginning of his last
descent—albeit in the garden—into unhappiness. The angels
question her treatment of the pilgrim and she answers with
blazing words. She intends her answer for him, she says,

⋇ perchè sia colpa e duol d'una misura.   (108)

After all, he was born not only with natural gifts but also
with divine gifts (109-114). The language now becomes
crucial.

⋇ "I recognise the tokens of the ancient flame." (Here Dante, in
seeing Beatrice, pays final tribute to Virgil by adapting *Aeneid*, IV,
23: Adgnosco veteris vestigia flammae.)

⋇ so that sin and sorrow be of one measure.

✻ questi fu tal ne la sua vita nova,
virtualmente, ch'ogni abito destro
fatto averebbe in lui mirabil prova.
Ma tanto più maligno e più silvestro
si fa 'l terren col mal seme e non colto,
quant'elli ha più di buon vigor terrestro.

(115-120)

Dante's wasting of the gifts of his "vita nova" is compared
to a garden or landscape going to ruin—a ruin which can
ultimately render the land even more rich and fertile. Here,
in brief, is the whole doctrine of the *Purgatorio*: a place
where you recognize and profit by past errors; where under
the eyes of God but completely through your own will,
you develop the potentialities to become a total human
being. All men potentially are "terren" "del buon vigor
terrestro"; but only when they have reaped and harvested
what is best within them can they achieve that *paradiso
terrestre* which is the symbol of their self-created inner order
and fertility.

The other element to notice in Beatrice's speech is that
the *vita nova* of the pilgrim, referring surely to that early
period of Dante's life when he realized Beatrice could lead
him to God, is associated with the "rich and fertile earth"
part of the image. Here Dante knots up the associations of
the earthly paradise with a new life. In order to enjoy a
"new" *vita nuova* in Heaven, the pilgrim must recapture
some of the innocence and bliss that was his during that
"old" *vita nuova* in Florence. The pilgrim's first moment

✻ this man was such in his new life potentially, that every good
talent would have made wondrous increase in him.

But so much the more rank and wild the ground becomes with
evil seed and untilled, the more it hath of good strength of soil,

of deeper insight occurs in Canto XXXI. Under Beatrice's questioning, he breaks down and confesses to his past lapses. This verbal confession is, of course, the true realization of sin, for in so speaking, he is facing what is within. Then, at her command, the pilgrim looks up and sees the angels and then the Lady herself (76-81). She is turned toward the griffin, the image of Christ, in a hieratic indication of her function as a guide to the realms of Bliss.

> ⁑ Sotto 'l suo velo, ed oltre la rivera
>   vincer pariemi più se stessa antica,
>   vincer che l'altre qui, quand'ella c'era. (82-84)

This is the moment of insight. The pilgrim now finally sees Beatrice as she is. And how does the poet convey to us the new perception? He says Beatrice now outshines her old self even more than she once outshone all the other women (of Florence, we assume). The index to Beatrice's brilliance, or the pilgrim's perception, is the "old" Beatrice of the *Vita Nuova*. That is the standard by which he judges, for "antica" in line 83 echoes "antica fiamma" of XXX, 48 and compresses all the sensations concerning the early Beatrice into one final moment. In fully realizing how bright she was then, he realizes how much more brilliant she is now. This, of course, means the pilgrim is finally *seeing* Beatrice, is finally obeying that

"Guardaci ben! Ben son, ben son Beatrice" (XXX, 73)

which was a plea, a command to see her as she once was so as to see her as she is. And yet, at this instant of en-

---

⁑ Under her veil and beyond the stream, to me she seemed to surpass more her ancient self, than she surpassed the others here when she was with us.

lightenment, Dante the pilgrim reaches his darkest moment. It is now that he feels the nettles of remorse and compunction (XXXI, 85). Better than any other time in the poem, the pilgrim understands the meaning of sin and Hell; what he has wasted, what he has lost, how wrong he was; for now he has a vision of that Beatrice to whom, in every sense, he was unfaithful. All this consciousness floods in on him and it is too much (XXXI, 86-87). He faints, and because he has finally understood his sins, when he regains consciousness he has been through Lethe and tasted its waters. The first stage of his renewal is completed.

The pilgrim is now shown the pageant Church and Empire in Canto XXXII and told its significance in XXXIII. But, for our examination of the garden, a tercet in the midst of XXXII is most important. Beatrice says to the pilgrim:

> ⚹ "Qui sarai tu poco tempo silvano;
> e sarai meco sanza fine cive
> di quella Roma onde Cristo è Romano." (100-102)

Here, in the midst of the spectacle, Beatrice is promising the pilgrim citizenship in the City of God as a consequence of his self-cultivation in the Garden. This tercet makes two very important points. It emphasizes again the fact that Eden is not an end, but a most important way station on the journey to a greater end. The tercet also sums up the two dominant external landscape (and thus inner spiritual) images of the poem—the garden and the City. It "plants," as it were, the City in the garden. This point will be further

---

⚹ "Here shalt thou be short time a forester, and with me everlastingly shalt be a citizen of that Rome whereof Christ is a Roman."

treated shortly in our examination of the final "landscape" of the poem.

Now let us see how the themes of the garden, new life and green vegetation, are summed up. We must understand that through his vision of the final pageant and his drinking of Eunoë, Dante has finally achieved that total fulfillment of self which was initiated when Virgil gave him crown and mitre at the end of Canto XXVII. The pilgrim, in a sense, has lived up to the garden by bringing his inner life into accordance with his free, fertile and innocent surroundings. For this garden is not a reflection of the pilgrim's inner state as it was, but as it should have been; and only now he is in harmony with it. The pilgrim's final emergence to a new level of insight and being is summarized in appropriate garden imagery in the last lines of Canto XXXIII:

> *Io ritornai da la santissima onda
> rifatto sì come piante novelle
> rinovellate di novella fronda,
> puro e disposto a salire a le stelle. (142-145)

In this imagery of budding foliage, Dante tells us how the pilgrim was now pure and disposed, i.e. felt himself entirely ready, to ascend to Heaven. In the words "rifatto," "novelle," "rinovellate," and "novella," we see the poet for the last time imaging that process of renewal that the pilgrim underwent in Eden. We hear the last, triumphant echoes of the *vita nuova* now again made new. As the pilgrim wasted the rich and fertile soil of his other "vita nova" (XXX, 109ff.) and so lapsed into sin, now his life is *rinovellata*; and like the branches of a green and budding tree, such as

---

* I came back from the most holy waves, born again, even as new trees renewed with new foliage, pure and ready to mount to the stars.

we would expect to find in Eden, he aspires to the celestial paradise.

The pilgrim has fully become part of the garden and therefore he is ready for the ascent to the City.

WE HAVE said that all the landscapes of Hell and Purgatory are either defective or incomplete versions of the terrestrial paradise. But the terrestrial paradise is itself only an image of the celestial paradise. The garden of Eden simply reflects the City of God. And, therefore, it should be no surprise to find one last landscape in the *Divina Commedia,* that celestial vista of which the terrestrial garden is the earthly image. We find this landscape in *Paradiso* XXX.

Beatrice first included the idea of the City as part of the successful cultivation of the Garden (XXXII, 100-102). Now, in *Paradiso* XXX as the pilgrim progresses into the Empyrean and Beatrice smiles on him with ineffable loveliness, there is the final vision of the City of God, the abode of blessed souls. The vision is divided into two parts. The first, preliminary vision runs from lines 61-81. Here the City of God is described in none other than earthly paradise terms. The pilgrim sees a river which flows

> ˟ intra due rive
> dipinte di mirabil primavera. (62-63)

From the river come sparks which light in the flowers, and look like rubies set in gold. There are sweet odors (67) and jewels again (76) suggested through metaphor. Now the river is Grace, the sparks angels, the flowers souls. However, what is important is that in this vision of the celestial community sustained by the grace of God, the poet has

˟ betwixt banks painted with marvellous spring.

included many of the motifs of Christian earthly paradises—
water, flowers, springtime, and indirectly, sweet odors and
jewels. We have come to where the City and Garden will
finally merge. Or we think we have. But Beatrice tells the
pilgrim that

> ※ "Il fiume e li topazii
> ch'entrano ed escono e il rider de l'erbe
> son di lor vero umbriferi prefazii." (76-78)

There is nothing wrong with them; Dante's sight, as has
been the case so often with so many in the past, is defective.
Therefore, in order to "disnebbiar" his vision once and for
all, the pilgrim dips his eyelids in the river, and like people
who take off disguises and thus change but remain the same,

> ※ così mi si cambiaro in maggior feste
> li fiori e le faville, sì ch'io vidi
> ambo le corti del ciel manifeste. (94-96)

The vision of the City as an earthly paradise has yielded to
the true vision, just as the terrestrial paradise yielded to the
celestial paradise. In the last analysis, the garden by which
all was found wanting is now seen to be an incomplete
image of the City. Incomplete does not mean misleading or
defective; it means that nothing else can finally stand for
the City. A soul must see for itself. Matelda said she would
uncloud the pilgrim's sight. And yet as it happens so often
in this poem, as in life itself, the full import of what we

※ "The river and the topaz-gems that enter and go forth, and the
smiling of the grasses are the shadowy prefaces of their reality."

※ so changed before me into ampler joyance the flowers and the
sparks, so that I saw both the two courts of heaven manifested.

try to do does not dawn on us until long after the deed. The fog is only dispelled with direct sight of the sun.

The City is now revealed, but we should not assume that the idea of the Garden is abandoned. The City is first spoken of as an amphitheater with tiers (112-114) and then, in the next tercet, as a rose (115-117). The rose-image is extended in lines 124-126:

> ✲ Nel giallo de la rosa sempiterna,
> che si dilata ed ingrada e redole
> odor di lode al sol che sempre verna,

and the language of growth, odor and perpetual spring brings back the essential elements of the Garden. Then immediately Beatrice exclaims:

> ✲ "Vedi nostra città quant'ella gira:" (130)

it is almost as if the poet were consciously alternating images of the Garden and the City. Finally, the City includes all; it is amphitheater and rose. Here, where will and desire are one, where perfect stillness creates perfect motion, the twin images of Garden and City are married in the final, luminous vision.

THE pivotal landscape of the poem remains, however, the terrestrial paradise. In this garden of freedom within order, the innocent life of man before the Fall and the blessed life of the soul in Heaven are both imaged. The past and future of the race are concentrated and symbolized in the garden.

✲ Within the yellow of the eternal rose, which doth expand, rank upon rank, and reeketh perfume of praise unto the Sun that maketh spring for ever.

✲ "See how large our city sweepeth!"

And, though no two men ever have the same soul and therefore the same journey, the garden of Eden is the *locus* and symbol for the personal redemption of Dante the pilgrim. We see his past awakened so that his future will be secure. We watch Matelda kindle the Florentine *vita nuova*; and we follow her as she leads the pilgrim to Beatrice, the "ancient flame" who, when seen properly, will lead the soul to a new life at the source of all flame and light, God Himself.

In a study concentrating on the earthly paradises of the Renaissance epics, it might strike some strange to begin with a consideration of Dante's garden of Eden. Yet insofar as Dante's garden emphasizes the responsibility of a man, in his essential uniqueness, to conduct himself, it is already in spirit a Renaissance garden. Furthermore, though not all the earthly paradises in the Renaissance poems are false or enchanted, those that are will be found wanting by some higher standard. And as a master-image of that standard, the Eden of Dante serves us well.

BIBLIOGRAPHY · CHAPTER TWO

The literature on Dante has reached proportions only a team of IBM machines could tabulate, and thus I include in this note only those items which are helpful in approaching Dante, and particularly the *Comedy*, and those studies which bear on the *Purgatory* and the earthly paradise.

For the medieval antecedents and intellectual background of Dante's writing, K. Vossler's two-volume *Mediaeval Culture: An Introduction to Dante and His Times*, tr. W. C. Lawton (New York, 1929) and H. F. Dunbar's *Symbolism in Medieval Thought and Its Consummation in the Divine Comedy* (New Haven, 1929; reprinted Russell and Russell, New York, 1961) are basic; so are E. Moore's *Studies in Dante*, published in four series by the Clarendon Press (Oxford, 1896-1917) on the scriptural and classical background to the *Comedy*. A basic introduction to Dante is M. Barbi's *Life of Dante*, tr. P. Ruggiers (Berkeley, 1954), though this has been recently superseded in many respects by the comprehensive volume of T. G. Bergin, *Dante*, Riverside Studies in Literature (Boston, 1965), where one will find lucid treatments of the poet's life, times, and works. A general manual on Dante is U. Cosmo's *A Handbook to Dante Studies*, tr. D. Moore (Oxford, 1950).

Dante has not been neglected by the makers of critical anthologies; in D. C. Heath's series, see I. Brandeis' *Discussions of the Divine Comedy* (Boston, 1961), with essayists ranging from Boccaccio to T. S. Eliot, noteworthy among them being Malagoli on Dante's language, Gilson on Beatrice, Tate on imagery and imagination; for Prentice Hall's ubiquitous *Twentieth Century Views*, J. Freccero has edited *Dante* (Englewood Cliffs, 1965), the essays of d'Entrèves on Dante's politics, Poulet and Father Foster on philosophy, Spitzer on the language of *Inf.* XIII being remarkable treatments; and for the Indiana University Press, M. Musa has edited *Essays on Dante* (Bloomington, 1964), which includes a new translation of the Letter to Can Grande. E. Auerbach and C. Singleton are represented in all three anthologies, and their writings though very different, have been probably the most influential of recent times. Auerbach's *Dante: Poet of the Secular World*, tr. R. Manheim (Chicago, 1961), originally published in 1929, is a masterly work, particularly illuminating on the early Dante; his study of "Farinata and Cavalcanti" in *Mimesis*, tr. W. Trask (Princeton, 1953) is, of course, his best known essay on Dante's style and structure. For all of Auerbach's writings on Dante, see the "Bibliography of the Writings of Erich Auerbach" in *Literary Language*, pp. 395-405. Singleton's works include his subtle and eloquent *An Essay on the Vita Nuova* (Cambridge, Mass., 1949), and *Commedia: Elements of Structure, Dante Studies 1* (Cambridge, Mass., 1954) and the *Journey to Beatrice, Dante Studies 2* (Cambridge, Mass., 1958).

Also on the *Comedy*, one should read the very personal but constantly stimulating study by C. Williams, *The Figure of Beatrice* (London, 1943).

On the *Purgatory*, I have found the notes and commentary in Dorothy Sayers' translation of that *cantica* (The Penguin Classics, Harmondsworth, 1955) lucid and helpful, and there is much good sense contained in W. W. Vernon's *Readings on the Purgatorio of Dante* (London, 1907) and J. S. Carroll's *Prisoners of Hope, An Exposition of Dante's Purgatorio* (London, 1906). Singleton's *Dante Studies 2* is concerned with *Purgatory*, as is B. Stambler's perceptive *Dante's Other World* (New York, 1957).

On the earthly paradise at the top of the mountain, there are a number of briefer studies. A. Graf's *Il Canto XXVIII del Purgatorio, Lectura Dantis* (Firenze, 1902) takes us through the garden much in the way Graf brought us to it in his *Leggende e Miti*; and similar to Graf's and Coli's work on the paradise myth is B. Nardi's "Intorno al sito del Purgatorio e al mito dantesco dell'Eden," *GD*, 25 (1922), pp. 289-300. P. Gamberà's "La Topografia del Viaggio di Dante nel Paradiso Terrestre," *GD*, 9 (1902), pp. 126-127, is helpful as a guide to the path of the pilgrim. In English, there are various treatments of Dante's landscapes and use of Nature. For Ruskin's interesting comments, reprinted from his *Modern Painters*, Vol. III, "Of Mediaeval Landscape" (1856), see *Discussions*, ed. Brandeis, pp. 33-41; also L. O. Kuhns, *The Treatment of Nature in Dante's Divina Commedia* (London and New York, 1897), esp. pp. 51-54, for a list of important landscapes. T. G. Bergin examines the landscapes of the *Inferno* in "Hell: Topography and Demography" in *Essays*, ed. Musa, pp. 76-93; and there is a general treatment by

122   *Bibliography*

J. Wilhelm, "Zum Problem der schönen Landschaft in Der Divina Commedia," *Dante-Jahrbuch*, 39 (1963), pp. 63-79. H. Hatzfeld's "About Direct Aesthetic Approaches to the *Commedia*" in the special Dante issue of *Books Abroad*, May (1965), pp. 19-24 gives a summary of recent criticism of Dante's landscapes (esp. pp. 22-23) and provides some further bibliography. All of these studies touch on the earthly paradise, while R. Poggioli deals exclusively with it in his "Dante Poco Tempo Silvano: Or a 'Pastoral Oasis' in the Commedia," *Eightieth Annual Report of the Dante Society* (Cambridge, Mass., 1962), pp. 1-20, as does Singleton in *Dante Studies 2*, Chapters ix-xiv. Also bearing on the garden, though not strictly from the point of view of landscape, are two articles in *Italica*, 42 (1965): Stambler's "The Confrontation of Beatrice and Dante: *Purgatorio* XXX*," pp. 61-97, and A. Paolucci's "Art and Nature in the *Purgatorio*," pp. 42-60.

For further bibliography, see Cosmo's *Handbook*, Bergin's *Dante*, esp. the "Bibliographical Note," pp. 299-304, and the "Selected Bibliography" in *Dante*, ed. Freccero, pp. 181-182, where those journals with detailed and recent bibliographies are also cited.

CHAPTER THREE

The First Renaissance Earthly Paradises

THE literature of the Renaissance turned man's sense of life's ambiguities back upon life itself. It studied the difference between illusion and reality, for instance, by dealing in illusion and reality. The obvious example is Elizabethan drama, constantly concerned with disguises, madness as an illusion or new reality, false identities, incantations and magic—with the implications of the metaphor that the world is a stage, that life is a setting for illusion. What seemed was constantly examined from the viewpoint of what "was." This in turn only started the cycle again, for every affirmation demanded a question, and reaffirmed man's sense of conflict, elusiveness, division. It could be exhilarating but also exhausting, and depressing, this sense of limitless and endless possibility whose darker side was fearful flux and mutability.

It is no accident, nor simply because of humanistic admiration for the ancients, that the men of the Renaissance elevated the epic above all other genres. For the epic alone had the size and scope to encompass what poets felt about life. And so most of the great epics of the Renaissance are tales of journeys, crusades, wanderings, pilgrimages, explorations—all leave-takings in search of a home, of something permanent, final, and fixed. Whether paladins left their sworn king and pursued elusive feminine beauty (to their disgrace, madness, or death); or sailors left Portugal to find India; or crusaders left Europe to recapture Jerusalem; or knights left the Queen's court in search of honor

and glory; the search was out across the world and the mind
to find tranquility, Truth or heroic glory.

The finished products of these poets will themselves tell
us something of the ceaselessly shifting inner world of the
Renaissance. I say "finished products"; but how many
Renaissance epics were finished? The *Orlando Innamorato*
never was; the *Orlando Furioso*, enormous, kaleidoscopic,
and complete was, strictly speaking, meant to finish the
Innamorato. And the *Furioso* itself is continued, or followed,
by those *Cinque Canti* which were published after Ariosto's
death. (This is not to speak of the revisions and additions
the *Furioso* went through between its first publication in
1516 and its final edition in 1532.) The *Gerusalemme
Liberata* was completed in twenty cantos, but Tasso (because
of his critics and his conscience) rewrote the *Liberata* and
called it the *Gerusalemme Conquistata*. *The Faerie Queene*,
like the *Orlando Innamorato*, was never finished, though
Spenser's poem ends with the *Mutabilitie Cantos*, the best
ending an unfinished Renaissance epic could have. Finally,
even though *Paradise Lost* was finished, Milton was not; he
went on to *Paradise Regained*. For the poets of the Renaissance, nothing was ever quite done with, nothing was truly
final—in art as well as life.

I · PETRARCH

It is in Petrarch we first sense the inner *agon* of the
Renaissance as it is expressed in literature; and his dilemma
is best embodied in a garden which occurs in the first of
the six *Trionfi*, the *Trionfo d'Amore*, chapter iv. The first
three chapters recount the procession of those held captive
by Cupid, the God of Love. The spectacle is told by a nar-

rator who himself is taken captive by a lady at the precise middle of chapter iii:

> ✡ con parole e con cenni fui legato. (91)[1]

The rest of the chapter is a recital of the torments of the lover and the disdain of the lady. This is not, however, simply a reworking of the *fin amors* of Langue d'Oc, for the lady is elevated by the Christian ideal of chastity, not exalted by a troubadour's poetic myth. Christianity haunts this poem and gives resonance and anguished depth to the plight of the narrator and his fellow sufferers. The narrator suffers not only from the pangs of Cupid-love, but also from the knowledge that this love is *wrong*.

In chapter IV, the narrator reviews all those who had previously written poetry in praise of such love, and then refers obliquely to his own love verse. A hint is dropped that Cupid, and what he represents, will himself be conquered just as his captives are now (ll. 88-93), but before that Triumph over Cupid, all Love's slaves are taken to the garden of Venus:

> ✡ Giace oltra, ove l'Egeo sospira e piagne,
> un' isoletta dilicata e molle
> più d'altra che 'l sol scalde o che 'l mar bagna:
> nel mezzo è un ombroso e chiuso colle

✡ by words and gestures I was bound fast.

✡ There lies beyond, where the Aegean sighs and weeps, a little island delicate and soft, more so than any other which the sun burns or sea bathes; in the middle is a shady and enclosed hill with such

[1] All Italian citations are from *Le Rime Sparse e I Trionfi*, ed. E. Chiòboli, Scrittori D'Italia (Bari, 1930).

con sí soavi odor, con sí dolci acque
ch'ogni maschio pensier de l'alma tolle.   (100-105)

This island presents a Renaissance amalgam of previous traditions: the ancient Isles of the Blessed, the late-classical bowers of Venus are combined with the Christian (and pagan) ideal of a benign garden atop a beautiful mountain.[2] However, the mountain is enclosed in shadow, and the paradisiacal aspect of the place is tempered by the suggestion of line 105: amidst the beauty, one's humanity is overcome. This classic Renaissance garden presents what poets from Ariosto to Spenser will expand—the beautiful-seeming earthly paradise which in reality is a dangerous and deceptive place where man's will is softened, his moral fiber unraveled, and his soul ensnared. It is the garden where insidious luxury and sensual love overcome duty and true devotion.

The challenge lies not only in combating these gardens and what they represent, but also in recognizing them; for they offer a life of love and ease which may well be evil, but is also profoundly appealing. Exercising great attraction, these paradises offer satisfaction for deep, almost buried needs. The gardens are therefore most dangerous precisely in the area they are most appealing—in their inducements to the senses, in their promise of rest, in their invitation to relax. This kind of danger is conveyed by Petrarch's line, "ch'ogni maschio pensier de l'alma tolle." A man is tempted to let down his guard, to succumb to the desire for security

---

gentle scents, such sweet waters, that it deprives the soul of every manly thought.

[2] Here, in the last line, which is echoed over and over in the epics of the Italian Renaissance, we can discern the dangerous, seductive quality of the enchanted garden. Venus has begun to acquire some of the traits of Circe, her isle of Cyprus those of Circe's island of Aeaea.

and female domination which the garden promises. Man is weakened in such a place; duty, honor, country, loved ones—God Himself—are forgotten in this paradise, in the arms of the woman who animates the place. Much of this attitude is developed in later poems, later paradises. But in Petrarch the problem is defined.

The dominant twin characteristics of the ancient and medieval Christian earthly paradises were their desirability but inaccessibility. These traits were measured in terms of time and space (though, of course, understood metaphorically as well). The garden was good and beautiful and harmonious, but distant, remote or lost. The same qualities pervade the garden of Petrarch, but two changes have occurred. The place is no longer supposed to be morally beneficial, and it is no longer measured in "literal" terms. The garden's meaning is now wholly metaphorical; it is viewed entirely as the referent for an inner state. The garden is the scene for the struggle between warring elements within a man's soul, and the garden is itself the symbol for one of the soul's segments: that part which loves ease, pagan luxury, classical learning, earthly goods. This impulse is dangerous to the Christian life, and it must be opposed by the knowledge that the Church is the only way to the true paradise. The garden must be opposed by some sign, or design, of permanence, stability, absolute value.

> * Questa è la terra che cotanto piacque
> a Venere, e 'n quel tempo a lei fu sagra
> che 'l ver nascoso e sconosciuto giacque.
> (106-108)

* This is the land that so pleased Venus and was sacred to her in that time when the truth lay hidden and unknown.

Petrarch sums up the problem: this *is* Venus' place, and all
it implies. It *was* sacred to her before the Truth was known.
The trouble is, the Truth now is known, and yet the narrator finds himself there. The evil place has tremendous
attraction, and in the later descriptions of the landscape, the
poet does full justice to the garden's corrupt influence, but
also to its desirability (ll. 121-129). An earlier tercet
schematizes the narrator's dilemma:

> ⚹ et anco è [the garden] di valor sì nuda e magra
> tanto riten del suo primo esser bile,
> che par dolce a i cattivi, e a i buoni agra.   (109-111)

The situation is described in terms of sweet and sour, good
and bad. But it is fraught with paradox: what was once
sweet is now sour to good men, and sweet only to the bad.
The poet-narrator knows this clearly, not because he is good,
but because he has succumbed to the evil sweetness, and
is bad.

> ⚹ In così tenebrosa e stretta gabbia
> rinchiusi fummo, ove le penne usate
> mutai per tempo e la mia prima labbia.
>
> (157-159)

Like the heroes of later Renaissance epics, the narrator will
pass through and break out of this paradise turned dungeon
of the mind; but certainly not without anguish and expense,
and—perhaps, perhaps—not without some lingering regret.

⚹ and even though of worth it is so bare and poor, it keeps so much
of its first lowly state [i.e. pagan quality] that it seems to the wicked,
sweet, and bitter to the good.

> ⚹ In such a gloomy and narrow cage
> we were enclosed, wherein my hair
> and my face were changed by time.

II · POLIZIANO

A variation on this Renaissance dilemma of the senses and spirit inspires the *Stanze per la Giostra* of that most accomplished and graceful of humanists and poets, Angelo Ambrogini, called Poliziano (1454-1494). Written (and never finished) to celebrate the tournament of Il Magnifico's younger brother Giuliano, the poem's first book tells of Giuliano's devotion (like Hippolytus') to the hunt, of Cupid's efforts to inflame the youth with love, of Giuliano's meeting with Simonetta Cataneo (in whose honor the tournament was held), and Cupid's subsequent victorious return to Venus' realm on the island of Cyprus. The rest of the book is concerned with an elaborate description of the landscape, the palace of Venus and the mythological paintings which adorn it. The second book, only about a third as long as the first, recounts Venus' plan to inspire Giuliano to hold a tournament, the dream which carries this message to him, and Giuliano's prayer to Venus and resolution to act. The poem is a masterpiece and though the pace is leisurely, we are pleased to linger.

It is the *tone* of the poem which is so distinctive. The love personified by Venus and Cupid (and their garden) is not overtly opposed to Christianity, but it is presented as debilitating, restrictive, decadent. A strain of melancholy runs through the music of the *Stanze*. The melancholy tone contrasts with the *carpe diem* verse which occupied so much of Lorenzo's, and his circle's, time. Perhaps the mood of the *Stanze* is the other side of a *carpe diem* attitude. Poliziano seems to be saying: If you do not seize love while you may, then it will, my friend, seize and stifle you. Beneath the elegantly buffed surface, the poem tells of an enervating love whose essence, not surprisingly, is embodied in a garden.

In Book I, the poet prepares us for the lesson of the garden of Venus by presenting Giuliano in the act of hunting. This activity is virile, pleasurable, and, above all, free. A man makes his own choice and pits himself against the natural world. It is a life which Poliziano compares to the splendid existence of the Golden Age, joyful and free (stanza 20), before things started to decay, and

> ✲ Lussuria entrò ne' petti e quel furore
> Che la meschina gente chiama amore. (21)[3]

But Cupid, relentless in his duties as Archer and Inflamer, is petulant and piqued at Giuliano's attitude:

> ✲ E chi non ubbidisce alla mia legge? (23)

Poliziano's world is not one where we expect to hear ominous notes, and yet—"legge" caps a stanza of Cupid's boasting and implies the constrictive quality of Love. This is as close to a sense of conflict as we will come, but such an undercurrent contributes to the melancholy beneath the smooth surface.

After Giuliano is inflamed with love, Cupid goes home. He has completed his "vendetta" (68), and again, in "vendetta," placed at the head of an octave, we sense pettiness, spite, dominance for its own sake. The account of Venus' isle and garden, which crystallize the poet's vision

✲ Wantonness entered the human breast, and that fury
Which the miserable people call love.

✲ And who does not obey my law?

[3] All Italian citations are from *Le Stanze L'Orfeo e Le Rime*, ed. A. Momigliano (Torino, 1921); numbers in the text refer to the stanzas of Book I.

of love, is long, lush, glittering, conventionally but master-
fully done. Of all the traditional paradise elements, let us
look at just one: the mythological frescoes which adorn the
place. They depict many traditional scenes (one of which,
the birth of Venus, always invites comparison with Botticelli,
as indeed Poliziano always does), but what is noteworthy is
that none of the scenes of love is particularly happy. The
birth of Venus is lovely, yet it begins with the mutilation of
Cronos (98-99). We see Europa, "frozen with fear and
sorrow," calling in vain for aid (106); Jove changing shape
to seduce various unwilling ladies; Daphne fleeing (109),
and Arriana lamenting (110). There is a portrait of Bacchus
and his rabble of satyrs (111); of Silenus drunk (112); of
Proserpine hysterical at the moment of abduction (113); of
Hercules

> ✻ veste di feminea gonna:
> Colui che 'l mondo da grave cordoglio
> Avea scampato, et or serve una donna   (114)

and of monstrous Polyphemus pining for Galatea (115-
118). Each subject is described usually in an octave whose
first four lines present a lovely vision, and whose last four
lines then shatter the illusion. Poliziano presents, gracefully,
limpidly, swift successive visions of love. But there is no
gaudium in these portraits, either for the beloved, or indeed,
the lover. (In fact, beloved and lover are usually presented
as hunted and hunter, an ironic variation on Giuliano's free
and joyful activity.) What we see is only the relentless,
domineering pressure of the power of Love. Stanza 119 ends

> ✻ dressed in a feminine gown:
> He who had saved the world
> From terrible affliction, now serves a woman.

the passage on the murals. It is worth quoting in its entirety because its own structure and statement illustrate what we have been saying.

> ⁕ Intorno al bel lavor serpeggia acanto
> Di rose e mirti e lieti fior contesto;
> Con vari augei sì fatti, che il lor canto
> Pare udir negli orecchi manifesto:
> Nè d'altro si pregiò Vulcan mai tanto,
> Nè 'l vero stesso ha più del ver che questo:
> E quanto l'arte intra sè non comprende,
> La mente imaginando chiaro intende.

The tone is uniformly smooth, but the charming vision conjured up by the first four lines is very different from the implication of the last four. The second half of the octave says that what we have seen is the truth; superficially this means that Vulcan has made his murals well (as Poliziano has made his octaves well). But the statement also means, and here the irony is delicate but razor-sharp, that this is the true picture of love—a furious denial of the self. The last couplet, which could stand as an epigraph to so much of the poetry of the Italian Renaissance, merely underscores Poliziano's irony, and his substantial meaning. The poet leaves it to the reader to imagine and understand what a

⁕ Around and beside the handsome work snake
Roses and myrtle and happy flowers entirely;
With various birds, so made that their song
Seems definitely to ring in the ears;
Nor does Vulcan value anything else as highly,
Nor does truth itself have more truth [reality] than this:
And whatever the art does not include within itself
The mind, imagining, understands clearly.

brutal thing this tender-seeming love inspired by the Boy really is; that little Boy

✂ Dolce in sembianti, in atti acerbo e fello;   (120)

"Sembianti" and "atti," ultimately words and deed, illusion and reality. It is in the intuition and manipulation of the split between them that Poliziano's irony operates; it is from that gap that his melancholy, and Ariosto's futility, and Tasso's dis-ease, and even Spenser's current of despair, all flow.

We need not dwell on the final indictment of the garden, or rather the love it embodies, which is the sickly, decadent caste Poliziano gives the place. The byplay between the principal inhabitants of the garden, the sources and embodiments of this kind of love, makes the situation very clear (see stanzas 121-125). Mars is lying with his head in Venus' lap; she is smothering him with kisses, and he gazes at her,

✂ Pascendo gli occhi pur della sua faccia.   (122)

"Pascendo" helps set the tone of the whole scene. It seems to imply coarse appetite, for "pascere" is the verb which refers to the way animals eat, as distinct from the human activity denoted by "mangiare."[4] The couple is sprinkled with flowers by cupids; and then Cupid himself falls upon his mother's neck. She seizes him and kisses him and asks the news. With this last "quadro d'amore," so to speak, with

✂ Sweet in looks, in acts bitter and wicked.

✂ devouring the eyes right from her face [i.e. feeding on her eyes].

---

[4] This word also appears in subsequent gardens; Tasso borrows it from Poliziano, and Spenser—as "depasturing"—from Tasso; see below, pp. 203, 278.

the participants in close, sweaty, possessive embrace, Poliziano ends Book I. No comment is needed. The kind of love inspired by Venus, set in and symbolized by her paradise, is clear to the mind that imagines.

III · MANTUAN

Not all gardens or paradises of the Renaissance are ambiguous in the way Petrarch's or Poliziano's are, however. The traditional earthly paradise still found its poets, and it found them where we would expect—in the Church. The Church was by no means dead in the Renaissance, nor was religion. Of course, that it was alive in a secular and worldly way offended the less skeptical North and led not simply to reform, always urged in the South, but to Reformation. The Church was alive as a spiritual force as well; this is one of the very reasons the Renaissance was such a time of inner uncertainty, multiple allegiances, monumental (sometimes desperate) syntheses. Many Renaissance poets, like Petrarch and Ariosto, belonged to minor orders; these benefices were mainly a source of income, but their spiritual implications were never entirely lost. The Latin that Petrarch, Poliziano, Ariosto and Tasso (to mention only a few Italians) read and wrote so well was assuredly the language of Virgil and Ovid, Horace and Cicero, but it was also the language of the Church. We saw how Latin carried the image of the earthly paradise from the pagan and early Christian past to the thirteenth century. We know that it was only the late medieval vernacular accounts which began to convey man's sense of separation from the traditional blessed garden. As it was of the Litany, so Latin was the language of incantation which could summon the traditional garden in Eden. Latin, in a sense, preserved the

Church, as the Church preserved it; and in this Latin the Christian earthly paradise survives into the Renaissance.

To find this earthly paradise we look to a Mantuan, a lover of Virgil whose townfolk put his bust beside that of the Roman poet; an author much admired in his time whose eclogues influenced generations of schoolboys and poets, not the least among them Spenser; but a man also six times vicar general, and finally in 1513, prior general of the Carmelites; a monk intimate with Leo X, who urged reform, was venerated in his own day, and canonized in the last century: Giovan Battista Spagnoli, known in English as Mantuan (1448-1516). Son of a Spanish father and Brescian mother, Mantuan wrote over 50,000 lines of Latin verse, almost all of it on religious subjects. He is a man of the Renaissance, but not in any modern sense a "Renaissance man."

There were no divided allegiances in Mantuan's soul. The Church, the Virgin—in spite of his love for the ancients —absorbed his life. Among his many other works, Mantuan wrote seven poems on saints entitled *Parthenices*. The *Parthenice Secunda*, on the life and passion of Saint Catherine of Alexandria, is in three books, the third of which contains the long account of the earthly paradise.[5] An angel visits the place in order to gather food for Saint Catherine, who is imprisoned in Alexandria.[6] Although Mantuan in the *Eclogues* shows a wide reading in classical and modern secular poets,[7] and although his love of Virgil

[5] Written probably at Rome in 1488 and printed at Bologna, 1489. See *The Eclogues of Baptista Mantuanus*, ed. with intro. by W. P. Mustard (Baltimore, 1911), p. 28, n. 8.

[6] The earthly paradise passage is found in *Opera*, 3 vols. bound as 2 (Paris, 1513), vol. I, fol. cxxxii *verso* to cxxxiii *recto*.

[7] *Mantuanus*, ed. Mustard, pp. 57-58.

is proverbial, it is striking that his garden of Eden in the *Parthenice Secunda* shows little pagan or classical influence. There is, to be sure, a thorough admixture of pagan names (Pelion, Ossa) but this seems to be the only concession to Renaissance Humanism. Mantuan's earthly paradise, situated in the east, high, high on a mountain, is described in scrupulously traditional Christian detail. The account opens with the venerable formula:

> ⁑ Est locus aeoos phoebi nescentis ad ortus
> Arduus attollens vicina cacumina caelo. . . .

In spite of the reference to "phoebi," the opening echoes the descriptions of Eden found in the early Christian poets, especially Victor and Avitus. Like the garden of Dracontius, Mantuan's contains medicinal fruit ("sunt medica mala"); and like all the traditional Christian paradises, there is a slight breeze blowing through every conceivable fruit and flower, over green grass, past the fountain and the four rivers. There are, the poet assures us, no lions here,

> ⁑ non serpens; nec cauda scorpius unca.

And, we might add, there are no Virgilian tags, no allusions to Ovid, no hint of Elysium or Henna's field. To the first of the *Parthenices*, Mantuan affixed an apology for poetry in which, among his predecessors in the art of versifying, he numbered Prudentius, Paulinus of Nola, Ambrosius, Bede, and Juvencus.[8] These Christian poets, most of whom de-

---

⁑ There is a place toward the gardens of the rising sun in the upper air,
A lofty place, raising its tree tops up to the sky.

⁑ no snake; nor hook-tailed scorpion.

[8] *Ibid.*, p. 58, n. 69.

scribed the earthly paradise, and their followers were the
models for this man who also had the Gonzaga for patrons,
and Bembo's father, Mantegna, Pico della Mirandola, and
Poliziano, among others, for friends.[9]

Through such a poem as the *Parthenice Secunda*, the
traditional Christian image of the earthly paradise survived
into the Renaissance, and achieved wide circulation.

IV · ARIOSTO

In the year Mantuan died, 1516, Ludovico Ariosto (1474–
1533) published the first edition of the *Orlando Furioso*.
With its appearance, a tremendous new force, destined to
influence epic poetry and theory for many years, engaged
the Renaissance imagination. However, this brilliant poem
was not simply a beginning; it was also, in a definite sense,
an ending. Ostensibly, the *Furioso* completed the *Orlando
Innamorato* of Matteomaria Boiardo; but of course it did
more than that. The *Furioso* also resolved conflicting or
parallel traditions into a totality whose form and tone would
never be possible again. The poem's sprawling, seemingly
haphazard episodic structure delighted readers for generations, but the reemergence of Aristotle's *Poetics* as the gospel
of poetic, and epic, theory meant that such structure could
never be entirely condoned. The elegant, fantastic, ironic
surface and tone of the *Furioso*—regardless of superimposed
allegories or apologies—could never again be wholly acceptable (even if understandable) to a Europe in ferment over
the Reformation. If we see the poem as an ending, it is
fitting that its publication should precede the ninety-five
theses by one year.

The literary background, of Carolingian and Arthurian

[9] *Ibid.*, pp. 22-24, 26.

material, of Franco-Lombard epics and immense classical learning, is too well known to need rehearsal here. What is pertinent is the gradual deepening of man's sense of bewilderment and despair as he attempts to reconcile the values of the past with the implications of the present and future. Here the undercurrents of elegant, though not necessarily conventional, melancholy in Petrarch and Poliziano are given an ironic outlet in Ariosto. The size and seemingly chaotic structure of the *Furioso* reflect the world seen not merely in flux, but of flux. In the meantime, the polished surface, the elegant, precise octaves, the knowing tone, maintain the image of cohesion and order at work upon the unstable material. The gap between the surface and the substance of the poem, between seeming order and felt mutability, is not a rift which the poet creates unwittingly, or into which he falls. The split is indeed the very subject of the poem, and no one is more aware of it than Ariosto.

In fact, Ariosto seems to be aware of everything, and that is the level upon which his much celebrated irony operates. Ariosto is constantly examining experience with experience; he is constantly turning attitudes, statements, codes, visions—in short, appearances, words—back upon themselves. The old chivalric code is always being examined by its behavior under stress and the limitations of chivalry in the modern day emerge as one of the themes of the poem. Love as an ideal of physical or spiritual existence is repeatedly subjected to scrutiny, and countless episodes reveal its shortcomings, delusions, absurdities. Things never are what they seem. There is too much going on, impinging, underlying, ever to allow one man's set of standards or absolutes the final say. Between what seems and what is, lies either the sane, middle path, open to a few, or the bitter road of futility and delusion, taken by most. And yet—perhaps both ways are finally the same; perhaps the road to sense is also the same as the path to non-sense. Perhaps the only answer or standard or guide to life is that there is no answer, guide, or standard. What is finally most important is that man be tolerant—that is, that man be forever aware of the many possibilities, contingencies, new realities which can exist under a single, simple-seeming guise.

This spirit of tolerance, however, does not ever manifest itself in the poem as simple, iconoclastic glee; nor, one should add, as sentimentality, bitter cynicism, or tired resignation. Rather, it reveals itself in a mingling of acceptance and regret; acceptance of the fact that nothing on earth can be regarded as fixed or finished or, finally, even true; and regret at the loss of codes of behavior which seemed to deal with the complexities of man's existence. I do not mean, as so many have said, that Ariosto is just the perfect cynic or the poet of a hopeless amorality. Such views are vast oversimplifications. Ariosto has definite moral norms by which he measures behavior; and they appear clearly in the passage we will examine in a moment. But he does not present these norms as dogmas, as Imperatives; in fact, he does not *present* them at all. Like everything in Ariosto, they appear obliquely, as implicit yardsticks to measure our vanity and delusions.

It is important, I think, to notice how in Ariosto the poem is constantly examining the poem; how poetry, as a process and a reflection of life, is always examining itself. The power or sense of illusion is repeatedly used to expose delusions, and thus the reader is always warned against taking literature (or life) at face value. Put another way, one could say that from Dante to Leopardi, Italian poets have been intensely realistic about illusions. It is that quality above all which informs the *Furioso*.

GIVEN the totally pervasive irony of this type of mind, I think, therefore, it is no accident that the only really sane character in the *Orlando Furioso* appears insane; the only one with sense deals in nonsense; the only secure person, not killed or seduced or violently disillusioned, is without fine illusions, ideals, or nobility: is, in short, the image of the poet—Astolfo.

When we meet Astolfo, he has indeed been trapped by Alcina and now resides in the myrtle. This was a state of affairs Ariosto inherited in part from Boiardo, but Ariosto uses the situation to advantage. For through his experience, Astolfo seems to have learned the futility of love and chivalric endeavor; he has learned to be aware, and wary, in a way no one else in the poem ever approaches. Astolfo tries to impart his wisdom to Ruggiero, but to no avail. Thereafter, Astolfo moves through the poem totally unencumbered by the illusions or the aspirations and hopes which beset the others. With his horn, book, horse, and lance, Astolfo is the complete yet unassuming master of magic. He is often foolish, to be sure, but never a fool. He is the still eye in a storm of absurdity; the grotesque and silly and pathetic, and even deadly, transpire around him, but never touch him. Astolfo is the master of his environment: the knight who comments warily on chivalry, the lover who knows better than to expect too much of love, the magician who is unawed by magic, he is like the poet, who comments, or is the filter for comment, on the poem and the nature of art. Like Ariosto, Astolfo is the supreme and superb ironist, more so because he does not seem so, unobtrusive yet ubiquitous, soaring above all creation, a figure from outside the world of the poem (through an etymological mix-up, this Old French character is now an Englishman) yet intimately related to the main characters, and action, of the poem. Like the poet, Astolfo knows everything (or can find everything out: the poet "reads" Turpin; Astolfo uses his magic book) but never seems to *do* much. And like the poet, Astolfo is the benign master of illusion without illusions himself, the constant antithesis of all that is viewed seriously, the comic, clownish, superficial-seeming man who knows profound, even deadly, truths. Astolfo is the genius of the *Orlando Furioso*, the poet looking at himself with irony. Ariosto never takes Astolfo seriously, because Ariosto knows there is nothing to be gained from taking anything, especially himself, too seriously for very long. In fact, it is this very quality which makes Ariosto a serious poet.

Astolfo, therefore, represents the all-knowing, omnipresent, gentle master of ironies; Alcina is the malignant manipulator of illusion, the corrupter of spirits; and Ruggiero stands for all those characters, and readers, who must walk the path in between. Because he knows less than Astolfo, Ruggiero is in need of education, and still capable of action. Ruggiero, with his incomplete awareness of the world, can still discern a road where Astolfo would see an intersection. Ruggiero must run the risk that the road is not what it seems to be; that it, in fact, leads to a trap where there seemed only a green field. This kind of pattern is established early in the *Furioso*, and occurs in that deceptive earthly paradise, the garden of Alcina. An examination of the garden in Cantos VI and VII will reveal some of the general preoccupations of the poem, and will also introduce us specifically to the first of the enchanted gardens of the Renaissance epic.

THE island of Alcina episode is one of incantation set in the traditionally remote but beautiful place. In Canto VI, stanzas 20 to 25 emphasize its beauty in conventional terms, often with echoes from previous poets.[10] The remoteness of the island, reminiscent of the Islands of the Blessed, the Fortunate Islands, of Venus' or Circe's isles, is also stressed (stanza 25). Upon arriving on the island, Ruggiero takes off his armor (24). This act marks the beginning of that emasculation Petrarch warned of, for the knight has already been seduced by the appearance of the place into leaving himself literally vulnerable.

Ruggiero has hitched the hippogriff to a myrtle bush. Suddenly the beast is frightened, for the myrtle begins to speak (27-28). The tone is melancholic, self-pitying, gentle: "Se tu sei cortese e pio."[11] Polydorus and Pier della Vigna

[10] For instance, "l'erboso smalto" (the grassy enamel) echoes the "smalto" of Dante's *Inferno*, IV, 118 and *Purgatorio*, VIII, 114, and allows Ariosto to imply the falsity and artificiality of Alcina's island before Ruggiero (or the reader) is aware of it. Later Camoens, *Os Lusíadas*, IX, 21, calls Venus' island "esmaltado," while Ronsard, *La Franciade*, III, 544 refers to "un riche émail de fleurs," and Milton uses the adjective in *Arcades*, 84; *Lycidas*, 134; and *Paradise Lost*, IV, 139—"gay enamell'd colors." In Marvell, what was a conventional descriptive term has become a process:

He gave us this eternal Spring,
Which here enamells every thing. (*Bermudas*, 13-14)

which converts Bermuda into a Christian Island of the Blessed.

[11] "[If] Thou courteous art and good. . . ."

All Italian citations are from the *Orlando Furioso di Ludovico Ariosto*, ed. N. Zingarelli, 6th ed. (Milano, 1959). All translations are from

are the models for this voice in a tree, but here a touch of absurdity spells all the difference. "Lieva questo animal da l'arbor mio." There is also, in the first words of Astolfo, a reference to Ruggiero's "cortesia." (The important implications of "pio," suggestive of Aeneas, are not expanded until Canto VII.) Through mention of Ruggiero's "cortesia," chivalry is established as the young knight's outstanding quality and becomes one of the episode's main concerns.

Ruggiero blushes (29) at his error, and says he did not know the rough bark hid a human spirit. The blush reinforces the portrait of the chivalrous young man who realizes he has broken the code by hitching his horse to a man. And Ruggiero's words introduce what we knew would be one of the other main themes to the episode: things are not necessarily what they seem to be. After the chivalry of Ruggiero is stressed in the next two octaves (he swears by his lady (31) and Astolfo mentions "cortesia" again in 32) we begin to see the poet's method. He wishes to praise the d'Este family by revealing their "ancestor" in such a favorable light, but he also wants to establish in Ruggiero that very quality which will prove his greatest weakness. Bradamante is alluded to not only because she is his lady love, but also because her presence in the foreground of Ruggiero's mind renders her dismissal from his thoughts, under Alcina's influence, all the more striking.

Astolfo now begins to speak. His tale is the essence of the episode, for it deals with the split between what seems and what is. For instance, what he thought was a whale

---

Ariosto's Orlando Furioso, tr. W. S. Rose, 2 vols. (London, 1824; rev. 1858). I have used the reprint of 1892; my additions or alterations are indicated by brackets.

turned out to be an island; what he thought was a lovely lady turned into a vile enchantress; the reciprocal true love between them was, after all, only a form of imprisonment. Even the way the tale is told—a teller within a teller within a teller, Alcina (39) or informers (42) within Astolfo within the poet or narrator—offers an image of what the tale is about. Each mode of discourse presents another version of the truth; and as we, as readers, pass through the discourses, we observe the many removes from reality which stand for the truth. Astolfo, or Ariosto's, brand of illusion—magic manipulated for its own sake or the sake of a point—is tacitly contrasted, as we progress, with Alcina's brand of magic whereby illusion is manipulated for the sake of the gap between appearance and substance. Alcina does not want to delight or educate; she wants to trap a man into believing that what seems is. In this way he becomes accustomed to surfaces and she can gain control of his spirit.

Alcina (and Morgana) are said to be unnatural daughters, while their sister, Logistilla, was a real, or natural, daughter. Alcina is also called a "fata" (42), and thus differs from her predecessors in a garden because she has the added dimension of a sorceress, of Circe. Alcina is an unnatural creature who can suspend or pervert Nature's laws, and thereby counterfeit or falsify Nature's face. Alcina and Morgana are contrasted to Logistilla as evil is to good, as appearance as false illusion is contrasted to appearance as the reflection of truth. Here is the point upon which the moral of the whole episode, and much of the poem, turns.

The plight of Astolfo, as he was seduced by Alcina, is conveyed by certain key words. "Veder" (46) is one; "pareami" (47) is another. Astolfo, in a Renaissance twist on the medieval *topos* of true love entering through the eyes, was fooled by what he saw and by what seemed, to the point that Alcina became the source and goal of all illusion.

> * Ogni pensiero, ogni mio bel disegno
> In lei finia, né passava oltre il segno. (47)

As we shall see in a moment, a man who bases his existence on illusion becomes, so to speak, not himself. Stanza 48 expresses Alcina's apparent devotion to Astolfo, while conveying Astolfo's real status as her slave. The difference between what is stated and what is implied is another way in which Ariosto interweaves his meaning into his method.

Astolfo is trying to educate Ruggiero in the difference between illusion and reality, art and life, and in the fate of those who confuse them or take one for the other. As an example of the situation, Astolfo has used his love affair with Alcina. Now, as a further example of the fate of those who confused the accidental with the essential, Astolfo reveals to Ruggiero the true nature of the island and, incidentally, the real character of its chief inhabitant. The beautiful-seeming isle, so striking in stanzas 20-23, is actually made of disillusionment. That is, all the rocks, trees, flowers, grass are really disillusioned lovers, lovers who have lost their illusions about Alcina, and with them, lost their humanity. This is one way in which a man is not himself when he bases his existence on falsity. To possess a blind faith in the superficial, Ariosto seems to be saying, means that one's substantial, intellective soul—the attribute which distinguishes man—is secretly corroded and defiled. So it is with the lovers of Alcina; they have become their mistake and

> * In her my every fancy, every hope
> Centered and ended as their common scope.

now embody the deception to which they fell prey. They seem to be beautiful objects of Nature, but in reality they are only beings which have lost their human nature. The lovers, so to speak, mistook a satyr for Hyperion, and now they are left with neither. Because once they failed to exercise discrimination, now they have lost the power of discrimination, and worse—the gift of believing in illusion. This is the true disillusionment. It is not bitterness or recrimination; it is Astolfo's condition, the state of total awareness. Perhaps here is a key to what is meant by the much-celebrated Renaissance fullness or completeness of man. It did not mean being Hyperion (as opposed to a satyr); for, as Dr. Faustus learned, that too could be an illusion. Rather the expansive totality existed in knowing about both extremes, being aware, as we have said, of the spectrum of possibilities in life, and of the split between word and deed, gesture and action, appearance and reality. To some writers, it also meant being aware of the futility of trying to overcome, or ignore, this gap; it meant simply enduring our going hence even as our coming hither.

Astolfo tries to impart this sense of awareness to Ruggiero, and in stanza 52 tells Ruggiero to beware of Alcina. Ruggiero will believe he has risen "sopra ogni mortal" and then, if he is not careful, he will actually sink beneath mortality—"o in fiera, o in fonte, o in legno, o in sasso." But Astolfo, perhaps reflecting the poet's feeling, does not really hope to persuade Ruggiero to beware the allurements of Alcina (53). He does not permit himself the illusion that man can learn so easily, or overcome so quickly, the dangerous power of sensual or superficial attractions. Astolfo wants to arm the at this point literally unarmed Ruggiero, but the tone of octave 53, like the tone of the whole poem, is not very hopeful.

All Astolfo has said hitherto has been in the nature of a rehearsal for what Ruggiero will now perform. But it is evident that Ruggiero understands only one side of what Astolfo has said.

> ✳ Si dolse assai che in steril pianta e grama
> Mutato avesse la sembianza vera: (54)

Ruggiero does not understand that under the appearance of the plant, Astolfo spoke mortal truths about Alcina and the island, just as a poet speaks truth through the illusions of art. All Ruggiero acquired from Astolfo was a superficial warning about a certain sorceress; he did not acquire an ironic sense of life, a taste for the self-reflecting, self-regarding kind of vision which must ultimately underlie noble intentions if a man is to survive.

Stanzas 55 and 56 portray the knight about to set out with a solemn determination to flee Alcina's realm. He is warned of a crowd of people who will attempt to impede his ascent of a certain "colle." In stanza 57 we see Ruggiero on foot. Like Guyon for much of Book II of *The Faerie Queene*, Ruggiero is a pedestrian knight whose education in courtesy—in this case, in its limitations—is part of the poem's point. Yet Ruggiero's very decision to walk indicates indecision, and this vacillation in the young knight's mind is clarified when he says: "Io passerò per forza, s'io non fallo." The two, neatly antithetical units of the line represent Ruggiero's hesitancy. The poet's only comment is "Ma vano era il discorso." All "discorsi" are in vain if they are made with-

---

✳ [He] Lamented much the sad Astolpho, turned
  From his true form, to barren plant and rude.

out a proper awareness of the world and all the possibilities within it.

Ruggiero arrives at a city which resembles the exterior of Claudian's Bower of Venus. Here the ambiguities about the gold façade (59) are central. The narrator says it is gold, then by mentioning alchemy he casts doubt on the gold, and then he casts doubt on the doubt. Finally, he says it is gold and accepts the appearance for reality. We are in the vacillating, innocent mind of Ruggiero, as the next stanza (60) makes clear. The knight thinks he has never seen the city's like. The narrator is guiding us through the whole cycle of deception again; Ruggiero is acting out what he and Astolfo have already been through in words. Only the words were largely lost on Ruggiero. Before, the whale was demonstrated to be an island, the island said to be made up of false Nature; and yet Ruggiero knows no better than to accept the city on the island at face value. We are watching a young man flunk his course.

Stanzas 61 to 65 recount the battle between the knight and the emanations of the city, those citizens who embody, in grotesque reality, the unnatural, distorted, crippled spirits which live within or beneath the city's handsome appearance. Here is a crucial point in Ruggiero's performance. The narrator says that if the knight had used Atlante's shield, if he had used "frodo," illusion (67), he would have overcome the ugly realities. But Ruggiero's innocent, i.e., simple-minded, unaware, code-bound, chivalry, his controlling frame of vision, demands he grapple with things as they appear. Thus he disdains to use the magic shield and its powers, and thus (68), his noble vulnerability is exposed and magic will be used on him. "Sia quel che può" is the dry comment of the narrator. Ruggiero must learn to deal with illusion, art, artifice, if not in it. In the meantime, his traditional strength, chivalry, is emerging as his new weakness.

Suddenly two creatures appear. Ruggiero judges them by their "gesti" and "vestire" (68) to be ladies come to help him.[12] But the poet's irony operates on these ladies, as it did on the gold, in the last three lines of stanza 69:

> ✼ Bisognerebbe aver occhio divino
> Per far li lor giudizio; a tal saria
> Beltà s'avesse corpo, e Leggiadria.

This seems to be the old technique of creating a vision and then elevating it by appealing to a higher quality—in this case the eye of God which alone could judge their beauty. But the lines also suggest that only an infallible standard could tell whether or not the ladies had any substance at all. The ambiguity is left open, and that is the point.

Ruggiero blushes again (70), just as he did at stanza 29: again a repetitive incident, again an index to Ruggiero's innocence. Before the myrtle was not simple myrtle. Now, what seems to the knight to be a warrior rescued by two maidens is by the blush set in an ambiguous context. Then it becomes clear: as Astolfo had thought himself master when he was really a slave, so now the rescuers are really the conquerors. The ladies appeal to Ruggiero's chivalry by their "atto humano," for which he is grateful, and to his sensuality. Ruggiero's code of knighthood and notions of

---

> ✼ [One] would need a surer sense than mortal sight
> To judge between the two. With such a mien
> Embodied Grace and Beauty would be seen.

[12] It is interesting to note that these same two maidens, Beltà and Leggiadria, helped entice Giuliano in *Le Stanze*, I, 45.

love, his superficial self, are lulled by flattery and thus, gradually, his essential self is endangered.

Stanza 71 presents the same kind of ambiguous attitude toward the diamond columns of the city which we noticed in reference to the gold façade (59) and the maidens (69). Again the surface is accepted as substance. In the next octave, we have a vision of lewd maidens in green skirts and wreaths, and Ruggiero is made to enter a "paradiso." This "paradiso," though the word automatically recalls it, is most certainly not an Eden; it is an ancient Elysium on the order of Tibullus': a place for "danza" and "gioco" (73). The externally lovely paradise is thus implicitly qualified by the echoes of pagan delight and Venus' bower; and in stanza 74 its deceptive and dangerous quality pivot on the word "par" (seems) in the second line. This is the poet's indication that Ruggiero is still unaware of his situation.

The knight is then symbolically disarmed in stanza 76. The hippogriff is taken away from him. This creature, emblematic of the knight's stature, is also a symbol of what Ruggiero does not understand—the ability to soar, to see, to control magic to a beneficial end. Ruggiero lost his mount because, one feels, he was never really in control of it, or the situation. In stanza 77 the ladies flatter his chivalry (ll. 5-8) and thus widen the chink in his spiritual armor. Then he is asked to combat Erifilla, another seeming test of chivalry which is actually a trap for his soul. Ruggiero progresses through these repetitive incidents as if he were penetrating to the essential core of the island. The irony of his situation is that once he has reached this core—Alcina —he has only arrived at the final source of all that is false.

Erifilla, mother of many of the grotesques Ruggiero met before, represents that stinginess of spirit which a true

knight is expected to overcome. The fact is presented clearly
enough, but the deception for Ruggiero lies in the fact itself. In overcoming the obvious, in conquering, as a knight
should, that quality of repression of noble spirit, Ruggiero
surrenders something deep in himself. He indicates the
limits of his own code of chivalry by surrendering himself
to the ladies' notions of chivalry; for he has been trapped
by a world which manipulates, but no longer truly believes in, the chivalric code. In overcoming the obvious, he
has succumbed to the superficial and overcome nothing
(79-81). As a digression, we might briefly note that this
episode helps illuminate what Ariosto meant by that famous
line in Canto I:

> [*] Oh gran bontà de cavallieri antiqui! (22)

The line is ambiguous. Ariosto is aware of the merits, but
also the limitations, of chivalry in the world. He knows
the code is outmoded, yet there is regret that such absolute
standards must necessarily be corroded by the shifting, relative context of life. If this explication seems to want the
line, and the poem, both ways, that is because Ariosto seems
to want to have everything, or seems to see everything, both
or many ways.

AT THIS point Canto VI ends. The themes of chivalry, and
to an extent, love, have been outlined. We have the context
of the garden as a place of illusory deception postulated;
and we have noted the image of the City again—now as the
Citadel of Unreason. What remains is to mesh themes and
context in the persons of Ruggiero and Alcina. Before beginning, however, the poet pauses to survey the tale thus

[*] Oh! goodly truth in cavaliers of old!

far. As usual, the comment is ambiguous and oblique. Stanzas 1 and 2 of Canto VII say that a vulgar audience, unaccustomed to believing in what is beyond their immediate experience, cannot accept the fantastic. But a courtly audience, such as was reading or perhaps listening to the poem, will understand and believe what they hear. This is a seemingly handsome compliment to the lords and ladies at the expense of the masses. But, beneath the compliment lies a comment on the relationship of art to audience, illusion to life. It is the courtly listeners who are like—indeed, some supposedly "descended" from—Ruggiero, and who are most liable to accept the superficial or chivalric appearances. This very audience is most likely to be trapped by what seems, just as they probably accepted these two stanzas for the compliment they apparently offered. As Astolfo tried to educate Ruggiero, so the poet is constantly trying to educate us by broadening the poem, involving us as readers or hearers, implicating us through our reactions. As we read, or hear, we become wary; we learn to suspend judgment; we are educated and therefore begin to discern patterns. Ariosto enlightens us by his techniques as well as by his content.

Erifilla, whom Ruggiero now fights, is in fact an ally of Alcina. Her bejeweled appearance, gaudy like the city or even the trappings of Ruggiero's new horse, is the link in the alliance of surface appearances and exposes Erifilla as a creature of the island. The knight, however, so intent on his duty, sees nothing of this; he does not even react to Erifilla's gesture (5) of showing her shield in a parody of what he should have done with Atlante's shield. The two fight (6-7) until the ladies shout ("gridar," which seems a strong verb for Beltà and Leggiadria), and the combat is over. Then we realize why they cry out; these maidens control Ruggiero. He is their creature. And they demonstrate the means of their control when they immediately flatter his chivalry again (stanza 7, ll. 5-8). As they undermine him, Ruggiero sinks deeper and deeper into the situation, and the ladies corrupt deeper and deeper sources within him. The movement from isle to City to Elysium to the last palace in a field (stanza 8 *et seq.*) plots the movement of his progress toward Alcina and his total ruin.

Alcina appears suddenly, as did the maidens. It is almost as if illusions appear when a man has deceived himself to the point where he will believe in them. Stanzas 11-15 are concerned with her appearance. Beside Circe, many ladies underlie this description of Alcina, notably Simonetta of the *Stanze* and Emilia of the *Teseida*. But Ariosto introduces the proper distinguishing trait in her appearance very early, the note of artificiality which sounds in:

> ✻ Di persona era tanto ben formata,
>   Quanto me' finger san pittori industri   (11)

and this quality of artifice, of almost mechanical falsity, is maintained throughout her description. In stanza 13 we have another reference to "paradiso," which harks back to Canto VI, 72, and reminds us that the false garden of Alcina is the best symbol of Alcina.

Ruggiero is inflamed at the sight of her, and moreover pinpoints her attractiveness for precisely the *wrong* reason:

> ✻ Ben si può giudicar che corrisponde

> ✻ Her shape was so excellently formed,
>   As only industrious painters know how to feign.

> ✻ yet might the observing eye of things concealed

A quel ch'appar di fuor quel che s'asconde.   (14)

This is the mistake that began with thinking that myrtle was myrtle. Stanza 16 contrasts Astolfo's warning and Ruggiero's disbelief that one so beautiful could be so bad. This recapitulation of Alcina's evil, coming as it does after a list of her beautiful qualities, reminds us of her true, ambiguous nature. It also indicates the gap between what seems and what is, and prepares for Ruggiero's final downfall. That downfall, after which all else follows easily and swiftly, is signaled in stanza 17. In this octave of rationalization, it is important to notice that Ruggiero begins to change *internally*, for it is his inner self which is corrupted by his faith in external appearance. The first sign of his essential corruption is his notion that Astolfo was changed for a good reason, signifying that Ruggiero already totally accepts the morality of changing a man into a plant. Then comes Ruggiero's judgment that Astolfo told a lie, followed by Ruggiero's thought that Astolfo was a hypocrite and spoke from jealousy. In this brilliant stanza of psychological probing, we watch Ruggiero's mind squirming as if caught in a trap. We also begin to realize that a man creates his own illusions, that a man creates that Hell he carries in him. Most of all, we watch Ruggiero acquiring a frame of mind which either perverts what is natural (the truth about Alcina) or accepts unnatural perversions (Astolfo's condition).

The bait has been taken and the trap snaps shut. Bradamante is forgotten "per incanto" (18)—a dismissal to which Alcina is agent but to which Ruggiero is also willing accomplice. Chivalry has met the dark side of a world of contingencies and has, in the person of its bravest exponent,

---

Conjecture safely, from the charms revealed.

failed the test. When the knight accepted the aid of Alcina's maidens in his battles, he lost the struggle for self-mastery and self-awareness. The poet now switches his attention to the subject of love. To begin with, love is linked with "invenzioni, e poesie" and "fantasie" (with the vaporous or potentially deceptive) in stanza 19; with mythological and obviously sexually oriented allusions in stanza 20; and with decadent Ovidian love-play and courtly assignations in stanza 21. Love, in three octaves, is shown to exist in Alcina's realm under many guises, but always to have lust as its basis. From this premise, the affair of Alcina and Ruggiero proceeds to its logical conclusion.[13]

Ruggiero now awaits Alcina in his chambers (20-23); his impatience reveals itself as lust (24), and he is tormented by "vani disegni" (25). The pattern of a life based on illusion, chivalric or amorous, is tormented by vain discourses, vain imaginings and is, in short, a futile and empty existence. In stanza 27, the single phrase "successor d'Astolfo" is applied to Ruggiero, and in a flash it reveals the irony of the situation. The great knight is now no better off, as a lover or a hero, than the semi-serious paladin. All the suspense and irony has been building up to the exalted love language of the first six lines of stanza 27. The whole Petrarchan arsenal thunders out the cosmic beauty and power of their love, and then suddenly:

✶ Salta del letto, e in braccio la raccoglie,

✶ He leaps from bed and folds her to his breast,

---

[13] This is not Ariosto's only view of love in the poem, but it represents the basic truth about love in its harshest light. Ariosto's attitude toward love seems to be similar to his attitude about religion: it is best not to ask too many questions, or expect too much.

Né può tanto aspettar ch'ella si spoglie. (27)

Within the context of the love theme, within the octave itself, the contrast between words and deeds, appearances and reality, is emphasized again. Alcina comes to Ruggiero in nothing but a sheer silk gown ("zendado") and a mantle (28). The mantle goes, but the sheer shift somehow remains. Under it she appears lovely, but she always is seen through such a veil. At this moment, her very person of course symbolizes the situation of which Ruggiero never seems aware.

Having embraced illusion and falsity, Ruggiero is totally their pawn. Through his presence, Ariosto satirizes court life, which he had observed at first hand, in stanzas 30-32. The codes of love, the secrets known to all, particularly the reliance upon clothing as an index to value—all these false attitudes and kinds of behavior are etched in three octaves. Much is made of the hunting indulged in by the court, a pastime that serves two purposes: it emphasizes the triviality of life in Alcina's realm, and it provides the opportunity, and continuity, for a break and shift in the narrative. Bradamante is now seen hunting Ruggiero as Ruggiero and Alcina are left chasing small game. When we last see the lovers, they are fishing. The tale of Alcina has come full circle; for this is the same activity in which Alcina was engaged when first Astolfo saw her (VI, 38). Then, as now, there was always prey at hand, poor fish who were once faithful paladins.

The poet switches briefly to Melissa and Bradamante, and we learn—in this major shift in discourse—another truth, another irony. Atlante, who loves Ruggiero like a son, sent the young knight to Alcina's island for safety.

Nor waits until the lady be undressed.

In fact, it is Atlante's magic that ensures Alcina's love (44). There is a major irony in the fact that good intentions often create the worst situations, that magic is divine but unpredictably demonic. But the immediate irony is that Alcina is a slave to Atlante much as Ruggiero (or Astolfo) is a slave to Alcina. Thus, nothing is constant in this world; all turns back upon itself. Magic operates against magic, one illusion contrasts with another, and there is no final reality. Art, like life, is a process or progress from one illusion to another. Supposedly the wise man knows this and withdraws. The only problem then is that one misses out on life, which for all its pitfalls is nevertheless always presented as attractive.

Melissa requests Bradamante's magic ring of reason in order to save Ruggiero. Why does she want this ring? In her reason:

※ "Per trar del regno effeminato e molle"   (48)

we hear once again an echo of Petrarch's insight into those enchanted gardens which:

※ Ogni maschio pensier de l'alma tolle.

Melissa changes a demon into a horse, and mounts. But she is careful to take the ring from her finger so as not to undo her own magic. This is a realistic touch typical of Ariosto's fantasy. It shows us, under the soaring imagination, the shrewd, hard mind which is always aware of possibilities; it reveals to us a master of illusion who knows better than to let his art become master of him. Through the figure of Melissa, we see a benign intention putting

※ [To bring him] From that effeminate, soft realm

※ deprive the soul of every manly thought

illusion to good use (50). This is part of the lesson Ruggiero never conned.

Melissa (in the appearance of Atlante, so as to better speak the truth) appears to Ruggiero and finds him much changed. His essential corruption has manifested itself in his new appearance which, though to some might indicate excellence, to the true, discerning eye bespeaks inner corrosion. Indeed, the landscape, soft, musical and lush, sets the scene for the meeting and projects Ruggiero's inner state (53). What is the knight's condition? His clothes tell the whole story.

> ✲ Il suo vestir delizioso e molle
> Tutto era d'ozio e di lascivia pieno,
> Che de sua man gli avea di seta e d'oro
> Tessuto Alcina con sottil lavoro. (53)

He is the very picture of the spiritually emasculated man; for into the fiber of his being, Alcina's subtle work has woven its soft threads. But Ruggiero reminds us of more than Petrarch's and Poliziano's soft lovers in an earthly paradise; Ariosto has a greater design in mind. Early in Canto VI, Astolfo called Ruggiero not only "cortese" but "pio," (28). The potential of that second adjective is now about to be exploited.

Ruggiero here reminds us of Aeneas, another strong man deterred and softened by a woman's wiles, a woman who was also under a love spell. Melissa finds Ruggiero as Mercury found Aeneas:

> ✲ His fine, soft garments, wove with cunning skill,
> All over, ease and wantonness declare;
> These with her hand, such subtle toil well taught,
> For him in silk and gold Alcina wrought.

✕ atque illi stellatus iaspide fulva
ensis erat, Tyrioque ardebat murice laena
demissa ex umeris, dives quae munera Dido
fecerat, et tenui telas discreverat auro.
(*Aeneid*, IV, 261-264)

The correspondence between the two heroes holds right down to the detail of the ladies weaving gold into the fabric. This Virgilian echo is carefully planted by Ariosto, for it provides resonance and weight to his statement that

✕ Così Ruggier fu ritrovato, tanto
Da l'esser suo mutato per incanto. (55)

And the Virgilian allusion also furnishes a pattern for the rest of the Ariostean episode. As Mercury, reprimand in his voice, asked Aeneas if this was his duty, so Melissa (as Atlante) demands of Ruggicro:

✕ "È questo dunque il frutto ch'io
Lungamente atteso ho del sudor mio?" (56)

Then, as Mercury reminded Aeneas of his destiny (272-276), Melissa reminds Ruggiero of his (61). Indeed, at this point, Melissa's language makes Ruggiero sound like a second Aeneas. Perhaps Ariosto thought that if the d'Este did not see the Virgilian parallel imbedded in the verse—and there

✕ And lo! his sword was starred with yellow jaspers,
and a cloak hung from his shoulders ablaze with
Tyrian purple—a gift that wealthy Dido had wrought,
interweaving the web with thread of gold.

✕ So was Rogero found, within that dell,
Changed from his former self by potent spell.

✕ "Is this the fruit at last
Which pays my tedious pain and labour past?"

was ample reason to believe such a subtle touch might well escape the male members of the family—then his encomiastic duties would be best served by making the Ruggiero-Aeneas parallel more obvious. At any rate, to round the parallel off, both Aeneas (279-280) and Ruggiero (65) react to their chidings in the same way and are speechless. This parallel also serves as an excellent example of how classical material was borrowed and transmuted by Renaissance artistry. Both the *Aeneid* and the *Orlando Furioso* are the richer for it.

The ring reveals Alcina, as she really is—ugly, foul, and loathsome—to the sight of Ruggiero. The long simile (71-72), notably the only heroic simile in the entire Alcina episode, underscores the revelation and solemnizes its meaning. The simile, of the little boy and the once prized, now rotten and rejected fruit, is literally apt. Ruggiero has been a little boy, innocent and uneducated, naïve and trusting, and the fruit which seemed so fine and is now so rotten that the boy spurns it, is precisely Alcina, that fair-seeming but actually much-handled delicacy of the deceptive earthly paradise. Ruggiero not only sees Alcina for what she is, but more importantly he sees her method, her art, and he understands her power (73-74). Thus Ruggiero finally learns what Astolfo tried hard to teach him: be wary of the world; adapt, bend, use illusion when necessary. Ruggiero now uses Alcina's methods on her—which in capsule is a description of the whole technique of the poem. He lies about his motives for trying on his armor; "finse," "finse," says the poet in stanza 75. Ruggiero is learning. It is also worth noting that as he learns, he is literally, as well as metaphorically, rearming himself.

Ruggiero's education is well on its way when he takes

up his magic shield again, that shield, Ariosto is careful to
point out,

> * Che non pur gli occhi abbarbagliar solea,
> Ma l'anima facea sí venir manco,
> Che dal corpo esalata esser parea. (76)

The shield, which not only dazzles the sight but strikes at
the soul, represents the conjunction of superficial glitter and
essential power. As we know, Ruggiero should have used
the shield before. Now at least he knows enough to use the
property—magic as a means to a good end—which it
potentially represents. "Fingendo," Ruggiero flees the palace
"lascivo e molle" (79). Perhaps as a sign of his new maturity,
Melissa gives him Astolfo's horse (77). The hippogriff,
though, is reserved for the master himself, who will soon
reemerge from the myrtle.

The triumph of Ruggiero, or Ruggiero's teachers, comes
when he finally does use the shield. In Canto X, 49ff.,
Ruggiero is pursued by Alcina and her followers. He exposes the shield (on the advice of Logistilla's boatman), and
this is the beginning of the end for the sorceress. Her fleet
in disarray, she and her realm are vanquished; for she who
had the power to suspend or reverse Nature now sees her
realm, as the poet says, "sottosopra volto" (53). However,
Alcina cannot die, and like Despair or Malbecco as jealousy
in *The Faerie Queene*, she continues, we feel, to exist as a
force in the world. She is always somewhere. Ariosto knows

> * which, espied,
> Not only dazzled the beholder's sight,
> But seemed, when its silk veil was drawn aside,
> As from the body it exhaled the sprite.

better than to think she could disappear, or that we could do without her.

Ruggiero arrives at Logistilla's realm, and we are meant, of course, to contrast this paradise with Alcina's. The jewels of Alcina's island were either fake or simply shiny; here they are real, and their brilliant surface gives a true reflection of a man's inner self (59). Perhaps the quality of Logistilla's kingdom is best caught in these lines on her garden:

> ✻ Ma quivi era perpetua la verdura,
> Perpetua la beltà de fiori eterni,
> Non che benignità de la Natura
> Si temperatamente li governi;
> Ma Logistilla con suo studio e cura
> Senza bisogno de moti superni
> (Quel che agli altri impossibile parea)
> Sua primavera ognor ferma tenea.　(63)

Unlike Alcina's, this garden is the antithesis of illusion. Here there is no flux, no shifting, shimmering snare of appearance. The repetition of "perpetua," "perpetua"—coming to rest in the "primavera" of the last line—recreates a garden where there is no fatal gap between what seems and what is. Logistilla's garden represents that state of soul which has found constancy and peace in a world of change. We notice

> ✻ But here the verdure still is permanent,
> Still permanent the external blossoms are;
> Not that kind nature, in her government,
> So nicely tempers here the genial air,
> But that, unneeding any influence lent
> By planet, Logistilla's zeal and care
> Ever keep fast (what may appear a thing
> Impossible) her own perpetual spring.

further that Logistilla has created and tended the garden herself, without any outside help, magic or divine. This is a product of herself, created out of and sustained by Logistilla's inner being. No trick, no incantation informs this garden, but only the lady's own "studio e cura." And finally, it is significant that the real selves of those knights reduced by Alcina come to Logistilla's garden upon their release. Here one is oneself; here the vital, radically sane connection between inner and outer man finds expression (64).

And yet, only one or two days pass before the knights decide to leave (65). Man is restless in this garden of everlasting peace. By nature, and in order to function as a man, he needs the challenge and the context of contingency, of danger and deception which may lead to glory and honor. The final irony of the gardens is that Alcina's will always be attractive and alluring, Logistilla's always somewhat, like virtue, bland, pale and, though immutable, a little dull. Life is most seductive where we are weakest. So the knights decide—back to "l'arme, gli amori,/Le cortesie, l'audaci imprese," back to the dangerous games of love and war.

There is, of course, one other garden of scope in the poem: the true earthly paradise (Canto XXXIV, 48 *et seq.*). Hither comes Astolfo, and meets St. John and the prophets Enoch and Elias. The description of the place, drawing heavily on Dante's garden of Eden, is in the traditional mode. Here the blessed live above corruption and await the Judgment Day. The spiritual significance of this garden, however, is not particularly emphasized, and it functions mainly as a peaceful, uncorrupted prelude to the landscape of the Moon. There Astolfo, man of nonsense, manipulator of the hippogriff, horn, book and lance, retrieves the wits of Orlando and surveys the wreckage—as only he could—of all our worldly illusions.

It is only after we have read the poem, seen the peace of Logistilla's garden or the benign serenity of the true earthly paradise, that we begin to take the full measure of Alcina's garden. Dangerous and corrupting though it certainly was, false and deceptive though its illusions were, Alcina's garden remains as the image of a way of life which man can never wholly reject. He cannot reject it because it is so much a part of himself; it represented something reprehensible but profoundly enjoyable. Its danger lay not in what it did to you, but in what it allowed you to do to yourself. Though Alcina's paradise embodied a way of life which should be avoided, it also embodied something which can never be destroyed; and, therefore, no other garden virtuous or divine, in this poem devoted to the world, can ever replace it.

Ariosto's gentle yet all-pervasive sense of the futility of human affairs must always be seen in relation to Alcina's garden. The garden teaches us that all deception is largely a matter of self-deception, and that no matter how strenuously we try to disagree, the final illusion is to think life would be at all bearable without illusions.

BIBLIOGRAPHY · CHAPTER THREE

GENERAL

Here I have included those works which have proved most useful as general background for a study of Renaissance literature, with particular reference to Italy and to the epic. Most of the works have their own bibliographies.

For the European cultural background, with an historical emphasis, see F. Heer, *The Medieval World: 1100-1350*, tr. J. Sondheimer (Cleveland, 1962), C. H. Haskins, *The Renaissance of the Twelfth Century* (Cambridge, Mass., 1927), and the works of Huizinga, notably his *The Waning of the Middle Ages*, first published in 1924, and now most readily obtainable in the translation of F. Hopman in the Anchor Book edition (Garden City, n.d.). For works with more emphasis on culture and literature, see C. S. Lewis, *The Discarded Image, An Introduction to Medieval and Renaissance Literature* (Cambridge, 1964) and C. Dawson's collection, *Medieval Essays* (first published, London, 1954; reprinted in Image Books, Garden City, 1959), esp. Chapters ix-xi. One should also see the very good study of D. Hay, *The Italian Renaissance in its Historical Background* (Cambridge, 1961).

Discussions of the Renaissance abound. For the term and its meanings, one should see the interesting essay by Huizinga, "The Problem of the Renaissance," first published in 1920 and included in *Men and Ideas*, pp. 243-287, and the most sweeping treatment of the subject, W. K. Ferguson's *The Renaissance in Historical Thought, Five Centuries of Interpretation*. Of course, J. Burckhardt's classic, *Die Cultur der Renaissance in Italien* (Basel, 1860), now available in many editions and translations, is still an indispensable work.

On the topic of travel and exploration during the Renaissance, which had so much influence on the literature of the period, see J. H. Parry, *The Age of Reconnaissance*, Mentor Books (New York, 1963) for a history of the explorers; for a fine review of travel literature in the Renaissance, see R. H. Pearce, "Primitivistic Ideas in the *Faerie Queene*," *JEGP*, 44 (1945), pp. 139-151.

For art history and Renaissance culture, see the studies of E. Panofsky, *Meaning in the Visual Arts*, Anchor Books (Garden City, 1955);

Studies in Iconology (New York, 1939), and *Renaissance and re-nascences in Western Art* (Stockholm, 1960). Also see E. Wind's, *Pagan Mysteries in the Renaissance* (New Haven, 1958), J. Seznec's *La Survivance des Dieux Antiques* (London, 1940), tr. by B. F. Sessions as *The Survival of the Pagan Gods*, Bollingen Series, XXXVIII (New York, 1953), and, important for considerations of the garden, K. Clark's *Landscape into Art* (first published London, 1949; reprinted as Beacon Paperback, Boston, 1961), esp. Chapters i-iv. Finally, there is the important study by R. W. Lee, "*Ut Pictura Poesis*; The Humanistic Theory of Painting," *The Art Bulletin*, 22 (1940), pp. 197-269.

On the intellectual and particularly philosophical currents of Renaissance thought, one should see the works of P. O. Kristeller: *The Classics and Renaissance Thought* (Cambridge, Mass., 1955), expanded in his *Renaissance Thought*, Harper Torchbook (New York, 1961); the many essays brought together in *Studies in Renaissance Thought and Letters*, Edizioni di Storia e Letteratura (Roma, 1956); and his recent *Eight Philosophers of the Italian Renaissance* (Stanford, 1964). E. Cassirer's famous study of Renaissance philosophy has been translated by M. Domandi as *The Individual and the Cosmos in Renaissance Philosophy*, Harper Torchbook (New York, 1963). For selections, in translation with critical introductions, from Petrarch, Valla, Ficino, Pomponazzi, and Vives, see *The Renaissance Philosophy of Man*, ed. E. Cassirer, P. O. Kristeller and J. H. Randall, Jr. (Chicago, 1948). Kristeller and Randall provided a valuable review of this material up to a certain point in "Study of the Philosophers of the Renaissance," *JHI*, 2 (1941), pp. 449-496.

For discussions of diplomatic, religious, political, intellectual, and art history; of revaluations of the concept of the Renaissance; and of English and Continental literature, see the three collections of essays: *The Renaissance: A Symposium* (Metropolitan Museum of Art, 1953; Harper Torchbook, New York, 1962); *Facets of the Renaissance* (Los Angeles, 1959; somewhat expanded, Harper Torchbook, New York, 1963); and *The Renaissance, A Reconsideration of the Theories and Interpretations of the Age*, ed. T. Helton (Madison, 1964). Each has six essays and provides good bibliographies in the notes.

On the general topic of classical culture and influence in Renaissance literature, G. Highet's *The Classical Tradition*, Galaxy Books (New York, 1957), esp. Chapters v-xii, contains general information; a survey is provided by D. Bush in *Classical Influences in Renaissance Literature* (Cambridge, Mass., 1952) which are lectures dealing with what Bush handled in his *Mythology and the Renaissance Tradition in English Poetry* (Minneapolis and London, 1932); for this study, I have used the new revised edition, Norton Library (New York, 1963). One should also consult his latest collection, *Prefaces to Renaissance Literature* (Cambridge, Mass., 1964; Norton Library, New York, 1965). One should also see R. R. Bolgar, *The Classical Heritage* (Cambridge, 1954; Harper Torchbook: New York, 1964).

For English literature of the Renaissance, one should see the volumes in the Oxford History of English Literature: C. S. Lewis, *English Literature in the Sixteenth Century excluding Drama* (Clarendon Press, 1954) and D. Bush, *English Literature in the Earlier Seventeenth Century 1600-1660*, rev. ed. (Clarendon Press, 1962) where there are full bibliographies. A. Barker in *Literary Views*, ed. Camden, offers "An Apology for the Study of Renaissance Poetry," pp. 15-43, a densely written cogent review of much recent Renaissance scholarship. Finally, one should see E. W. Tayler's *Nature and Art in Renaissance Literature* (New York, 1964); the topic is traced from its classical and medieval origins into the Renaissance and examined in detail in representative works of Spenser, Shakespeare, and Marvell.

For Italian literature of the Renaissance, see the standard histories in the Storia Letteraria d'Italia series: V. Rossi's *Il Quattrocento*, revised by A. Vallone (Milano, 1954), and G. Toffanin's *Il Cinquecento*, fifth rev. ed. (Milano, 1954). Here one will find good chapters on the main figures of the fifteenth and sixteenth centuries, and excellent bibliographies.

The best study of the epic is T. M. Greene's *The Descent from Heaven*, cited above p. 92. Here one finds chapters on all the epic poets of the Renaissance, as well as antiquity. There is also Sir M. Bowra's *From Virgil to Milton* (London, 1945). On the romantic epics of the Italian Renaissance, see R. M. Ruggieri, *L'umanesimo cavalleresco italiano* (Roma, 1962) and, for all the views of F. De

Sanctis on the subject, *La Poesia Cavalleresca*, ed. M. Petrini, Scrittori d'Italia (Bari, 1954).—Though it reached me too late for inclusion in all the proper places, a recent study by R. M. Durling, *The Figure of the Poet in Renaissance Epic* (Cambridge, Mass., 1965) includes chapters on Boiardo, Ariosto, Tasso and Spenser.

MANTUAN

For Mantuan, see *The Eclogues of Baptista Mantuanus*, ed. W. P. Mustard (Baltimore, 1911), which contains an excellent introduction to the man and his works; also V. Zabughin, "Un Beato Poeta," *Arcadia, Atti dell'Academia*, I (1917), 61-90. In his forthcoming study of the Brief Epic, Professor Stewart Baker will have a detailed chapter devoted to Mantuan.

ARIOSTO

A good biography of Ariosto is G. Toffanin's *La Vita e Le Opere di Ludovico Ariosto* (Napoli, 1959); this is the most recent edition. In English there is only the old study by E. G. Gardner, *The King of Court Poets* (New York, 1906).

For the literary sources and antecedents of the *Orlando Furioso*, one must consult P. Rajna's *Le Fonti dell'Orlando Furioso*, and the splendid critical apparatus in the *Orlando Furioso*, ed. L. Caretti, and the *Opere Minori*, ed. C. Segre, Vols. 19 and 20 in *La Letteratura Italiana* (Ricciardi; Milano and Napoli, 1954). The notes to the *Furioso*, contained in the *Opere Minori* volume, are indispensable for anyone interested in the sources of Ariosto's imagery and his literary allusions. See also G. B. Bolza, *Manuale Ariotesco* (Venezia, 1868).

There are good bibliographies in Toffanin, *Il Cinquecento* after the two chapters devoted to Ariosto; in the *Opere Minori*, ed. Segre, pp. xxii-xxv; and in Toffanin's *Vita e Opere*. For general guidance, see W. Binni, *Storia della Critica Ariostesca* (Lucca, 1951) and R. Ramat, *La Critica Ariostesca dal Secolo XVI ad Oggi* (Firenze, 1954) which covers items from many countries; and G. Fatini, *Bibliografia della Critica Ariostea 1510-1956* (Firenze, 1958). The best general criticism in Italian is in the works of Toffanin, and in A. Momigliano's *Saggio su L'Orlando Furioso* (Bari, 1925; 1959).

One might also consult the volume *L'Ottava d'Oro* (Mondadori, 1933), a collection of 39 essays on Ariosto and his works commemorating the 400th anniversary of the poet's death. The quality of the essays is not consistently high; there is Fascist propaganda and a few prose poems, but many of the essays are sound, and A. Momigliano's "Nell' Isola di Alcina," Chapter xii, pp. 289-312, is particularly interesting for what concerns us in this study.

In English, Ariosto is often mentioned but seldom written about, largely, one fears, because he has acquired a reputation for superficiality and frivolity. One can understand Dr. Johnson's reference to Ariosto's "pravity" (in his *Life of Milton*), but it is astonishing to find a distinguished scholar like J. W. Bennett telling us at this late date that Ariosto has "nothing more profound on his mind than the amusement of his readers . . ." ("Genre, Milieu, and the 'Epic-Romance'" in *English Institute Essays 1951*, ed. A. Downer [New York, 1952], p. 111.) Suffice it to say that, like many rumors, this one too is false. There are a few scattered pages in Lewis' *Allegory of Love*, 301-303 and *passim*, which can be read to support Mrs. Bennett's view, though they need not be; comments in G. Hough, *A Preface to the Faerie Queene* (London, 1962), Chapter ii; the very acute introduction by R. Gottfried to his *Ariosto's Orlando Furioso, Selections from the Translation of Sir John Harington* (Bloomington, 1963), pp. 9-20; much information on Ariosto in England in M. Praz, *The Flaming Heart* (Garden City, New York, 1958), pp. 287-307; a good article by R. M. Durling "The Divine Analogy in Ariosto," *MLN*, 78 (1963), pp. 1-14; and an incisive chapter in Greene, *The Descent from Heaven*, pp. 112-142.

There are some other items indicated in *Harington's Furioso*, ed. Gottfried, p. 12; and Ramat, *Critica Ariostesca*, p. 235, cites studies concerned with source-and-influence study.

On Alcina as a traditional figure, see Rajna, *Fonti*, pp. 182-184; also Bolza, *Manuale*, p. 15, where the reference to Boccaccio's *Teseida* should read XII, 53. Also, for Alcina as well as her sisters in later poems, see M. Y. Hughes, "Spenser's Acrasia and the Circe of the Renaissance," *JHI*, 4 (1943), pp. 381-399.

CHAPTER FOUR

The Earthly Paradise and the Christian Epic

A RIOSTO first published the *Furioso* in forty cantos in 1516. When the definitive 46-canto version was published in 1532, the poem was, in certain respects, already out of date. In the intervening years, events in Europe had made it impossible to write such a poem again. After the impact of the Reformation, no poet could afford, as Ariosto seemingly had, to ignore Christianity and its teachings. And after the reformation in Italian literature, no romance like the *Furioso* could be critically acceptable.

The whole atmosphere of the South became one of rigid rules and pressures. The Reformation brought an inevitable, wrathful reaction from the Church. Through the Curia, Index, Society of Jesus, and above all the Council of Trent, Rome sought to redeem itself as the repository of Truth. At the same time, through tracts, academies, polemics and feuds Italian critics were subjecting language and literature to the most rigorous and debilitating kind of formalization. From Vida's *De Arte Poetica* in 1527, the tide of poetics and "arts" and theories of poetry rose to Summo's *Discorsi* in 1600; and swelling and urging the tide were the editions, commentaries, and translations of Horace's *Ars Poetica* and, above all, Aristotle's *Poetics*. The twin pressures of cleric and critic, the true interpretation of the Word and the proper application of words, were at once contradictory and congruent. Poets were confronted at different levels of their minds with classical rules and Christian teachings, both demanding, as dogmas, to be accommodated. Accommodation, or reconciliation, became a necessity, and from this necessity sprang the invention of the Christian epic. At once aesthetically correct and spiritually edifying, this synthetic construct was rarely satisfying, for the poems, indeed the poets, were asked to do too much. In Tasso and his *Gerusalemme Liberata* we shall see the noblest attempt to confront and reconcile all the sets of rules; in Camoens and his *Os Lusíadas* we shall witness a very different solution to the same problem. Both of these poets, however, were writing their epics in the 1570's; to see them in proper perspective, particularly Tasso with whom we are most concerned, we must examine briefly the evolution of epic poetry from the beginning of the century. The best place to start is by considering Trissino.

I · TRISSINO

Giangiorgio Trissino (1478-1550) was a typical, all-purpose man of letters in whom we can see the development of the literary attitudes of the times. He was an early theorist, and published four *Discorsi* on poetry in 1529. During his lifetime he wrote two more, published posthumously in 1563, and their increasing reliance on the *Poetics* is a barometer of the critical pressures of the early sixteenth century. Trissino relied on Aristotle in practice as well as theory; indeed, in this respect he was a pioneer. His play, *Sophonisba* (1515), was perhaps the earliest tragedy of the modern era to be written according to Aristotelian rules for drama. It was not a great success. But this did not dampen Trissino's faith in himself or Aristotle, and he went on to write an epic according to Aristotle's precepts.

His motivation needs a note of explanation. Italian critics, in spite of Aristotle's relative neglect of the epic, had decided there was no Italian epic which conformed to the Philosopher's rules. The only real candidate for honors as an epic was the popular and enchanting *Orlando Furioso*. But the *Furioso* violated every canon of critical judgment. For one thing, the people liked it, a sure sign to the "dotti" that it had no theoretical value; for another thing, it obviously had no beginning, since it was ostensibly a continuation of Boiardo's *Orlando Innamorato*. Furthermore, its mad, dashing, delightful scenes broke the sixteenth century's two cardinal rules for epic poetry: Aristotle's statement that narrative poetry should treat of a single, unified action; and the current doctrine that profit and instruction, not delight and pleasure, were the proper ends of poetry. These two basic objections, on the grounds of aesthetic theory and "official" morality, were further buttressed by an appeal to Aristotle's rule of verisimilitude. Aristotle had said that "since the poet, like a painter of animals or any other maker of likenesses, is an imitator, he must always imitate some one of the three aspects of things: either as they were or are, or as men say they are and they seem to be, or as they ought to be." He goes on to say that there are "two kinds of error in the art of poetry," and one is "to imitate or [write] of impossible things."[1] Into this category of the

[1] I use the translation of the *Poetics* in *Literary Criticism Plato to Dryden*, ed. A. H. Gilbert (Detroit, 1962), p. 108, where Aristotle goes on to say that the error of imitating impossible things "is not germane to poetry"; here, as elsewhere, it is necessary to distinguish between Aristotle and his sixteenth-century adherents; what he said and what they, under his name, chose to follow are very often different things. On Aristotle's theory of narrative poetry imitating "one action that is whole and complete," see *Poetics*, 59a17 *et seq.*, Gilbert, p. 103; in the main, the six-

impossible, critics put Ariosto's marvellous—his flying horses and magic shields. However, because Aristotle had recommended the marvellous, and because it was clearly necessary for the epic, the marvellous was adapted into the Christian marvellous. This marvellous, probable and instructive, satisfied Aristotelian verisimilitude, the doctrine of profit and delight, and the morality of the Church.

Thus the arbiters of Italian literature disposed of what was then Italy's literary masterpiece, the *Orlando Furioso*, because it did not satisfy their rules; and to fill the void which resulted, Trissino went to work on a theoretically and morally orthodox epic. He took Procopius as a source and wrote a poem describing the successful efforts of the Byzantines, under Justinian and Belisarius, to drive the Goths from Italy. *L'Italia Liberata da' Goti*, composed in *versi sciolti*, occupied twenty years of labor, appeared in 1547-1548, encompassed 27 books, and was an immediate failure. The poem simply proved once again that, despite his knowledge of Aristotle's rules, Trissino was no poet. The unkindest cuts of all came from those critics who pointed out that the only passable parts of the poem were those imitated from Homer—and Ariosto.

---

teenth century seems to have adopted this statement as the rule for epic rather than Aristotle's remark that epic might interweave "dissimilar episodes in the action" (*Poetics*, 59b30, Gilbert, p. 105)—though Tasso is an obvious exception.

For discussions related to what is proper for poetry, and what is not, see *Poetics*, 51a36 *et seq.*, Gilbert, p. 81, on poetry and the universal; 60a26 *et seq.*, Gilbert, p. 107, on the improbable; and 61b9 *et seq.*, Gilbert, p. 112, on the impossible. These are all thorny matters in the *Poetics* and its Italian commentaries and translations, and my remarks are meant merely to indicate the general position of sixteenth-century criticism, particularly with reference to Ariosto.

Nevertheless, Trissino's epic demonstrates, in concentrated form, some of the problems epic poetry faced and some of the directions which it was to take. For this reason it demands our attention; and the best part of the poem in which to examine the trends of the times is that account in Books IV and V of the sorceresses Ligridonia and Acratia, and the enchanted garden of Acratia. Here is the earthly paradise of the *Italia Liberata*, a garden which looks back at Ariosto and, it has been suggested, forward to Tasso and Spenser.

First, briefly, the action. In Book IV, Belisarius' army is stationed at Brindisi, and eight knights set out on a mission. Along the way they meet a

> ˣdonzella/Tanto leggiadra . . .
> piena di fallaci inganni   (IV, p. 137)

whose name is Ligridonia.[2] She leads them, under false pretenses, to a fountain. There the knights meet Faulo, who overcomes them all, except Areto, and who sends the vanquished, under a spell, to Gnatia, the land of his sister Acratia. Areto returns to Brindisi and aid is dispatched in the persons of Trajano, Achille, Corsamonte, and Areto. These knights are also joined by an old man who is really the angel Palladio in disguise. The old man recounts the story of Queen Areta, who wept for her slain niece and whose tears created the fountain.

ˣChiunque beve

ˣvery graceful maid/ . . . full of deceitful tricks

ˣWhoever drinks

---

[2] All Italian citations are from *L'Italia Liberata da' Goti* (Paris, 1729), referred to by book number of the poem and page number of the edition.

Di sì dolce acqua, tutto si risana,
Onde è detta la fonte del sanajo.
E giova ancor quella santissim' onda
Contra ogni incanto, e ratto lo dissolve.   (IV, p. 146)

Acratia, the chief sorceress, has Faulo guard the fountain
so no one may benefit from its virtues and she can reign
unchallenged.

Now follows an incident which catches, in part, the spirit
of the Alcina interlude. As Astolfo told Ruggiero to use a
magic shield to overcome Alcina, so the old man tells the
knights to use a magic shield with Faulo. But Corsamonte
says no.

⁎ Veramente a me non piace
  Vincer con artificio, e con inganni,
  Ma per viva virtù, per viva forza.   (IV, p. 148)

Corsamonte, like Ruggiero, refuses to use artifice; he would
rather rely on his native might and chivalric virtue. Like
Ruggiero, Corsamonte immediately falls prey to the sorceress,
while Trajano, who has accepted "il buon soccorso" (IV,
p. 149), is the knight who eventually saves the day. In this
incident, Trissino copies Ariosto and grasps, in a rudimentary
way, the principle of heroic limitation and the necessity of
manipulating illusion. Illusion here of course is sanctified
by its source—the angel in disguise.

Of that most sweet water, becomes entirely healed,
Whence it is called the fountain of health.
And that greatly blessed water is still potent
Against every charm, and immediately dispels it.

⁎ Truthfully I do not like
  To conquer by artifice and by tricks,
  But rather through natural virtue, natural strength.

Heroic Corsamonte is duped by Ligridonia, but the other knights overcome Faulo. In Book V, Areto is left on guard, Trajano and Achille bathe in the "fonto del sanajo," and the angel, now revealed, leads the baptized paladins to Acratia's land. On the way, Palladio gives a long (V, pp. 166-171) description of the garden and palace. This technique of prophetic discourse is again copied from Ariosto (Astolfo's speech to Ruggiero) and anticipates Tasso. In the angel's description of the land of Gnatia, Trissino incorporates literally all of the traditional earthly paradise and bower of Love motifs. According to Palladio, green lawns, a fountain, and pliant maidens, inviting the visitor to lascivious games, first greet the eye. Through walls of alabaster and crystal, doors of crystal and gold open into a courtyard; there rich loggias overlook the lawn; frescoes, "che pajon vive," adorn the walls; and lords and ladies, served by boys and girls "che pajon messagier del paradiso" (V, p. 168), satisfy all their appetites.

Through doors we move beyond to an earthly paradise of odoriferous groves and warm, languorous streams. The angel's remark is that " 'l sol non vide mai cosa piu molle" (V, p. 169), and here "molle" is used, as it was in Petrarch and Ariosto and will be in Tasso, to suggest the corrupt quality of a garden life. Beyond again, says the angel, is the room of Acratia, and off it open bejeweled alcoves whose main appointments are beds. Each little alcove looks out onto yet another garden where, against a background of scented flowers and green grass, there is a fountain full of silver fish, groves, mild animals, singing birds, and every type of fruit and tree. This maze of delights, gardens alternating with palaces, symbolizes the loss of true self in sensual excess and is modeled on the seductive, ever-receding pleasure places of Alcina's isle. Indeed, the parallel between the gardens, and the ladies, is maintained by Trissino throughout. Acratia, like Alcina, exists at the center of the whole garden, the ultimate source of all depravity, and when Acratia is finally exposed as essentially ugly, we are invariably reminded of Ruggiero's perception of Alcina's ugliness.[3]

However, there is one difference in the treatment of the gardens and the sorceresses who animate the gardens. Astolfo never tells Ruggiero how ugly Alcina really is; he only emphasizes the false beauty of the island. Palladio, on the other hand, does reveal something of Acratia's real nature by describing her personal bower which is closed to everyone else. By implication her true self is mirrored in

> *una selva orrenda,
> Ove son l'erbe livide, ch' odore
> Mandano d'assa fetida, e di solfo.
> E questa orribil selva è circondata
> D'un gran muro di ferro, e quindi s'esce
> Per un sol uscio picciolo, e coperto
> Di amare ortiche, e di pungenti spine.   (V, p. 170)

> *a ghastly forest,
> Where there is livid grass which sends forth
> The smell of asafoetida and sulphur.
> And this horrible forest is surrounded
> By a great iron wall, and thus one leaves
> By one lone, small exit, covered
> With bitter nettles and with prickly thorns.

---

[3] The episode, however, is much coarser in Trissino than in Ariosto. Ruggiero sees through Alcina with the help of a magic ring (*Orlando Furioso*, VII, 72); but Acratia is seized by Trajano who "levò la gonna/ Di lei, mostrando le secrete parti" (V, p. 175) (lifted her skirt,/ exposing

In this interesting passage, Trissino figures forth Acratia's real inner corruption and evil through a garden which is in direct contrast to the pleasure parks around it.[4] This personal bower is seen at the center of the other gardens, the ugly source of all beautiful illusions.

Acratia's personal bower is inaccessible to all under her spell, but it is transparent and penetrable to those bathed in the "fonte del sanajo." On this note, the angel's discourse ends. The knights then arrive at Gnatia. While the angel becomes a dove and flies over the wall, the knights make a cross with their swords and rush through a gate (V, pp. 171-172). They have no trouble in finding Acratia's bower, storming it, and capturing the sorceress. Once Corsamonte and the rest are freed, Acratia is exposed as foul and filthy, and is eventually turned over to Queen Areta.

The garden of Acratia resembles Ariosto's isle of Alcina in its use of traditional paradise motifs and through its use of common themes and structure. But it differs from Ariosto's garden by incorporating the Christan marvellous, and by implicitly contrasting Acratia's values with Christian virtues. Thus the episode in the *Italia Liberata* illustrates two characteristics of epics to come. On the one hand, they will continue, despite Aristotelian rules and Counter Ref-

---

her secret parts). Here Spenser does seem to be adapting from Trissino, for the exposure of the falsely beautiful Duessa as a foul hag is very similar (*The Faerie Queene*, I, viii, 46-50).

[4] This technique is also used by Ronsard in *La Franciade*, III, 1,303-1,310, where the foul garden of Jealousy is a symbol of her physical and spiritual ugliness; he then passes to a description of Jealousy herself (1,310-1,324). See *Oeuvres Complètes*, ed. P. Laumonier, Société des Textes Français Modernes (Paris, 1950-1952), Vol. XVI. In this passage, Ronsard follows closely Ovid's account of Envy and her cave, *Metamorphoses*, II, 760-805, and this description may have also influenced Trissino.

ormation morality, to be greatly influenced by the *Orlando Furioso* and the traditional material it embodies; on the other hand, the epics of the sixteenth century will make greater efforts to incorporate the values and symbols of Christianity and the moral attitudes of the Counter Reformation Church. Epic poets are now obliged to take greater risks than Ariosto, for instance, ever was, and as a result, their poems exhibit greater weaknesses than does the *Orlando Furioso*. The Christian epic is the product of divided times, and the epics in the latter half of the century reflect the strain. As intellectual and religious divisions exhaust men, exhaustion and the quest for peace and rest become themes more deeply imbedded in the poems themselves. Indeed, it is as places of peace and relaxation that the island paradises of Tasso and Camoens make their greatest appeal.

II · TASSO

Torquato Tasso was just eight months old when Paul III summoned the Council of Trent with the bull *Laetare Hierusalem* (November 19, 1544). There is perhaps a note of ironic fate here, for the image of Jerusalem was to haunt the precocious Jesuit educated young man and was to animate his greatest work, the *Gerusalemme Liberata*, which was completed in 1575. The image of Jerusalem perhaps underlay that other event we date from 1575, the visible commencement of Tasso's mental derangement. The religious pressures which could be released through art could not be controlled in life.

Though he was only thirty-one when he completed his epic, the road to the finished poem had been a long one. For besides the religious tensions, Tasso had to cope with a bewildering variety of literary obstacles in the form of theories, strictures, admonitions and examples good and bad. By the time he was twenty, Vida, Trissino, Daniello, Giraldi Cinthio, Muzzio, Fracastoro, Minturno, Partaneo, and Scaliger had all published major works dealing with poetics in general and the epic in particular. And by the time Tasso was twenty-six, he had witnessed eight attempts to write an Italian epic worthy of Aristotle's rules and learned men. For following Trissino's *Italia Liberata* had come Alamanni with *Girone* (1548), Giraldi Cinthio with *Ercole* (26 cantos in 1557; the other 22 were promised but never appeared), Pigna with *Eroici* (1561), Cattaneo with *Amor di Marfisa* (1562), Tasso himself with *Rinaldo* (1562), Bolognetti with *Costante* (1565), Oliviero with *Alamanna* (1567), and Alamanni's posthumously published *Avarchide* (1570). And Tasso had seen all the efforts go for naught.[5] Hovering over this mass of theory and practice were the twin spectres of the pagan aesthetician and the Council of Trent, while in the distance stood the polished, mocking figure of Ariosto.

What was the aspiring young epic poet to do? Follow the rules of Aristotle or the successful, subversive example of Ariosto? Write of a single action, or multiple actions? Use ancient history or contemporary events? Classical matter or Christian material? Observe the rules of verisimilitude

---

[5] See V. Vivaldi, *Prologomeni . . . sulle Fonti della Gerusalemme Liberata* (Trani, 1904), chapters i-ii. What was worse, all these poems failed in different categories; for as Vivaldi points out (p. 17), they fell into three classes: poems made of romance material, written according to epic rules (*Girone, Amor di Marfisa, Avarchide*); a poem dealing with heroic material, infused with romance, written according to epic rules (*L'Italia Liberata da' Goti*); and poems seeking classical epic unity through the action of a single hero (*Ercole, Eroici*, and to an extent, *Rinaldo*).

or frankly employ the marvellous and miraculous? Did one compose according to truth, by rules, or did one invent? Should one appeal only to the "dotti" or could one also appeal to popular taste (and posterity)? Was it best to follow Aristotelian theory and be right, or Platonic inspiration and be read? And finally, was the proper end of poetry profit and instruction, or delight and pleasure? These and many other questions confronted Tasso, and he tried to answer them in a manner typical of his critical age. He wrote both epic theory and epic poetry.

The first treatise of theory was *Discorsi dell' arte poetica e in particolare sopra il poema eroico*. Though not published until 1587 at Venice, these discourses were written perhaps as early as 1564[6] and were read at Ferrara in 1570. After, and according to, this theory came the *Gerusalemme Liberata*. Begun in the early '70's, it was finished in 1575 and published, while Tasso was confined to Sant' Anna, in pirated editions in 1580-1581. Tasso never did authorize an edition of his great poem. What he did finally publish himself was a "corrected" version, the *Gerusalemme Conquistata*, in 1593. His final theoretical work, called simply *Discorsi del poema eroico*, appeared the following year. In their moralizing and dogmatism, these last *Discorsi* and the *Conquistata* reflect the religious and literary pressures to which Tasso had succumbed. Whereas the young poet strove to be right, the middle-aged poet was now content to be correct.

However, from a reading of his discourses, the outline of Tasso's theory of the epic emerges clearly. An epic poem, he believed, is one which, according to the rules of verisi-

---

[6] Angelo Solerti thinks 1567 is closer; see his *Vita di Torquato Tasso* (Torino-Roma, 1895), I, 121-123.

militude, imitates a segment of Christian history neither too modern nor too ancient. The poem has a beginning, a middle, and an end, is neither too long nor too short, and is concerned with a single, unified action told with a multiplicity of diverse episodes. The poet is free to invent, use the marvellous (which meant essentially the Christian marvellous), change historical particulars and treat any subject, including love, as long as he does not alter the origin, outcome or outstanding events of his historical action. Of course, the events, and the action in general, had to be noble and illustrious. Finally, Tasso believed that such a poem had as its end instruction through delight: "È dunque ... la poesia imitazione delle azioni umane, a fine di giovare dilettando."[7]

This epic theory, reconciling Aristotle, Church, and Ariosto, unified, moral and multiple action, as well as many other questions, is a monument to Tasso's greatest gift—the ability to synthesize and integrate diverse materials. It is this same gift which enables him, with classical rules and models, to write an avowedly Christian poem. The

⅍ Poetry is, therefore, . . . the imitation of human actions whose goal is to instruct by delighting.

[7] Tasso's treatises on poetry are conveniently found in *Opere*, ed. G. Rossini (Pisa, 1832), Vol. XII. The final position of Tasso on delight and profit, cited above, is from *Del poema eroico,* I (*Opere,* XII, p. 15) and means there is an aesthetic delight to poetry and an ethical or moral delight. The first is pure pleasure, the second is pleasure in virtue; each is an end in itself, but aesthetic delight is also a means to the end of moral delight. Tasso's statement is a standard Renaissance fusion of Aristotle and Horace's dictum that "The poet's aim is either to profit or to please, or to blend in one the delightful and the useful" (*Ars Poetica,* 333ff., in *Literary Criticism,* ed. Gilbert, p. 139). For Tasso's earlier position on this question, in *Dell' arte poetica,* see *Opere,* XII, p. 229.

Gerusalemme Liberata, adhering to Tasso's theory, is a great technical and structural achievement, and is the most serious effort of the Italian *cinquecento* to reconcile the many levels of classical culture with Counter Reformation Christianity. However, what Tasso lacked was an imaginative vision commensurate with his technical skills and genius as a theoretician. The conflicts which he reconciles in his poem's structure remain unresolved at some deeper level. The epic remains the final victim of the divisions it so brilliantly dramatizes and desperately tries to overcome.

The *Gerusalemme Liberata* is organized around the classical distinction between town and country, City and Nature. Most obviously City and Nature function as structural principles according to Tasso's theory of unified yet episodic action. Thus the single, unified and unifying action of the poem concerns the recapture of Jerusalem and is centered around the City. The episodes, meant to offer structural relaxation from the main action, are scenes of surcease from the fighting at the City and are set in nature. Erminia's pastoral interlude and Armida's garden are episodes of this sort. We can see here how the City represents the center of a man's duty, nature a place for the evasion of that duty and for the pursuit of personal comfort and satisfaction. The traditional distinction between City and Nature becomes emblematic of the classical conflict between duty, or honor, and love. The structural poles of the poem function as sources for antithetical value systems.

It is as the center not merely of action but of true moral value that the City functions most importantly in the poem. For Jerusalem is the center of a Crusader's duty precisely because it is the Holy City, simulacrum of the City of God. By doing battle for the City, by overcoming the external enemy, the pagans, a man achieves inner salvation. On this level, the natural world represents the values of a very different way of life, the life of ease and pleasure. The City is the way to eventual inner redemption through physical conflict, Nature the way to immediate inner peace through the avoidance of physical struggle. Therefore the City and Nature function on two separate but allied levels: in the conflicts between men, the structural and narrative level, the City is the center of action and proper duty, and nature is a place of escape; in the conflict within a man, the spiritual or moral level, the City is the source and symbol of Christian value and salvation, and nature represents the joys and principles of an alternative way of life. But, this is a Christian poem and thus whether we are dealing with the conflicts between men or the conflict within a man, the City is always the norm by which all is judged. The City is always the ultimate center of action, the true source of value. Tasso has taken the classical categories of town versus country, duty versus love, and placed them in a framework of Christian morality. City is always superior to nature, duty to love, redemption to rest. In short, it is physically and morally better to live in a state of Grace than a state of Nature.

Throughout the poem, Armida is the figure who represents all that is inimical to the City and Christian endeavor. Early in the poem she is introduced as the representative of the obvious enemies of the City. This occurs in Canto IV when her wizard uncle, Idroate, at the instigation of Pluto, persuades the beautiful sorceress to try and seduce Goffredo and bring chaos to the Christian camp (26). Here Tasso equates the pagan as heathen and classical (Pluto), with the demonic and magical and sees them all, through Armida, as opposed to the City. In Canto X, Armida is associated specifically with the natural world (62-70). According to a knight, she inhabits a beautiful garden wherein (like Circe) she changes men's shapes and wills (66) and induces in them a "vano e torbido sogno" (67). This preliminary association of Armida with nature anticipates, of course, the great garden episode of Cantos XIV to XVI.

In this episode, Tasso presents us with the greatest structural deviation from the main action and the most concentrated image of an alternative to the City way of life. Rinaldo, the greatest Christian champion, is pictured as shirking his duty to City and God by dallying in the garden with Armida. The garden promises him, and others, total ease, total relaxation; it is a world predicated on completely different principles from the City. Here Tasso brilliantly dramatizes, through the picture of a Christian in the arms of a pagan, the essential conflict within the poem: what is the proper source of peace? Should one serve God or serve oneself? Is it better to redeem the spirit or indulge the senses? Throughout the garden episode, Tasso demonstrates that he knows what the answer should be, that he is aware the proper source and goal of one's responsibilities lies beyond oneself. And to this end, he constantly condemns the garden by the moral standards of the City and returns Rinaldo at last to the main action. But he tries to do more; he tries to salvage Armida while condemning her garden way of life. He has Armida fall in love with Rinaldo so that, through this love, he can prepare for her redemption. Tasso wants ultimately to reconcile her with the City, and in this way finally resolve within Rinaldo the conflict between City and garden, duty and love. This final resolution of the conflict dramatized in the garden is never achieved and the *Gerusalemme Liberata* remains divided at its core. However, this is anticipating too much. Let us first see how Tasso's version of the earthly paradise functions within the framework of his Christian epic.

The actual garden of Armida is visited in Canto XVI by the knights Carlo and Ubaldo who have gone in search of Rinaldo. However, Tasso begins to discuss the garden in Canto XIV, and we must begin here in order to see the garden in proper perspective. In XIV, the conflict between City and garden as sources of value and as states of body and soul is made with special reference to Rinaldo and Armida by the dream of Goffredo.

The leader of the Christians sinks into a deep sleep and has a vision of a

> ✻ cittadin de la città celeste   (XIV, 7)[8]

in the form of Ugone. Goffredo says he wants to be released from his "carcer terreno" and asks that he be put on the true path. Ugone replies that Goffredo is indeed on "la via verace" (12), and he obviously implies that by discharging one's duty to Jerusalem, one will eventually achieve the Celestial City. However, says Ugone, there is one who is not on the true path:

> ✻ sol che richiami dal lontano essiglio
> il figliuol di Bertoldo io ti consiglio.   (12)

> ✻ citizen of the celestial city.

> ✻ Only from Exile young Rinaldo call;
> This give I thee in Charge; else nought at all.

[8] All Italian citations are from *Torquato Tasso Poesie e Prose*, ed. S. A. Nulli (Milano, 1955). All subsequent translations are from *Jerusalem*

Rinaldo is seen to be in exile, from duty, from community, from salvation, and the image of exile starts a whole chain of associations involving City and garden. What we notice immediately is that Rinaldo, known to be with Armida "ne l'ozio e ne l'amore" (17), is the first among Goffredo's "compagni erranti" (18). And Rinaldo is "errante" in the double sense of being wrong (in "errore," 17) and being a wanderer. Thus, to live in the garden is seen as existing in spiritual exile. By leaving the realm of Grace for the world of Nature, Rinaldo has wandered off the true path and into a state of moral error, a world of lies. Wandering, which for all Renaissance epic poets was the emblem for spiritual uncertainty, is here linked to a definite moral code.[9] City and garden are set up as opposing moral norms, with the City as the true center and source of value and the garden as a way of life based on physical and moral error.

For the rest of Cantos XIV and XV we shall be, along with Carlo and Ubaldo, slowly immersed into the garden world, and we shall gradually approach the garden itself as a place and as a corrupt state of soul. As we draw near, Tasso will acquaint us with two aspects of the garden: the tremendous attraction which the place has as a source of fulfillment and rest, and the way in which the very attractiveness of the place is emblematic of its immoral principles and corrupting powers. Like all false earthly paradises, the

---

Delivered, tr. E. Fairfax (London, 1749), with my additions or emendations in brackets.

[9] Thus, the only way back to Grace later is through redeemed Nature (Mount Olivet, XVIII, 12-15), in spite of demonic Nature (the Enchanted Forest) which the renewed Christian recognizes as only another form of his previous enchantment. Consequently Rinaldo disregards the apparition of Armida in the Enchanted Forest, XVIII, 18 *et seq.*, because he now sees through the falsity, and the illusions, of his garden life.

garden of Armida is condemned precisely where it is most enchanting. Its apparent virtues are its essential vices.

WHEN Carlo and Ubaldo leave the Christian camp on their mission, the first person they meet is the old man of Ascalona. From stanza 50 of Canto XIV to stanza 71, the old man recounts the story of Rinaldo's flight from the City, his seduction by Armida and her love for him. From stanzas 72 to 76, the old man anticipates, point for point, the action of Cantos XV and XVI.[10] In providing background to the garden and warning the knights about what they will encounter, the old man's discourse has a definite cautionary tone and function. In this respect, it is modeled on the discourse of Astolfo to Ruggiero and Palladio to Achille and Trajano. However, the old man is important for more than what he tells about the garden; he is equally instructive as a foil to Armida. Both the old man and Armida are magicians, and both practice their arts. The old man, however, is a convert to Christianity and uses his skills for good, while Armida is untouched by Grace and uses her powers to corrupt.

The old man lives in a magnificently decorated underground cave:

> ˟ E ciò che nutre entro le ricche vene
> di più chiaro la terra e prezioso,
> splende ivi tutto: ed ei n'è in guisa ornato
> ch'ogni suo fregio è non fatto, ma nato. (48)

> ˟ All what is bred in rich and pretious Vein
> Of wealthy Earth, and hid from mortal Eyes,
> There shines; and fair adorn'd was ev'ry Part,
> With Riches grown by Kind, not fram'd by Art.

10 Canto XIV, 72 on the guide anticipates XV, 45; XIV, 73 on the

His surroundings are real, as opposed to artificial, true as opposed to false. The surroundings reflect the values of the man, and thus the distinction between the artificial and the real, like all distinctions in the poem, is given a moral implication. To live in an artificial world is to live in a world based upon values other than the City's values. This is, of course, exactly what Armida's world will be, a garden whose artificiality is the source of its beauty but also the symbol of its moral unreality, its false values.

Tasso has made this distinction between the artificial and real, and implied its moral significance, even before the old man starts his discourse to the knights. As soon as the old man speaks, however, he demonstrates Armida's fatal power to seduce and corrupt in the same terms. Rinaldo, in his flight from the Christian camp, had killed some of Armida's warriors and had left his own armor behind. In this way, he hoped to escape unnoticed. Armida, however, was fearful that the Christians sent to find Rinaldo would reach him before she could take her revenge. Therefore, she put Rinaldo's armor on a headless pagan corpse, hoping in this way to deter those following him. To insure the deception,

> ⁒ Non lunge un sagacissimo valletto
> pose, di panni pastorai vestito,
> e impose lui ciò ch'esser fatto o detto

> ⁒ . . . near the Corse a Varlet false and sly
> She left, attir'd in Shephard's homely Weed,
> And taught him how to counterfeit and lie,

---

monsters anticipates XV, 47-51; XIV, 74 on the fountain anticipates XV, 53-57; XIV, 75 on the maidens anticipates XV, 58-66; XIV, 76 on the labyrinth and the lovers anticipates XVI, 1-2 and 9-24.

fintamente doveva: e fu esseguito.
Questi parlò co' vostri, e di sospetto
sparse quel seme in lor ch'indi nutrito
fruttò risse e discordie e quasi al fine
sediziose guerre e cittadine. (55)

Here Armida's power to make the artificial appear the real, the evil seem the good, is seen as it operates specifically through the natural world. She is able to make the unnatural pass for the real. This has disastrous consequences, because once one accepts her imitation of reality for the real thing, one finds one has accepted a world of completely false values. The Christian soldiers are tricked into accepting artificial nature (the bogus shepherd) for a real shepherd, and once they do, they no longer know what is right or wrong. Through Armida's power, nature is able to undermine the City's values; Tasso even uses a "natural" metaphor for the creation of civil chaos: "di sospetto/sparse quel seme in lor ch'indi nutrito/fruttò risse e discordie. . . ." The theme of artificial nature, symbolic of Armida's seductive charm and of the false principles of her moral values, is established long before we actually encounter the garden.

The old man's discourse also establishes another theme which is developed as we progress—the pagan, i.e. classical, quality of Armida's realm. We are told how, after Rinaldo swoons at the song of the siren (62-64) who has seduced him by appealing to "natura," Armida gazes at her vanquished enemy:

As Time requir'd; and he perform'd the Deed:
With him your Soldiers spoke; of Jealousy
And false Suspect he mongst them strow'd the Seed,
   That since brought forth the Fruit of Strife and Jarr,
   Of civil brawls, Contention, Discord, War.

✳ e 'n su la vaga fronte
pende omai sì che par Narciso al fonte. (66)

Not only does this classical allusion serve to contrast Armida's world, and love, with the main Christian concerns of the poem, but the image gives us an insight into the kind of love which animates this world. And as she shifts from being an enemy to a lover ("e di nemica ella divenne amante," 67), the implications of the Narcissus-image begin to expand; for she becomes now possessive and self-absorbed.

✳ Di ligustri, di gigli e de le rose
le quai fioran per quelle piaggie amene,
con nov'arte congiunte, indi compose
lente ma tenacissime catene. (68)

Here the themes of artificial nature and the pagan quality in her world are subtly joined by the poet. Armida can create, with her art, the strongest of chains from the most tender of flowers; and she takes those flowers from "piaggie amene," from a landscape which consciously echoes, ultimately, the "amoena virecta" of *Aeneid*, VI, 638. In short, Armida and nature are in league at every level in their effort to overcome Rinaldo and his devotion to City values. Yet we note here the curious ambiguity Tasso injects into his treatment of Armida and her world; for we are always

✳ on his Forehead gaz'd the Maid,
As in the Stream Narcissus doting lay'd.

✳ Of Woodbines, Lilies, and of Roses sweet,
Which proudly flow'red through that wanton Plain,
All platted fast, well knit, and joined meet,
She fram'd a soft, but surely-holding Chain.

sensible to the great beauty and charm of the lady and her surroundings even while, by City standards, we are being shown the paganism and potential corruption latent in her values and natural world.

Finally, Tasso's method as a moralist, as opposed to a psychologist, is apparent in this incident. We do not enter Rinaldo's mind as he is seduced and carried off to the garden (70-71), for he is still in his swoon. It is enough that he wandered away from the City and his Christian duty. His initial error is the source of all his subsequent errors. Implied here are the conflicts which Tasso never truly resolves in the poem: either a man is saved, through rigid adherence to absolute values and his sense of duty, or he is damned. He serves the spirit or he wallows in sensuality. There is no middle ground.

Having told the knights what to expect when they reach Armida's island paradise (71-76), the old man then gives them a magic shield (77). This shield is to be used so that Rinaldo may see his moral corruption, due to "amor indegno," reflected in its adamantine surface. This shield is an example of how the old man's magic, unlike Armida's, is in harmony with City values and therefore produces a true, not a false, image of reality. The knights, who are simply the agents for proper moral values in the garden episode, accept the shield as well as a book and a magic staff to help them through the labyrinth. Shield, book and staff are all examples of how pieces of traditional, romance marvellous can be invested with Christian value and thus integrated into the moral patterns of the Christian epic.

In Canto XV, the knights leave the old man and make their way toward the island-garden and Armida. Most of this canto is devoted to their long, long voyage in the bark of their guide. She is a young-looking old woman who, like the old man, is a "good" magician. Thus, as she takes them to Armida's isle, she serves again as a foil to Armida herself. The journey takes the knights even farther from the City, and serves as a geographical metaphor for Rinaldo's spiritual error. Once again, Tasso lets the twin themes of paganism and artificial nature imply a world of beauty and charm which is, at the same time, based on false, non-Christian values. For instance, the further they sail from the City, the deeper into the classical past the knights seem to go. First they pass "l'isole Felici" (35), home of

> * gli elisi campi e le famose
> stanze de le beate anime . . . (36)

and then, next to Armida's isle, they see "l'isola di Fortuna" (37). Tasso is able to associate Armida's isle with the naturally beautiful places of the ancient world while, on the moral scale of values controlling the poem, he places Armida's world far below the absolute standard of the City. The same double implication is found when the knights look up and see the way greenery and ice exist together, and the poet remarks:

> * cotanto
> puote sovra natura arte d'incanto. (46)

Here again, while reminding us that Armida's world is attractive, the poet reestablishes that it is a product of magic, a magic alien to the Christian values of the City.

From stanzas 47 to 56, the knights are engaged in climbing

* The Fields Elysian, as fond Heathen sayn,
Were there, where Souls of Men in Bliss remain.

* Thus Art can Nature change, and Kind subdue.

the mountain and attaining the plain at the top. On the way, they overcome—by means of the "verga aurea immortale" (49)—the snake, lion, and monsters which block their way. These creatures function as foils for the power of Grace in the magic staff. The point is, as the old man implied in his forecast of the beasts (XIV, 73), nothing can deter these knights, forewarned and literally forearmed, from the true path of duty—even when that path is in the midst of a hostile, or dangerous, world.

The greatest temptation to leave the path of duty comes when the knights reach the magnificent plain at the top of the mountain. Here air, odors, sun, climate, grass, flowers, and shade (53-54) all provide the setting for "il bel palagio" —an image of the anti-City—inside of which is the garden of Armida. The scene, reminiscent of so many gardens and bowers in classical literature, has some appeal for the tired knights:

> ✻ onde ne gian per quella via fiorita
> lenti or movendo ed or fermando i passi.   (55)

Then they see the fountain. It is fed by streams and a river, which in turn issues from a clear pool. The knights were warned by the old man not to touch the water of this place; one drop "inebria l'alma . . . e la fa lieta" (XIV, 74) with disastrous results. Thus they know that to succumb to the place means inner corruption, and they realize they must

> ✻ tener a fren nostro desio.   (57)

It is just as well, for before them they see spread a feast

✻ through those grassy Plains they scantly creep;
They walk'd, they rested oft, they went, they stay'd;

✻ [Hold] our Lust bridled with Wisdom's Rein . . .

on the banks of the lake, and in the water "due donzellette garrule e lascive" (58). It is these maidens who will present the greatest temptation, and will illustrate for us, here outside the walls of the garden, the fundamental attraction of the place—the principle upon which the whole garden life is predicated, and which the pagan, artificially natural garden world exemplifies.

The nude maidens are splashing, and racing each other, in the water. The knights are struck by them (59) and stop to watch. Although Tasso later implies that the girls did not see the knights immediately, here the implication lingers, in the verb "seguian," that the maidens knew they were being observed:

> * ed elle
> seguian pur i lor giuochi e i lor diletti.
> Una in tanto drizzossi e le mammelle
> e tutto ciò che più la vista alletti
> mostrò, dal seno in suso, aperto al cielo:
> e 'l lago a l'altre membra era un bel velo.   (59)

There is, in this portrait of the girls "ignude e belle," something fresh and appealing, and there is meant to be. We are as susceptible to it as the stern knights are. However, Tasso is not the unwitting admirer of such pleasures that so many critics have claimed him to be. For while relishing the scene, he also—here and throughout the episode—carefully shows us how much these pleasures appeal to the eye and ear. That is, he implies that this is a purely sensual,

* The Nymphs apply'd their sweet, alluring Arts,
And one of them above the Waters quite
Lift up her Head, her Breasts and higher Parts,
And all that might weak Eyes subdue and take;
Her lower Beauties vail'd the gentle Lake:

ultimately sterile kind of inducement whose sole object is to inflame but which has no greater goal than stimulation and titillation. It is a calculated inducement the maidens offer, a sly naturalness whose artificiality is in keeping with the surroundings. Here the poet implies all the seductive powers of artifice; later in the garden he will show us the false values artifice implies.

In stanza 60, there occurs one of the few similes in the garden episode: the girl rising out of the water is compared to the "matutina stella" rising from the waves, and the "dea d'amore" coming out of the ocean spray. Of course, the morning star and the goddess of love are both Venus, and here Tasso emphasizes the pagan and purely sensual quality of the maidens—and by extension, the garden to come. When the girl turns and sees the knights ("girò gli occhi"), we feel that she has known they were there the whole time and is now going to see how they reacted to "tutto ciò che più la vista alletti." Her subsequent display of modesty (61) is simply the maiden's equivalent of embellishing nature with art. The coyness is calculated, and so well calculated as to be charming. Therein lies its danger.

There now follows their siren song to the knights (62-64), and it echoes the song of the siren who seduced Rinaldo (XIV, 62-64) and anticipates the song of the Rose (XVI, 14-15). This song is meant to entice the ears as the naked coyness enticed the eye; and it makes the frankest appeal of the garden to the knights' most basic instinct and desire: sexual pleasure as a way to satisfaction, peace and contentment.[11]

[11] See T. M. Greene, *The Descent from Heaven* (New Haven, 1963), p. 216, for a brief, excellent discussion of the garden as a place of false peace.

* Questo è il porto del mondo, e qui è il ristoro
de le sue noie, e quel piacer si sente
che già sentì ne' secoli de l'oro
l'antica e senza fren libera gente.
L'arme che sin a qui d'uopo vi fôro
potete omai depor securamente
e sacrarle in quest'ombra a la quiete:
ché guerrier qui solo d'Amor sarete,   (63)

e dolce campo di battaglia il letto
fiavi e l'erbetta morbida de' prati.   (64)

The garden's great appeal is that it can soothe conflict and
care ("le sue noie"), which are the very terms whereby a
man wins salvation through the City. And the garden promises this peace because it holds out the *pleasures* of the golden
age. All one must do is surrender—symbolically by taking
off one's armor—to unchecked sensuality, give oneself up to
Amor rather than God, and make the bed the battlefield.
Then all care will pass, and life will be joyous and peaceful.
But it is that check which must be overcome, the "fren"
which the knights knew they must maintain (57), and
without which, so the maidens claim, the ancients lived their

* This is the Place, wherein you may asswage
Your Sorrows past; here is the Joy and Bliss,
Which flourish'd in the antique Golden Age;
Here needs no Law, here none doth ought amiss:
Put off those Arms, and fear not Mars his Rage;
Your Sword, your Shield, your Helmet needless is;
    Then consecrate them here to endless Rest;
    You shall Love's Champions be, and Soldiers blest:

The Fields of Combat here are Beds of Down,
Or heaped Lilies under shady Brakes;

full, free life (63). In the use of "fren" in the two contexts, Tasso allows us to understand the level of the garden's appeal while maintaining, in the background, the City's values.

Indeed, the maidens themselves, as they offer the garden's greatest delights, inadvertently refer to the standard of the City. "Questo" and "qui" recur over and over as they emphasize that *this* is the whole world, *here* is true peace to be found. But the maidens' insistence on *this* implies *that*, *here* implies *there*; and their claim that the garden is the whole world for body and soul only takes us back to the City, where life in the garden was regarded as exile from the real world. And their promise of peace in the isle-garden contrasts finally with Ugone's vision, from the Celestial City, of virtue as a mean reward and earth itself as an "isola" (XIV, 10), small and insignificant. This *contemptus mundi* vision is at the opposite end of the scale of values in the poem from the garden, yet it hovers over the maidens' song. Thus, while the knights are being tempted by the battlefield of love, they are also reminded of the plain outside Jerusalem; while they hear the invitation to pagan pleasures, unencumbered by arms, the sound of Christian duty rings in their ears; and while they are being promised peace through sensuality, the serenity offered by the City puts all into perspective. Tasso manages to provide us with a double vision: the garden on its own terms, and the garden as it is false by City standards. Thus, after all the garden's delights are glowingly presented, the maidens' invitations by act and look ("atti" and "sguardi," 65) are really seen as enticements to corruption:

* i cavalier hanno indurate e sorde

* [The knights harden and deafen their souls

l'alme a que' vezzi perfidi e bugiardi,   (65)

and the knights pass by.

In this incident, Tasso makes the appeal of the garden to man's instinct for rest and sensual ease as powerful as possible; but he still maintains clearly the relation of garden to City, and he conveys the fact that for all the appeal to the senses, the soul is ultimately at stake.

In Canto XVI, Tasso offers us the compelling corrupt garden of Armida as an image of the sensual life. Just as the garden is within a "ricco edificio" (XVI, 1), so this existence is completely closed off, artificial, and unnatural. The fallacy of appealing solely to sensation is that the senses can never be satisfied; they constantly demand new pleasures. A vicious circle results whereby man constantly indulges, and seeks new stimulation for, the senses. The greatest image of purely sensual love, as we shall see, is Narcissism. The inner spirit of man, which is supposed to find peace in this life, finds only frustration. There is never any essential peace in the garden, for there is no goal beyond the immediate satisfaction of sensual desire. In the City, man fought for a greater end than himself, and could eventually achieve a greater satisfaction. Here he seeks only to please himself, a false goal which leaves him with only the illusion of pleasure.

Nature in the garden is the embodiment of the false sensual life.

* acque stagnanti, mobili cristalli,

---

to the wicked, lying charms.]

* The moving Crystal from the Fountain plays:

fior vari e varie piante, erbe diverse,
apriche collinette, ombrose valli,
selve e spelonche in una vista offerse;
e quel che 'l bello e 'l caro accresce a l'opre,
l'arte che tutto fa, nulla si scopre.   (9)

Stimi (sì mesto il culto è co 'l negletto)
sol naturali e gli ornamenti e i siti.
Di natura arte par che per diletto
l'imitatrice sua scherzando imiti.
L'aura, non ch'altro, è de la maga effetto,
l'aura che rende gli alberi fioriti:
co' fiori eterni eterno il frutto dura,
e mentre spunta l'un, l'altro matura.   (10)[12]

Fair Trees, high Plants, strong Herbs, and Flowerets new,
Sun-shining Hills, Dales hid from Phoebus' Rays,
Groves, Arbours, mossy Caves, at once they view;
    And that which Beauty most, most Wonder brought,
    No where appear'd the Art, which all this wrought.

So with the rude the polish'd mingled was,
That natural seem'd all, and ev'ry Part;
Nature would Craft in counterfeiting pass,
And imitate her Imitator, Art:
Mild was the Air; the Skies were clear as Glass;
The Trees no whirlwind felt, nor Tempest smart,
    But ere the Fruit drop off, the Blossom comes;
    This springs, that falls; that ripens, and this blooms.

[12] "co' fiori eterni eterno il frutto dura" echoes the inscription over the
gate to Hell in the *Commedia*: "Dinanzi a me non fuor cose create/se
non etterne, e io eterna duro" (*Inferno*, III, 7-8). (Before me were no
things created, but eternal; and eternal I endure.) Armida's garden is a
hell for those who succumb to its way of life, for they, like the inhabitants
of Dante's hell, are trapped within the consequences of their own mistakes.

This is a world which images the life of sensuality, for it is at once vastly diverse, as if new sensation were constantly needed, and it is completely false. The elements of the landscape, flowers and the rest, reflect the quest for the new, the different, the untried. And because the landscape as a whole is a creation of magic, is "fatto," not "nato," it images the false principles and unnatural qualities of life in the garden. There is no real fertility here, but only the manufactured and false flowering of fruits and flowers. This is a hothouse, not a garden; it only imitates, but not duplicates, the world of the "secoli de l'oro," just as finally the garden life, based on false values, provides only the illusion of peace and satisfaction.

The danger of the garden lies in the fact that it does imitate some reality so well. Indeed, the garden is so cleverly made that nature seems to imitate her imitator, art. One risks taking the counterfeit for reality, which is emblematic of the temptation to substitute, on the basis of what it seems to promise, the indulgence of the sense for service to the spirit. What we finally see in this landscape so calculatingly made is that in the garden all distinctions between what is true and false, real and feigned, are collapsed. Beautiful and meretricious no longer can be told apart; and this landscape, of course, is simply a reflection of man's inner condition. Tasso finally seems to say that by living in the garden, error is complete. One has wandered to the point where, by accepting sensuality as an end in itself, one accepts a false moral standard; by living in an artificial world whose fertility is an index to its sterility, one lives in a spiritual state where what seems pleasure is only essential corruption. This paradox conveys the depth of the division within Tasso's own mind. He can see no gradations, no area where sensuality would be anything but false and unnatural. Indeed, there is here a kind of Puritanism of the imagination never found in Spenser and Milton.

RINALDO has accepted the way of error, and the knights must find him. As they move through the garden, Tasso gives us another indication of how one is never sure, in this world, what is and what is not:

> ˟Ecco tra fronde e fronde il guardo inante
> penetra e vede o pargli di vedere,
> vede pur certo il vago e la diletta,
> ch'egli è in grembo a la donna, essa a l'erbetta.   (17)

He lies, as if in flagrant disregard of all the moral hierarchies governing the poem, in her "grembo molle" (18) which is the symbol for soft sensuality in the garden. (See the old man's forecast, XIV, 76; and the mural of Antony in Cleopatra's lap, XVI, 7). Armida leans over him, her gown open, her hair blowing, sweat standing out on her face (18). Tasso manages to make the sight of the lovers at once captivating and corrupt. And through their lovemaking, he demonstrates, as he did in the landscape, the falsity of the sensual principles upon which the garden is based. Through the eyes of the knights, we watch sensual love as it is manifested through the eyes of the lovers. They gaze at each other, Rinaldo looking into her face,

> ˟e i famelici sguardi avidamente

> ˟'Twixt Leaf and Leaf their Sight before they sent,
> [And saw, or seemed to see,
> now saw for sure the wanderer and the charmer,
> for he lay in the lady's lap, and she was on the grass.]

> ˟His hungry Eyes upon her Face he fed,

in lei pascendo si consuma e strugge. (19)

Sensuality, here imaged in the eyes, brings no true peace; it provides the lovers with the situation, but not the satisfaction, of pleasure.[13] Here the promise of the maidens that man will find surcease from "noie" is shown to be false. Self-indulgence provides its own frustrations, its own conflicts, and offers no real rest. As he lies in her lap, Rinaldo sighs as if he were thinking:

⊁ 'Or l'alma fugge
e 'n lei trapassa peregrina.' (19)

In the midst of the attainment of sensual "peace," the soul continues to wander, continues to seek the source of true repose. And this is how man is fundamentally corrupted, for in his quest for bodily ease, he projects his soul into the object of desire and then loses himself entirely in what he falsely believes is the source of his contentment. Yet in reality he only worships himself. This is Narcissism, the sterile contemplation of an illusion which is only the self. And Narcissism results from indulging the senses for themselves alone.

Tasso shows this Narcissism in the next four stanzas and thus fully expands that image first applied to Armida by the old man (XIV, 66). Armida is completely absorbed in herself, Rinaldo completely absorbed in the woman into whom he has projected himself. Armida becomes Narcissus when she takes a mirror and gazes at her image:

> And feeding them so pin'd himself away;
>
> ⊁ his Soul had fled
> From his frail Breast to hers.

[13] See Poliziano's *Le Stanze*, I, 121 *et seq.*, where "pascendo" set the tone as the man of war reclined in the lap of the woman of pleasure.

> ✻ ella del vetro a sé fa specchio, ed egli
> gli occhi di lei sereni a sé fa spegli.   (20)

Her eyes are "sereni" because it is only in total self-absorption that she can find any pleasure. Rinaldo in her eyes sees reflected only himself, and these are the terms of his Narcissism. Through the symbol of the mirror, Tasso shows the lovers entirely dependent for their love on illusion: literally, the image of self; ultimately, the illusion that sensuality can provide contentment.

Rinaldo is completely corrupted, for in losing himself in sensuality, he has only become Armida's slave:

> ✻ L'uno di servitù, l'altro d'impero
> si gloria, ella in sé stessa ed egli in lei.   (21)

Sensuality only leads to self-love and spiritual slavery. Rinaldo pleads with Armida to look at him, to see his desires as the true image of her beauty (21), but Armida only laughs:

> ✻ Ride Armida a quel dir, ma non che cesse
> dal vagheggiarsi e da' suoi bei lavori.   (23)

She goes on enhancing her natural beauty by calculated effects, creating, like Horace's Pyrrha (*Odes*, I, v), in Davis Harding's phrase, her own kind of "sophisticated simplicity." All exists for Armida alone, and the tender battle of

✻ [From the glass, she makes a mirror for herself, and he
Makes mirrors for himself from her serene eyes]

✻ [One glories in slavery, the other in command,
She in herself and he in her.]

✻ And with that Word she smil'd, and ne'ertheless
Her Love-toys still she us'd, and Pleasures bold:

love promised by the maidens turns out to be only a futile
mockery of the main concerns of the poem (25). Rinaldo's
own ironic position is that here the greatest "campion de la
cristiana fede" (XV, 44) is unable even to move about the
garden when Armida leaves him:

> ✵ ch'a lui non si concede
> por orma o trar momento in altra parte. (26)

The "carcer terreno" of which Goffredo complained to
Ugone (XIV, 12) leads at last to the peace of the City of
God, where

> ✵ in angeliche tempre odi le dive
> sirene e 'l suon di lor celeste lira. (XIV, 9)

Here in the garden, one is trapped in a world whose counterfeit landscape only mirrors the false values and promises,
and frenetic self-absorption, of sensuality. One is trapped
in a frenzied world where nothing lasts:

> ✵ Cogliam la rosa in su 'l mattino adorno
> di questo dì, che tosto il seren perde (XVI, 15)

where the easy way to pleasure brings no pleasure at all,
but rather corruption of the spirit.

Petrarch said that such a life "ogni maschio pensier de
l'alma tolle." And this is what has happened to Rinaldo.
He has become a softened little boy, his head nestled in
the lap of the woman upon whom he depends for suste-

> ✵ The Youth remain'd, yet had no Pow'r to bend
> One Step from thence.

> ✵ The Angels singing hear, and all their Choir.

> ✵ Oh, gather then the Rose, while Time thou hast;
> Short is the Day, done when it scant began;

nance and guidance. Ubaldo implies later that Rinaldo has lost his manhood, and become a little boy, when he calls Rinaldo

> ✲ egregio campion d'una fanciulla. (32)

It is Ubaldo's duty to bring Rinaldo back to the true path of duty, and to a sense of his responsibilities to the City. To this end, he approaches Rinaldo and shows him his reflection in the magic shield.

> ✲ Egli al lucido scudo il guardo gira,
> onde si specchia in lui qual siasi e quanto
> con delicato culto adorno; spira
> tutto odori e lascivie il crine e 'l manto;
> e il ferro, il ferro aver, non ch'altro, mira
> dal troppo lusso effeminato a canto:
> guernito è sì ch'inutile ornamento
> sembra, non militar fero instrumento. (30)

The shield, adamantine and military, is the symbol of the City and is obviously meant to contrast with the "cristallo . . . lucido e netto" (20) which was the emblem of soft, sensual love. The shield reflects a true image of Rinaldo, not a false illusion, and he sees himself as effeminate and corrupt. He has become, like the garden, an artificial creation

✲ [noble champion of a little girl]

✲ Upon the Targe his Looks amaz'd he bent,
And therein all his wanton Habit spy'd;
His Civet, Balm, and Perfumes redolent,
How from his Locks they smok'd, and Mantle wide;
His Sword, that many a Pagan stout had shent,
Bewrapp'd with Flow'rs, hung idly by his Side,
So nicely decked, that it seem'd, the Knight
Wore it for Fashion-sake, but not for Fight.

("culto" in 30 echoes "culto" in 10), a counterfeit man whose appearance embodies the ideals he has adopted. Like Ariosto before him, Tasso is here recalling *Aeneid*, IV, 261-264, where Aeneas' mantle and sword were indices to his corruption. And like Aeneas and Ruggiero, Rinaldo is stunned at the revelation of his true self (31); while, like Mercury and Melissa, Ubaldo exhorts the soldier to return to his proper activities (32-33).[14] The desired effect is achieved, the City is reestablished as the true center of a knight's duty and devotion, and Rinaldo prepares to leave the garden.

At this point it is necessary to note that Tasso does not, like Ariosto, drop the parallel with *Aeneid*, IV. Tasso wants to reconcile this episode with the main action, and these lovers with the love of God. To do so, he audaciously extends the Virgilian parallel so that the parting of Armida and Rinaldo corresponds very closely to the parting of Dido and Aeneas.[15] The poet has two specific purposes in mind

[14] Rinaldo resembles Ruggiero in another respect, for like Ruggiero, he was lulled into taking off his armor upon his entrance into the garden world. In both cases, the gesture symbolizes the first stage of spiritual seduction; see *Gerusalemme Liberata*, XIV, 59, which corresponds even to the detail of the breeze to *Orlando Furioso*, VI, 24.

[15] Armida's speech, *G.L.*, XVI, 44-51, ll. 1-2, corresponds to Dido's, *Aeneid*, IV, 305-330; 51, ll. 7-8, and 52, ll. 1-2, show Rinaldo making efforts, like Aeneas, 331-332, to control himself. Rinaldo's speech, 53-56, ll. 1-4, has the same calm, slightly pompous tone as Aeneas' speech, 333-361. Dido's frenzy, 362-364, is matched by Armida's 56, ll. 4-8; while Armida's second speech, 57-59, ll. 1-4, corresponds in tone and images (of the male's cruelty) to Dido's second speech, 365-387.

The Italian at 57, ll. 4-8, corresponds to the Latin, 367-370; 58 corresponds to 371-379; 59, l. 1, corresponds to 380-381; 59, ll. 2-6 to 384-387, and 59, ll. 7-8, and 60, ll. 1-4, to 382-384. Dido, 388-392, runs off and swoons; Armida, 60, ll. 5-8, faints. Both Aeneas, 393-396, and Rinaldo, 62, ll. 1-4, experience the same sense of indecision before going to their ships.

here. Through the parallel with Dido, he hopes to ennoble Armida's passion, convince us of the depths of her feeling and thus salvage Armida from the false garden, and prepare—at least thematically—for her conversion at the end. Also, by associating Rinaldo with Aeneas, Tasso returns us to the main theme of the poem, and the locus of the lovers' eventual reconciliation, because Rinaldo, like Aeneas, is called by duty to a distant City. Here Rome lends its mythical weight to Jerusalem, and all the religious and heroic sentiments in the *Aeneid* are, in a sense, channeled into the First Crusade. Through this composite image of the City, episode is linked to main action, classical material is integrated into Christian theme, and love and its values are subordinated to duty and its ideals. Tasso also has managed to prepare for the salvation of Armida by showing her love to be mistaken, though sincere. Like the poem itself, this garden episode has begun (in Canto XIV) and ended (in Canto XVI) with the image of the City, and thus Tasso is able to incorporate the ancient garden world into the structural and moral framework of the Christian epic. All the ways in which the earthly paradise is false stem ultimately from its structural and dramatic opposition to the City.

Though the garden and City, episode and single action, are made to mesh on a technical, or narrative, level, we nevertheless feel that Tasso's imaginative vision is not completely coherent. We have noted how deep and conflicting were the attractions of City and garden values, and how Tasso seemed unable to envisage anything but total service to spirit or complete indulgence in sensuality. We felt that the temptation to pleasure was strong and could only be overcome by the most rigid adherence to Christian morality. There was, we suggested, a severity in his condemnation of sensuality which failed to recognize any area where sense and spirit, body and soul, could enjoy harmony and mutual bliss. Sex was either corrupting and unnatural, a kind of cloying courtly love—always tempting, never satisfying—or it was not at all. Critics have often claimed that for all his Christian morality and theme, Tasso was really of Armida's party, that he really believed more in sensuality than spirituality. These commentators point to the garden and its powerful portrayal of pleasure as their proof, but they overlook the fact that Tasso constantly condemns the garden precisely at those points—the lush landscape, the lovers' sensuality—where it makes its greatest appeal. Tasso's problem is not that he was more of Armida's party than God's; it was simply that he could see no way of radically reconciling the two. His vision, finally, did not include, like Dante's, a garden which would be acceptable to the City. The two poles were unalterably separate, and he could not duplicate in his imagination the synthesis he created in his epic theory and in the epic's structure.

Armida's conversion is Tasso's attempt to create a kind of Magdalen, to bring the object of sensuality into some kind of harmony with the demands of the spirit. But when Rinaldo asks Armida to forsake paganism (XX, 135), and she replies:

> ✻ Ecco l'ancilla tua: d'essa a tuo senno
> dispon, (136)

we wince. This echo of the words of Mary to Gabriel in Luke 1:38 ("Ecce ancilla Domini, fiat mihi secundum verbum tuum" in the Vulgate) is too forced. Indeed, there is some-

✻ [Here is your handmaiden; do with her
Whatever you wish]

thing desperate here in Tasso's effort to bring Armida into line with Christianity. The shift implied by these words is too great, and we are finally unconvinced of Armida's redemption. The inner conflicts which were dramatized so beautifully in the garden remain to haunt the poem.

THE *Gerusalemme Liberata* was one of the most concentrated efforts of the sixteenth century to incorporate the classical and romance materials into a Christian view of the world. And the garden of Armida demonstrates how the motifs from ancient literature, and the earlier Renaissance version of the deceptive paradise, were subsumed into Christian morality. In Armida's garden we were presented with a double view: the garden of delight which seemed sensuous and satisfying but was actually artificial and frustrating. Thus, pleasure could be suggested, made powerfully attractive, and at the same time condemned as illusory and immoral. However, Armida's garden represents only one way in which the Christian epic of the sixteenth century managed to turn traditional matter to Christian uses. There is a garden in a very different Christian epic of the 1570's which is emblematic of another solution to the problem of reconciling delight with instruction, pleasure with duty. This is, of course, the island paradise of Venus in Canto IX of *Os Lusíadas* by Luis Vaz de Camoens.

III · CAMOENS

Camoens' poem, published in 1572, has as its ostensible subject the voyage of Vasco da Gama to India and back. This was a topic which the author was peculiarly fitted to describe, for he spent from 1553 to 1570 as a sailor and explorer, and he visited most of the places touched by da

Gama and many, such as Borneo, which da Gama never saw. Thus, the poem, "glowing with the truth of experience" as Abercrombie puts it, is a monument of travel literature and a passionate, episodic story of the sea. And it is from Camoens' keen, accurate observations of things distant and strange that the poem derives its intensity, and it is from the massive presence of the ocean as background that the poem receives its radical sense of coherence and unity.[16]

Indeed, this intensity of description and the ocean setting are all that do hold the poem together, for in his celebration of da Gama—and through him, Portugal and Portuguese history—Camoens adopts a method which would have ruined the effort of a lesser poet. Camoens insists on using two sets of deities, one Christian, the other classical, as the

[16] See L. Abercrombie, *The Epic* (London, 1922), p. 97.

For Camoens, the sea was all those forces presented by the giant figure of Adamastor (Canto V) and Portugal's glory consisted in braving them. It is the passionate sense of individual and collective heroism, and the feeling that the sea is the proper scene for that heroism, that hold this poem together. When, at the end of Canto II, the King of Malindi is praising the Portuguese, he recalls the Titan's war on Olympus, and Theseus' and Pirithous' assault on the underworld, and he says:

> Se houve feitos no mundo tão possantes,
> Não menos é trabalho ilustre e duro,
> Quanto foi cometer Inferno e Céu,
> Que outrem cometa a fúria de Nereu. (112)

> (Great deeds on earth, of these the compeers fit,
> Have been, superb and fearful to endure.
> If they dared Hell or Heaven to engage,
> These others bore the brunt of Nereus' rage.)

The ocean, on which so much of the action or narration takes place, is for Camoens the battleground where glory is as desirable and dear as ever it was to those who attacked Heaven or Hell.—All Portuguese citations are from *Obras Completas*, ed. H. Cidade (Lisbon, 1947), Vols. IV and V; all translations of poetry from *The Lusiads of Luiz de Camões*, tr. L. Bacon (The Hispanic Society of America, New York, 1950).

means for telling his tale. At the outset, he explicitly states that his theme is the glory of Portugal (I, 10) and rigidly excludes traditional epic material as being fantastic, i.e. outside the "truth" of Portuguese history:

> ˣ As verdadeiras vossas são tamanhas
> Que excedem as sonhadas, fabulosas,
> Que excedem Rodomonte e o vão Rugiero,
> E Orlando, inda que fora verdadeiro.   (I, 11)

But then he offers us two vehicles for, or versions of, the "truth." There is on the one hand the tale of da Gama, and the history of Portugal, as the unfolding of a sublime Christian destiny under the watchful eye of God. The Portuguese are God's champions, and da Gama's expedition to the East is motivated by Christian, that is, aristocratic, imperialistic as well as religious, impulses. This is, in large part, another Crusade poem. On the other hand, there is elaborate pagan machinery, culled lovingly from Virgil and Ovid, which is buttressed by a wealth of classical allusions, echoes, topoi, and scenes from all the Latin (and neoclassical Italian) poets Camoens knew so well. The classical machinery is the vehicle for the other version of Portuguese history. Venus is pictured as the champion of da Gama and his crew, while Bacchus, who fears for his prestige in India, is their implacable enemy. Thus while the sailors pray to God, their fortunes are also dependent on the desires of the gods; and the result is often silly. For instance, shortly after we are shown a debate on Olympus where Venus disputes Bacchus (I, 30-35), we are presented

> ˣ So great and true those acts that they exceed
> Utterly all such fabulous fantasies,
> And Rodomont and the vain Roger too,
> And Roland's tale, even if that were true.

with da Gama haughtily expounding Christianity to the Moors (I, 64-66).

Greene has justly termed this "cosmic confusion,"[17] and to our modern eye it is the great weakness of the poem. Indeed, it reveals *Os Lusíadas* as weakest precisely where the *Gerusalemme Liberata* was strongest—in its structure. Yet Camoens is completely unconcerned by these bizarre effects and inconsistencies, and for most of the poem he makes no effort at all to marry the classical and Christian mythologies. He simply makes them live together as best they might. And Camoens does this because, to his mind, within his historical framework, there is no incompatibility between these two elements. He sees the pagan and Christian versions of da Gama's expedition as complementary, not clashing, because he is relying upon our awareness, and acceptance, of a literary convention. That is, that pagan elements are simply decorative, whereas Christian elements in art are essential. Thus, Camoens proposes two versions of da Gama's voyage, and ultimately, Portuguese history: the Christian, true, instructive version, and the pagan, mythical, delightful version. One is meant to teach us, the other to give us pleasure.[18]

Both versions of history come to the same, final "truth"— Portugal is the greatest nation of Europe—for Venus will

[17] Greene, *The Descent from Heaven*, p. 225.

[18] This reading, with the pagan elements used as ornament, is by no means inconsistent with sixteenth-century religious beliefs or poetic practices. Emile Mâle, in his masterly study *L'Art Religieux après Le Concile de Trente* (Paris, 1932) points out how the Church, having proscribed nudity in religious art, made its peace with the ancient gods: "Car il n'était pas possible, non plus, d'éxorciser les dieux, de les chasser des imaginations: il eût fallut en bannir, en même temps, Homère et Virgile; c'était une autre conquête à laquelle l'humanité ne pouvait renoncer; l'Église n'y eût pas consenti; car elle aima toujours cette antiquité qu'elle avait sauvée. La mythologie, devenue sans danger, restait un enchantement. Elle était pour le Chrétien, qui savait où était la vérité, le

triumph over Bacchus just as God will see da Gama to India and home again. The two versions of history have had this common theme from the beginning, and they finally come together at the end. When the two versions become one, it is the Christian, instructive version, naturally, which becomes dominant. The pagan simply merges into it, as delight did into instruction in Tasso's epic theory. Camoens had not meant anyone to take the pagan element seriously; it had simply been his concession, within his historical framework, to the pleasurable and fantastic. Venus and Bacchus

---

charme des heures de loisir, le délassement d'une vie sévère. Les Jésuites, qui étaient alors les grandes educateurs, en jugeaient ainsi" (p. 3).

Indeed, the Jesuit censor who passed on the poem in 1571 could have been the model for Mâle's generalization; for he said: "não achey nelles [the ten cantos] cousa algũa escandolosa nem contraria â fe & bõs costumes." (I did not find anything scandalous in them or contrary to the faith and to proper behaviour.) On the pagan elements in particular, he wrote: "somente me paraceo que era necessario aduertir os Lectores que O Autor pera encarecer a difficultade da nauegação & entrada dos Portugueses na India, vsa de hũa fição do Deoses dos Gentios." (Only it seemed to me necessary to advise the readers that the author, in order to stress the difficulty of navigation and entrance of the Portuguese into India, uses a fiction of the Gods of the Gentiles.) However, this Jesuit takes the view imputed by Mâle to most: "Toda via como isto he Poesia & fingimento, & O Autor como poeta, não pretenda mais que ornar o estilo Poetico não tiuemos por inconvieniente yr esta fabula dos Deoses na obra. . . ." (All the while, since this is poetry and pretence, and the author as poet does not pretend to do more than ornament the poetic style, we do not consider it improper that this fable of the Gods should be part of the work.) Text in *Obra*, ed. Cidade, IV, 1v. We need not believe, as he does, that the "Deoses dos Gentios sam Demonios" (the Gods of the Gentiles are Devils), but it is reasonable to assume that this ornamental function is all we are expected to see in the use of classical mythology in the poem. This view of the role of mythology applies particularly well to the Isle of Venus in Canto IX; for there, in the words of Mâle, Camoens gives us a scene which is explicitly meant to be "le charme des heures de loisir, le délassement d'une vie sévère."

could be made to have a bearing on Portugal's story, and so they were used; Rodomonte and Orlando could have no ultimate historical relevance, and they were excluded.

To us, the structure is flawed by these two mythologies, and the conventional resolution of the gods with God seems pat and tedious. However, by means of this convention and by a strict adherence to his historical matter, Camoens is able largely to integrate classical and Christian motifs. Though his methods may be outmoded, and his effects may be bizarre, his Christian epic nevertheless achieves a kind of imaginative unity which Tasso's much better constructed *Gerusalemme Liberata* did not have. We can best appreciate the virtues and defects of *Os Lusíadas* by examining that garden episode in Canto IX. There the pagan and Christian versions of history begin to merge into one final vision; yet here the sensual pleasure which was so condemned in Armida's garden is made compatible with Christian duty. The extremes of the poem find their most forthright expression in the island garden, and it is typical of Camoens' whole method that the most delightful and pagan episode should be made the source and pointer for the dominant Christian, historical theme.

The mariners have been successful in their expedition to India, and now they are on their way back to Portugal. Venus wonders how she can reward them for their labors on and against the sea (IX, 19-20), and she decides to prepare

[✕] algũa ínsula divina,
Ornada d'esmaltado e verde arreio;   (21)

[✕] a certain isle divine
Enamelled bright and green eternally.

Venus plans to create a pleasure island, made resplendent by Zephyr and Flora (40) where the homeward-bound sailors can take their ease. Among palaces, refreshments and nereids inflamed by love, the sailors will enjoy delights of a sort they have not tasted on their voyage. From stanzas 22 to 50 there is a description of how Venus, Cupid and Fame, who spreads the glory of the Portuguese among the Gods and sea nymphs, make the island ready. The sailors then watch the island approach them from across the sea (51-52) and finally they sail up on to it (53).

The island garden itself is described in exquisite, lush terms and is the obvious result of Camoens' wide reading in Latin and Italian poets. Burton was perfectly justified when he placed this garden among the great earthly paradises of Western literature.[19] First we are offered a panoramic view of the mountains, grassy vales and fountains (54), then a description of streams and lakes (55), and finally individual glimpses of many kinds of fruit (56). These stanzas owe much to Claudian's description of the field of Henna in *De Raptu Proserpinae*, but they have a sensuality and clarity all their own. The couplet on lemons is a most obvious, but delightful, example:

[19] Sir Richard Burton, *Camoens' Life*, 2 vols. (London, 1881), Vol. II, pp. 651-652, in answering objections to the scene of the nereids and sailors, remarks: "the same faults may be found with the Island of Calypso (*Odys.* v) and the Garden of Alcinous (*ibid.* viii); with the Elysium of Virgil (*AEn.* v) and Milton; with Dante's Terrestrial Paradise (*Purg.* xxxviii); with Ariosto's 'false Alcina's empery' (*O.F.* vi. 20, etc.); with Spenser's Mount Acidale (*F.Q.*, vi. 10) and with Tasso's Paradise of Armida (*Ger.* xvi.)." I have quoted this passage because the total point is well taken; I have not corrected the mistakes in reference and the misprints.

˟ Os fermosos limões ali, cheirando,
Estão virgíneas tetas imitando. (56)

The next stanza is a variation on the ancient "mixed forest" motif, taken from Ovid, *Metamorphoses, X,* and describes all the nonfruit-bearing types of trees.[20] The ancient garden motif of spontaneous fertility is expanded in 58-59, with special emphasis on more fruit, and is followed by a long description of the many kinds of flowers (60-63) and an account of the animals on the island and their harmonious existence. Both the spontaneous fertility and the animals were features of the Golden Age landscape and appear together in Horace's *Epode XVI.* Finally, the nereids are seen engaging in the traditional sports of ancient Elysiums— hunting or making music (64), as well as the pleasure which was a convention in Renaissance gardens—bathing naked in streams.

˟ Algũas, que na forma descoberta
Do belo corpo estavam confiadas,
Posta a artificiosa fermosura,
Nuas lavar-se deixam na água pura. (65)

However, here there is no hint of wantonness or sly sensual-

˟ And beauteous lemons breathe out perfume here,
And as they were the breasts of maids appear.

˟ Some, who upon the grace without disguise
Of their fair bodies hopefully relied,
Their artificial beauties put away
And, in the pure stream bathing, naked lay.

[20] For a discussion of the "mixed forest" *topos,* especially as it relates to the *locus amoenus* and the garden tradition, see Curtius, *Literature,* pp. 193ff.

ity in the nereids' bathing; and in this touch we see the whole difference between Alcina and Armida's island gardens and this one. Venus' garden is designed for pleasure of a real, not illusory, sort; and the nereids discard what they consider artificial beauty, "artificiosa fermosura," i.e. their clothing, to reveal frankly what is natural. These maidens, and their truly pagan garden, promise the same pleasure of the "secoli de l'oro" offered by the maidens in Armida's garden, but here the promise will be fulfilled.

The sailors go ashore prepared to hunt game (66-67), and then they see colors moving in the greenery (68). Veloso is the first to understand what is behind the trees, and after shouting to his friends (69), he concludes:

> ✻ "Sigamos estas Deusas, e vejamos
> Se fantásticas são, se verdadeiras!"   (70)

What began as a hunt for game becomes the game of hunting nymphs. The sailors are hounds, the girls the prey, and the analogy is maintained throughout much of the episode. This is not the first hint of cruelty underlying love; there were suggestions of it in Cupid's wounding of the nereids in preparation for the island (43; 47-48). However, the injection of a melancholic, sometimes almost savage, tinge to the love on the isle does not interfere at all with the sense of delight; it merely serves to save the scene from sentimentality or softness, and imply that the pleasures of the island are masculine ones, untouched by frivolity.

Camoens finally gives us an impression of the general scene through the particular episode of Lionardo, a sailor luckless in love and his pursuit of Efire, "exemplo de belleza"

✻ "Follow these goddesses, and let us find
Whether they be fantastical or true."

(76). She lets him get close, then flies again while he pro-
tests his true and abiding love on the run (75-82). But the
coyness and the chase have no other purpose than to make
the inevitable more pleasurable; and when the teasing has an
end, then, as Spenser was to say in the Garden of Venus
and Adonis, "sweet love gentle fits emongst them throwes."

* Oh, que famintos beijos na floresta !
 E que mimoso choro que soava !
 Que afagos tão suaves ! Que ira honesta,
 Que em risinhos alegres se tornava !
 O que mais passam na manhã e na sesta,
 Que Vénus com prazeres inflamava,
 Milhor é esprimentá-lo que julgá-lo,
 Mas julgue-o quem não pode esprimentá-lo. (83)

At this point Tethys, the loveliest of the nereids, tells da
Gama she will reveal the secrets of the universe to him, and
hand in hand they go up a "monte alto e divino" to where

* ũa rica fábrica se erguia
De cristal toda e de ouro puro e fino. (87)

This palace, which might have come out of any number of

* What famished kisses were there in the wood!
 What gentle sound of pretty lamentation!
 What sweet caress! What angry modest mood
 That into bright mirth knew sweet transformation!
 From dawn to noon such pleasures they pursued
 As Venus kindled to a conflagration,
 Which men would rather taste of than condemn.
 Rather condemn who cannot taste of them.

            * a splendid palace raised its head,
 Wrought all of crystal and pure gold and fine.

late-Latin bowers of Venus, is the scene of the leaders' love-making.

> ⋇ Ela nos paços logra seus amores,
> As outras pelas sombras, entre as flores.   (87)

In the union of Tethys and da Gama, we have symbolized Portugal's final mastery over the sea; and in the general scene of love and delight, Camoens conveys the Portuguese's sense of satisfaction, which is their reward.[21]

Camoens, however, does not leave this meaning implicit in the scene, for he must somehow reconcile this vision of sensual pleasure amid pagan surroundings with the Christian, historical framework of his poem. Therefore, he suddenly announces that all the previous scene is an allegory:

> ⋇ Que as Ninfas do Oceano tão fermosas,
> Tétis, e a Ilha angélica pintada,
> Outra cousa não é que as deleitosas
> Honras que a vida fazem sublimada.
> Aquelas preminências gloriosas,

> ⋇ She in her palace revels in love's powers,
> But her sisters in the shadows 'mid the flowers.

> ⋇ For Tethys, the sea nymphs with such beauty bright,
> And the painted Island of angelic kind
> Are nothing more than honors which delight,
> Whereby life is exalted and refined.

[21] Burton, who played a large role in the exploration of central and eastern Africa in the nineteenth century, puts this point well: "To speak as a traveller. The Isle of Love embodies the sense of self-esteem, the satisfaction, the revenge of success, and the 'rapture of repose' following a successful exploit full of difficulty, hardship, pain and danger. Every explorer knows it right well." *Camoens*, II, 653. In the fine phrase "the revenge of success" Burton captures the qualities of intensity and cruelty we sensed in the pursuit of the nereids by the sailors.

Os triunfos, a fronte coroada
De palma e louro, a glória e maravilha,
Estes são os deleites desta ilha. (89)

The explicit transformation of the island-garden into a frame of mind is then followed by two stanzas, probably derived from Cicero's *De Natura Rerum*, II, 24, of euhemerism which explains that all the gods

✝ foram de fraca carne humana. (91)

Camoens then ends the canto with a plea for men to perform their Christian duty to the king and their country (94-95), and he says that if they do,

✝ numerados
Sereis entre of Heróis esclarecidos,
E nesta "Ilha de Vénus" recebidos. (95)

Thus, the poet has made pleasure the reward of duty, and has found a way to incorporate the frankly pagan garden into a Christian morality. Out of this allegorization of the island comes Camoens' eventual reconciliation of the whole pagan machinery with his Christian theme. For in Canto X, after a sumptuous feast and a long prophecy of the Portuguese in India, Tethys takes da Gama higher up the mountain, across a field of gems (X, 77), and shows him a

---

And all pre-eminence at glory's height,
The triumphs, brows which palms or laurels bind,
The splendor and the wonder of it all,
These are the joys that in the Isle befall.

✝ Were all of them but feeble human clay.

✝ You shall stand
With splendid figures of heroic kind
And in the isle of Venus welcome find.

simulacrum of the Christian universe (78-79). She then proceeds to put all the pagan elements in the poem into proper perspective:

> ⅹ "Aqui, só verdadeiros gloriosos
> Divos estão, porque eu, Saturno e Jano,
> Júpiter e Juno, fomos fabulosos,
> Fingidos de mortal e cego engano.
> Só pera fazer versos deleitosos
> Servimos;" (82)

The process whereby the garden was transmuted into a state of heroic joy is completed as the purpose of the pagan mythology is made clear and the Christian vision of the universe becomes dominant. Camoens wants us to see that the role of mythology in the garden is like the role of mythology in the poem: the gods only prefigure God; the pagan material is only a way, a pleasant way, of telling a greater story. Thus, to Veloso's question about the nymphs:

> ⅹ vejamos
> Se fantásticas são, se verdadeiras,

Camoens would reply that they are both: though the nymphs are "false," they represent "real" rewards; though the isle is "fantastic," it provides a way of seeing the historical and cosmic "truth." Veloso's nymphs, like all the

> ⅹ "Here only gods of truth and glory dwell,
> For Saturn, Janus, Juno, Jove and I,
> From the beginning were but tales to tell,
> Feigned by blind, mortal ingenuity.
> We are mere themes for verses that please well."

> ⅹ let us find
> Whether they be fantastical or true.

pagan deities, are for both delight and instruction; the former way of seeing them leads simply to the latter, just as seeing da Gama's voyage by way of fable and mythology only offers a lesser version of the true Christian vision of the world and Portugal's important place in that world.

Those critics who claimed that the allegorical stanzas (89ff.) of Canto IX were surely inserted because of pressure from the Inquisition were unaware of the point of the garden of Venus, and it is no wonder they have been proved wrong.[22] For Camoens needed no urging to end Canto IX the way he did; the last stanzas simply reveal the moral basis of his poem. Portugal is the center of value in *Os Lusíadas* just as the City was in the *Gerusalemme Liberata*. Portuguese history is the standard by which men's actions are judged; whatever contributes to the glory of Portugal is therefore a Christian deed. In this way, Camoens can use all the pagan elements he wants, for they only recount in a pleasurable way the higher truth. However, what is most objectionable in the garden of Venus is the swiftness with which Camoens goes from his pagan premises to his Christian conclusions. The point of view may be valid, but its presentation is unsatisfying. This is perhaps the reaction that underlay the claims of those who saw Jesuitical interference at the end of Canto IX. They simply could not believe that a poet could go from such an aesthetically brilliant presenta-

[22] J. D. M. Ford, in his edition of *Os Lusíadas* (Cambridge, Mass., 1946) states: "There is no proof that the ecclesiastical censor who passed a favorable judgment on the poem of Camões suggested to the poet the present explanation that his phantasmagoria of gods, goddesses, and nymphs was pure poetic fiction" (p. 431). F. Pierce, in his article on the role of mythology in the poem, *CL*, 6 (1954), p. 108, n. 26, and p. 119, n. 31, cites those who have argued ecclesiastical interference, and those who have refuted the claim.

tion of a garden of delight to such a jarring reversal—unless he were forced to. Perhaps, it was the structure of the end of Canto IX that disturbed the critics; yet this is what disturbs us throughout the poem—the very same insensitivity and naïveté in the handling of pagan and Christian deities. In this way, the garden of Venus is emblematic of the whole poem; on one hand, we are enchanted with the rich, allusive verse and the scene presented, and on the other hand we are annoyed and finally repelled by the clumsy manner in which the poem is constructed and the various levels of mythology handled. We do not mind so much the conventional resolution of pagan and Christian as much as the way in which it is finally thrust upon us.

Camoens presents us with a Christian epic which finally leaves us with the same kind of doubts we felt about the *Gerusalemme Liberata*—the poem suffers from an imbalance between what it says and how it says it. In Tasso's case, the theoretical synthesis of pagan rules and Christian morality, and the structural tension and resolution of their analogues, garden and City, far surpassed the poet's integration of the inner conflict between pleasure and duty, pagan love and Christian honor. In the case of Camoens, however, we have the opposite situation. His inner means of making delight consonant with instruction, the love inspired by Venus harmonious with the love of God, finds no external or structural analogue. For in his narrative technique, the pagan and Christian mythologies are always clashing, and when by means of allegory and literary convention they do come together, the effect is at once too jarring and too pat. In short, the successful Christian epic proved an impossible task.

Still, the island-garden of Venus stands, by itself, as a

brilliant achievement, a typical, and yet unique, Renaissance earthly paradise. Like the gardens of the Italian epics, this garden indicates what is real as opposed to illusory, true as opposed to false; and it also tells us something about the relationship of love to duty, pleasure to honor. Again like all the other gardens, it is animated by a female figure and ultimately comes to represent a frame of mind, a state of soul. The difference between the garden of Venus and the gardens in the Italian poems is that this garden is controlled by a nationalistic and historical, not an ironic or moralizing, point of view. Camoens has a less complicated, more provincial view of the world; whatever is right for Portugal, is right. There is no irony to this garden, no revelation of ugliness beneath the beauty. There is no Circe here. Venus is for delight, not delusion. In the Italian gardens, illusion passed for reality, or tried to, because Ariosto and Tasso saw life as a much greater snare where change or temptation constantly led one astray; in the garden of Venus, however, reality finally insists that it is only a kind of illusion, a lower version of a higher reality. The whole garden, like the cypress trees, points

* onde é posto o etéreo Paraíso   (IX, 57)

because to serve oneself, if one is Portuguese, is not incompatible at all with serving God.

For all the common Renaissance themes in the garden of *Os Lusíadas*, we have in many ways a unique treatment of traditional material. The garden embodies a more satisfying image of existence than we found in Ariosto or Tasso because it springs, finally, from a more self-satisfied point of view. Though Camoens had seen much more of the

* Still . . . to ethereal [eternal] Paradise.

world than previous poets, he had a much simpler, more limited view of it, and his grand garden seems almost a throwback to the late-Latin bowers he evidently loved so much. Though it is intimately related to its Renaissance counterparts, the garden of Venus ultimately stands apart from the main tradition of earthly paradises. For, in fact, that main tradition truly goes from Italy to England, from the enchanted gardens of Alcina, Acratia and Armida to the Bower of Bliss of Acrasia.

BIBLIOGRAPHY · CHAPTER FOUR

For basic material on poetic theory and criticism in the Renaissance, see J. E. Spingarn, *A History of Literary Criticism in the Renaissance* (New York, 1899; I have used the edition of 1925); C. S. Baldwin, *Renaissance Literary Theory and Practice*, ed. D. L. Clark (Gloucester, Mass., 1959), reprinted from the Columbia University Press edition of 1939; G. Saintsbury, *A History of Criticism*, 3 vols. (Edinburgh and London, 1922), esp. Vol. II, Book IV, Chapters ii-iii; B. Weinberg, *A History of Literary Criticism in the Italian Renaissance*, 2 vols. (Chicago, 1961) and his essays in *Critics and Criticism*, ed. R. S. Crane (Chicago, 1952), esp. "Castelvetro's Theory of Poetics," pp. 349-371; B. Hathaway, *The Age of Criticism, The Late Renaissance in Italy* (Ithaca, N.Y., 1962); W. K. Wimsatt and C. Brooks, *Literary Criticism, A Short History* (New York, 1959), esp. Part II, Chapter 9 on "The Sixteenth Century." *Literary Criticism, Plato to Dryden*, ed. A. H. Gilbert (1940; reprinted by Wayne State University Press, 1962) has generous selections from some outstanding critics and theorists of the Renaissance, and good notes. V. Hall, Jr., has written a short study of the whole subject, *Renaissance Literary Criticism* (New York, 1945); his "Renaissance Poetics" in *EPP*, pp. 690-695, is a good survey and contains an excellent bibliography.

There are sketches devoted to Italian theory of the epic in W. L. Renwick, *Edmund Spenser* (London, 1925), Chapter i; E. M. W. Tillyard, *The English Epic and Its Background* (London, 1954), Part Three: *The Renaissance*, Section v; Hough, *Preface to the Faerie Queene*, Part I, Chapter iii: "A Note on Epic Theory." There is necessary information in Highet, *Classical Tradition*, Chapter 8, "The Renaissance: Epic," and a convenient descriptive summary in Spingarn, *History*, pp. 107-124. For specific and detailed treatment, see the works of Weinberg and Hathaway.

For general accounts of the fortunes, rise and influence of Aristotle's *Poetics*, see Spingarn, *History*, pp. 16ff., and 126ff., and Saintsbury, *History of Criticism*, II, 30ff.; for detailed treatment, see B. Weinberg's "From Aristotle to Pseudo-Aristotle," *CL*, 5 (1953), pp. 97-104, and his *Literary Criticism*, I, 349-423. Bibliography is provided in Toffanin, *Il Cinquecento*, p. 459, nn. 1 and 2; but his account of sixteenth-century Aristotelian criticism is perfunctory and riddled with mistaken dates of publication. One should also consult J. E. Sandys' three-volume *A History of Classical Scholarship* (Cambridge, I, 3rd ed., 1921; II-III, 1908), Vol. II, Book IV, Chapter xi.

For a listing of the principal editions, translations, and commentaries on the *Poetics*, see S. H. Butcher, *Aristotle's Theory of Poetry and Fine Art* (London, 4th ed., 1911; reprinted 1951), xxxvii-xl; this list can be supplemented by consulting L. Cooper and A. Gudeman, *A Bibliography of the Poetics of Aristotle* (New Haven, 1928). For further bibliographical material, see G. F. Else's "Classical Poetics" in *EPP* under (2) *Aristotle*, p. 134.

Robortelli's commentary on the *Poetics*, published in 1548, was the single most important factor in the rise of Aristotle's authority, and it has been treated by Weinberg in *Critics and Criticism*, ed. Crane, pp. 319-348.

Horace's *Ars Poetica* continued to enjoy a high reputation throughout the sixteenth century; see, for a good survey, M. T. Herrick, *The Fusion of Horatian and Aristotelian Literary Criticism 1531-1555*, Illinois Studies in Language and Literature, Vol. XXXII, 1 (Urbana, 1946). Herrick has a list of commentaries and paraphrases of the *Ars Poetica* from 1488-1576, pp. 110-111.

I. TRISSINO

On Trissino, see Toffanin, *Il Cinquecento*, pp. 446-450; for bibliography, p. 459, nn. 3-5 and *addenda*, p. 461. Selections from Trissino's *Discorsi* can be found in *Plato to Dryden*, ed. Gilbert, pp. 212-223.

For the influence of Acratia's garden on Tasso, see F. Ermini, *L'Italia Liberata di Giangiorgio Trissino* (Roma, 1895), pp. 252-255; and for the influence of this garden on Spenser's garden of Acrasia, a possibility given short shrift by most recent Spenser critics, see C. W. Lemmi, "The Influence of Trissino on the Faerie Queene," *PQ*, 7 (1928), pp. 220-223.

II. TASSO

The standard life of Tasso is A. Solerti's *Vita di Torquato Tasso* (Torino and Roma, 1895); there are two other volumes of documents, etc. There is also a new and excellent study in English by C. P. Brand, *Torquato Tasso, A Study of the Poet and his contribution to English Literature* (Cambridge, 1965) which gives an account of his life and comprehensive criticisms of his works; Brand is particularly illuminating on Tasso's style and language, and his notes provide a good review of Tasso scholarship and criticism. One might also consult *Torquato Tasso Jerusalem Delivered, Translated by Edward Fairfax*, ed. J. C. Nelson, Capricorn Books (New York, n.d.), xiii-xxxiv, for a useful introduction to the poet and his major epic, and a selected bibliography of works in Italian, German, French, and English. There is additional bibliography at the end of the Tasso chapters in Toffanin, *Il Cinquecento*, pp. 613-614 *ter*, and p. 625. The journal *Studi Tassiani*, published annually at Bergamo, contains detailed bibliography in every number.

For the sources, background and explications of literary allusions in the *Gerusalemme Liberata*, see the works of V. Vivaldi, *Prologomeni . . . sulle Fonti della Gerusalemme Liberata* (Trani, 1904). *La Gerusalemme Liberata Studiata nelle sue Fonti*: Vol. I, *Azione Principe del Poema* (Trani, 1901); Vol. II, *Episodi* (Trani, 1907). Also E. de Maldé, *Le Fonti della Gerusalemme Liberata* (Parma, 1910).

The best single study of the epic, as well as the rest of Tasso, is still E. Donadoni's *Torquato Tasso Saggio Critico*, 5th ed. (Firenze, 1963). For treatments in English of the *Gerusalemme*, see Brand, *Tasso*, Chapter iv; and Greene, *The Descent from Heaven*, pp. 176-219. These are the best. One might also consult Bowra, *Virgil to Milton*, Chapter iv, and Hough, *Preface to the Faerie Queene*, Chapter ii. Comments can be found in J. Arthos, *On the Poetry of Spenser and the Form of Romances* (London, 1956), pp. 92-183, on "The Italians" and in Tillyard, *English Epic*, IV, iii, 1. Finally, there is a good deal of shrewd commentary in J. A. Symonds, *The Renaissance in Italy*; see *The Catholic Reaction* (New York, 1887), II, 1-125.

For the background of the Italian epic, see particularly Brand, *Tasso*, pp. 56ff., and Vivaldi, *Prologomeni*, Chapters i-ii. On Tasso's critical and epic theory, see many of the works cited above and on page 227; the most detailed study is B. T. Sozzi, "La Poetica di Tasso," *ST*, 5 (1955), pp. 3-58.

On the background of Armida and her garden, see de Maldé, *Fonti*, pp. 151-203, and also the article by M. Fubini on "Armida" in the *Dizionario Bompiani*, VIII, 73-74.

There are comments on the garden in all of the critical works cited above; see also R. M. Durling, "The Bower of Bliss and Armida's Palace," *CL*, 6 (1954), pp. 335-347 on the gardens of Spenser and Tasso.

Some interesting observations on Armida, Alcina, and Circe can be found in Marino's *Dicerie Sacre, La Musica, parte tre*; see *Giovanbattista Marino, Dicerie Sacre e La Strage de gl'Innocenti*, ed. G. Pazzi (Torino, 1960), p. 293. Similarly in Marino's *Adone*, VI, 6.

III. CAMOENS

Still the standard life of Camoens, though partially superseded by later scholars, is W. Stork, *Luís de Camoens Leben* (Paderborn, 1890). The best sketches, with some criticism of his works, are found in A. F. G. Bell, *Luís de Camões,* Hispanic Notes and Monographs (Oxford, 1923), and in the latest Britannica (1963) where A. J. da Costa Pimpaõ has revised the earlier article by Prestage. The translations of *Os Lusíadas* by L. Bacon (New York, 1950) and W. Atkinson, Penguin Classics (Harmondsworth, 1962) contain general summaries of the poet's life and times. There is much valuable information of a scholarly sort in the editions of J. D. M. Ford: *Os Lusíadas* (Cambridge, Mass., 1946) and his facsimile edition of Fanshawe's translation (1655) (Cambridge, Mass., 1940). Surveys of the poet's life and works can also be found in G. Le Gentil, *Camoëns, L'Oeuvre Épique et Lyrique*, Connaissance des Lettres (Paris, 1954) and H. H. Hart, *Luis de Camõens and the epic of the Lusiads* (Norman, 1962), though Hart's book blithely mixes fact and legend, and should be approached warily.

All of the studies cited contain some bibliography, the most useful being that in Ford's edition of the Portuguese and Bell, *Camões*; for a recent and accessible bibliography of works in various languages, see G. C. Rossi, *Storia della Letteratura Portoghese* (Firenze, 1953), pp. 133-135.

The extensive use made by Camoens of earlier literature and of chronicles has been thoroughly investigated by J. M. Rodrigues, "As Fontes dos Lusíadas," *O Instituto*, 51 (1904)-60 (1913); there are 45 articles in all; additional comments of the Italian influence on Camoens is in V. Cioffari, "Camões and Dante: A Source Study," *Italica*, 25 (1948), pp. 282-293. F. de Figueiredo, "Camões: a épica portuguesa do século XVI," *ACABL* (Rio de Janeiro, 1943), pp. 201-231, places the epic in the context of subsequent Portuguese literary history.

Critical comment on *Os Lusíadas* is not very plentiful in English, though the poem has been a great favorite with translators. (There have been at least 17 English versions.) I have found particularly helpful the notes to Ford's edition of the Portuguese, and to a lesser extent those in Bacon's translation; and, though it is often eccentric, one should consult the commentary of Sir Richard Burton, found in Volume II of his *Camoens' Life*, 2 vols. (London, 1881). Bell's monograph, cited above, is useful, as is his *Studies in Portuguese Literature* (Oxford, 1914). The most acute criticism, though I think a bit severe, is in Greene, *The Descent from Heaven*, pp. 219-231; Bowra, *Virgil to Milton*, has a good chapter on Camoens. Though I have not been able to see it, an important topic is treated by N. H. Andrews, Jr., "An Essay on Camões' Concept of the Epic," *RLA*, 3 (1962), pp. 61-93. Finally, for a valuable survey of Camoens criticism and an interesting discussion of one of the most vexed problems in the poem, see F. Pierce, "The Place of Mythology in The Lusiads," *CL*, 6 (1954), pp. 97-122; this is particularly useful as it touches on the Isle of Venus and its role in the poem.

CHAPTER FIVE

Spenser

THERE ARE innumberable ways of approaching and interpreting *The Faerie Queene.* C. S. Lewis, for instance, sees it as a "fusion" of the two kinds of poetry, "the medieval allegory and the more recent romantic epic of the Italians," while Josephine Waters Bennett asserts that "Spenser owes more to Langland and the Ploughman literature of early English Protestantism than has been generally recognized. It is here, rather than in the Italian poets, that his deeper roots penetrate."[1] Others treat *The Faerie Queene* primarily as a document in the history of ideas, or as a series of myths or images, or as historical allegory, or finally as the "simple" allegory it often appears to be.

Book II, which will concern us because of Acrasia's Bower, presents the problems of approach in acute form. There are almost as many interpretations as there are critics. Some see the book in theological terms, others in terms of "natural ethics" as opposed to a Christian framework. There are those who read it in light of Plato and those who regard it as a commentary on Aristotle. The latter group then falls into three camps: those who consider Guyon's quest as an exposition of Temperance, as a commentary on Continence, or as both. Or consider another garden which will concern us briefly, the Garden of Venus and Adonis in

[1] C. S. Lewis, *English Literature in the Sixteenth Century, excluding Drama* (Oxford, 1954), p. 380; J. W. Bennett in *English Institute Essays,* ed. A. Downer (New York, 1952), pp. 124-125. For the subsequent topics mentioned, see references in the Bibliography.

Book III. Is this Garden's "source," its "meaning," to be found in Empedocles, Plato, Lucretius, Plotinus, the Florentine Neo-Platonists, Bruno, Golding's *Ovid*, or Renaissance commonplaces?

There are also those who seek to know whether Spenser's religious affiliations were Calvinist, Puritan, Anglican (if so, of what particular allegiance), or indeed pantheist, mystical or Catholic. There has been much speculation, and this too concerns our study of the gardens, about his view of Nature, and after Nature, Art. Finally, we have been offered many versions of the man engaged in writing *The Faerie Queene*: the scholarly Spenser, with texts open before him, and the hard-pressed civil servant Spenser, cribbing much of his learning from Comes' *Mythologiae*, Cartari's *Imagini*, and a variety of Renaissance dictionaries.

Many of these studies concerned with Spenser from the "history of ideas" approach sooner or later run afoul. For these scholars try to impose on Spenser an intellectual or "philosophic" consistency or unity which is simply not there; either they are forced to distort the poem to fit what they think *must* (i.e. *should*) have been Spenser's point of view, or they are compelled to admit that their sources are incomplete. Thus Frank Kermode, in a closely argued explication—by way of mythology and Christian doctrine—of Guyon's visit to the Cave of Mammon, finds that there is one detail for which he cannot account: "Proserpina's silver seat, or stool, in [sic] which Mammon urges the weary knight to rest and eat an apple. Had he done so, the fiend would have seized him. What are we to make of this stool?" Kermode says that "in common sense" it cannot be what commentators say: "an invitation to sloth"; then he shows how Upton thought it might come from accounts of the

Eleusinian mysteries by Meurs; how it cannot be from the
Hymn to Demeter (published only in 1780); and he finally
does not know what to do. "I should like to produce, but
cannot, Spenser's immediate source for this placing of a
punitive chair of oblivion in the garden of Proserpina; it is
in Meurs—too late, of course, and in a scholium of Aris-
tophanes, perhaps too obscure."[2] All this because "common
sense" (never elaborated upon) rejects reading the stool as
an "invitation to sloth"; as, in short, a stool. Why could
not Spenser have included a stool for the weary knight to
rest upon, should he be tempted to eat the golden apple?
Why a *silver* stool? Why not? This is Mammon's realm,
source of worldly riches and material temptations. What
better place to eat a golden apple than on a silver stool?

The rigorous consistency of philosophy or doctrine we
find in Dante, or even Milton, is simply not part of Spenser's
equipment or his genius. His *Faerie Queene* will not yield
to consistent historical, or moral, or mythological, or ethical
interpretation. Of course, it will yield to all of these approaches much of the time, but not to any one of them all
of the time. Perhaps it is a tribute to *The Faerie Queene*,
and an indication of where its appeal lies, that so many
differing, often contradictory or hostile approaches, can be
accommodated—indeed absorbed—by the poem. If so, it is
a tribute to the poem's scope, its breadth of vision, and inclusiveness of spirit. The existence of so many "sources" and

[2] F. Kermode, "The Cave of Mammon" in *Elizabethan Poetry*, ed. J. R.
Brown and B. Harris, Stratford-Upon-Avon Studies 2 (New York, 1960),
pp. 164-165. The metamorphosis of the "silver seat, or stool" into a
"punitive chair of oblivion" takes place in the sea-change from page 164
to 165 in Kermode's own text; this is how commentaries on Spenser
become themselves handbooks of Spenserian mythology.

"influences" and differing interpretations is simply proof of what we should, and in fact do, realize all along: this is a typical poem of the Renaissance which mingles the classical and Christian, the historical and mythical. It is eclectic, synthetic, and finally, as various and varied as life itself. It was written by a poet who was, like so many of the Renaissance men of letters, first of all a public official, whose interests were far broader than his scholarship, whose imagination happily transcended his immediate reading, and whose time was far too limited for all the recondite research he is sometimes assumed to have done. I do not claim Spenser used none of the sources or ideas scholars have provided; he was a man of culture, and he used many of them. But he was not finicky about where his material came from, any more than Shakespeare was, and his poetry is done no real service if it is constantly explicated by a new citation from Aristotle or Augustine or Thomas or Ficino or Castiglione or Elyot or any of the many others always adduced to clarify *The Faerie Queene*. Of course these people and many others shed light on the matter; of course there was a common body of knowledge and information and attitudes. But the prevailing tendency to read Spenser only in the light of intellectual history often tends to take us far, far away from the poetry—often never to return.

I am not asking for a return to reading Spenser as the "painterly" Prince of poets, valuable only for his effect as an opiate. But while *The Faerie Queene* is not the field of poppies Hazlitt, for instance, thought it was, perhaps neither is it the casebook for a history of Western Ideas, or Myths, that some modern commentators seem to think it is. It is one thing to say a poem is about the life of the mind; it is another to explicate the poem by supplying the poet's reading—by reconstructing the intellectual life of the poet's mind.

After all this, I must make my own biases clear. My Spenser is really a very conventional one; he who took the mood of the dream vision and the method of allegory from the French and English poets of the Middle Ages and mingled them with motifs, scenes, characters, and structure from the Renaissance poems of Boiardo, Ariosto, to some extent Trissino, and Tasso. In doing so, he created *The Faerie Queene*—that is, something very similar to its predecessors, and yet completely different. I see the poem as essentially part of the tradition of the romantic epic, especially because Spenser himself offers us evidence of his preoccupation with the Italians, both outside of his poem and within the poem itself.[3] I do not intend to hunt up more parallels or sources in the Italians, but rather simply to read the poem—particularly the gardens of Acrasia and Venus and Adonis—in the light of the traditions of the romantic epics and their gardens. I should like to make it clear that my primary aim is not to assess the value of one poet or poem in terms of another; I am not concerned with the kind of cultural competition which seems to stir some critics. Because Spenser had, among other things, the Italians on his mind did not mean he had no mind of his own; indeed, quite the contrary. He used everything he touched, and he

---

[3] I refer to the famous letter of Harvey's where he reminds Spenser of his intention "to emulate," indeed "to overgo" the *Orlando Furioso* with his *Elvish Queene*; see, in the edition I have used throughout, *The Complete Poetical Works of Spenser*, ed. R. E. N. Dodge (Cambridge, Mass., 1936), p. 773. See also Spenser's Letter to Ralegh, where the poet says that in portraying an excellent man in Arthur, he is following the examples of Homer and Virgil; Ariosto and Tasso. See Dodge edition, p. 136.

changed everything he used. The points of resemblance between Spenser and his Italian predecessors will serve finally to illuminate the vast differences between them; the garden-image will, of course, be our main interest. Before we examine some of the gardens in *The Faerie Queene*, however, we must first consider some of those larger areas of contrast between it and the Italian epics.

FROM the Italians, Spenser inherited not only motifs and structure, but also what we can term the materials of a point of view. He took, in general, the grand romance-image of questing, wandering heroic action in a hostile world. From Ariosto he appropriated the theme of illusion and reality as the result of magic, and he used it through the figures of Archimago, Duessa, and the witch (III, vii, 6 *et seq.*) who creates the false Florimell. All of these characters possess, or embody (in the cases of the first two), the power of making the apparent pass for the actual. From Tasso, Spenser directly inherited the tradition of heroic duty opposed to personal pleasure—the ethical categories which preoccupied the Italian so much. And through the Italians (and ultimately all the "Platonic" philosophy in the air), Spenser learned to equate the good with the real, the evil with the illusory; and he finally saw how a landscape could be the symbol of evil masquerading as the good. All these common themes, as well as motifs and the like, link *The Faerie Queene* to its Italian forerunners. What ultimately distinguishes the English and Continental poems, however, is the way in which the themes and motifs are handled, and the purposes underlying this treatment.

The Faerie Queene is one of the most religious of all the great Renaissance poems. It takes for granted all the religious *values* (as distinct from *doctrines*) which are so prominently espoused by the *Gerusalemme Liberata*. Spenser's poem, as we know from the Letter to Ralegh, has a professed moral, didactic purpose, and the allegory is its vehicle. *The Faerie Queene* is a Christian poem in a way the *Orlando Furioso* had no desire to be and the *Gerusalemme Liberata* could not be. Everything in the English poem is seen as under the eye of God. Spenser's God will not yield to classification any more readily than anything else in the poem,[4] but He is Protestant in the sense that He is remote, transcendent rather than immanent. He is manifest throughout His creation, but He is certainly not available the way the deity was in Tasso or Trissino. He is the principle of Order and Permanence which created the world, and He remains always above it. All men strive for Him but all men fall short; He sustains them, succors them, but—because they are fallen—is not familiar to them. In its character as a Christian poem, and in the relationship of God to the world, or better, of man to God, *The Faerie Queene* differs most profoundly from the Italian epics.

In those earlier poems, the conflicts, like their precise geography, were primarily of this world. And from the urgency of the conflict between what seemed and what was,

---

[4] C. S. Lewis has said that Spenser probably knew little of "technical theology," but that he "was certainly in his own way, a religious man. And also a religious poet. But the deepest most spontaneous, and most ubiquitous devotion of that poet goes out to God, not as the One of Plotinus, nor as the Calvinist's predestinator, nor even as the Incarnate Redeemer, but as 'the glad Creator' the fashioner of flower and forest and river, of excellent trout and pike, of months and seasons, of beautiful women and 'lovely knights,' of love and marriage, of sun, moon and planets, of angels, above all of light. He sees the creatures, in Charles Williams' phrase, as 'illustrious with being.' " *EA*, 14 (1961), pp. 115-116.

in Ariosto, or what one wanted to do and what one ought to do, in Tasso, came the energy, the immediacy, indeed the relevancy to our own feelings and situations. However, in *The Faerie Queene* the essential conflict is not of this world, and as a result there is no corrosive irony dissolving all into a masterful illusion of futile reality; there is no deadly opposition between pleasure and honor, delight and duty. The conflict in *The Faerie Queene* is between this world and the next; and all the mundane conflicts found in the Italians are absorbed or reconciled into this greater, cosmic tension between flux and permanence, mutability and eternity.

It is this conflict which haunted Spenser throughout his career. In *The Shepheardes Calender* we see the poet seeking to image the universe by encompassing time. By showing us the year in twelve eclogues, Spenser reflects the changes within a year, and the change that is a year; and at the same time he creates a

> Calender for every yeare,
> That steele in strength, and time in durance, shall
>   outweare.

Through the image of change, the poem mirrors eternity in two ways. It mirrors the ceaseless change to which man and his world are subjected, while, as an artifact, it rises above the process it describes and offers itself as permanent and beyond time.

The dilemma of man yearning for permanence in the midst of change also bursts out in the last two stanzas of *The Faerie Queene*. Here, after the claim of Mutability to rule Heaven as well as earth, and her rebuff by Nature, the first person suddenly intrudes;

When I bethinke me on that speech whyleare
Of Mutability, and well it way,
Me seemes, that though she all unworthy were
Of the heav'ns rule, yet, very sooth to say,
In all things else she beares the greatest sway:
Which makes me loath this state of life so tickle,
And love of things so vaine to cast away;
Whose flowring pride, so fading and so fickle,
Short Time shall soon cut down with his consuming
                                                    sickle.
Then gin I thinke on that which Nature sayd,
Of that same time when no more change shall be,
But stedfast rest of all things, firmely stayd
Upon the pillours of eternity,
That is contrayr to Mutabilitie:
For all that moveth doth in change delight:
But thence-forth all shall rest eternally
With Him that is the God of Sabbaoth hight:
O! that great Sabbaoth God, graunt me that Sabaoths
                                        sight.   (VII, viii, 1-2)[5]

Here, especially if we understand Sabbath, "rest," as well
as Sabbaoth, "hosts," we shall hear all of Spenser's weariness
expressed in the desire for the sight (site) of rest and
immutable peace.

This same note of weariness is often struck in *The Faerie
Queene.* For across the vast plains, through the wide woods,
into the light and the dark, to the top of hills and the
depths of caves, past castles and gardens, rivers and mountains, the knights are always searching, always hoping,

[5] In the last line, I have followed the punctuation given in the text of
Variorum, VI-VII, 181. For comments on emending Sabbaoth to Sabbath,
see *Variorum,* VI-VII, 315-316; also Dodge's edition, p. 809.

always *moving*. All the knights are searching for something —a beloved, a reward, a place—but all are essentially looking for something permanent. And they never really find it; no one, as we have the poem, ever really finds what he wants, or is ever finished. This is not just because the poem is unfinished; it is rather the nature of the world, of man's life. Perhaps had Spenser completed his poem, all the loves and all the quests would have been reunited at Gloriana's Court; but perhaps that Court would only have been, finally, an image of Heaven. For as the poem shows us, for better than six books, nothing can be achieved in this world that will not slip away; nothing can be done that time and change and chance will not undo again. Thus, there is a profound ambiguity in the world of *The Faerie Queene*: we are constantly presented with the rewards for the quest of virtue, health, honor, peace, and yet there is always a sense that the effort is self-defeating. In this way, *The Faerie Queene* includes more than the Italian epics. There is a greater spectrum of mood and experience; there are greater joys, and pleasure has at times a keener edge—and there is also a deeper fatigue, a more profound sense of despair beneath the surface. We find a vital serenity in *The Faerie Queene* which is evident in no other poem, but we also see this life, always, as a struggle, a trial, a long weary way to a goal which is by definition beyond life.

Because man is enmeshed in time as he struggles toward some state of soul beyond time, because all the quests in the poem are versions of man's one great quest for peace, we often hear the fatigue expressed by the characters involved. And because the sea is interwoven through the poem's imagery as the emblem of man's shifting, changeful state, Britomart's cry is typical:

> Huge sea of sorrow and tempestuous griefe,
> Wherein my feeble bark is tossed long,
> Far from the hoped haven of reliefe,
> Why doe thy cruel billowes beat so strong,
> And thy moyst mountaynes each on others throng,
> Threatning to swallow up my fearful lyfe? (III, iv, 8)

Closely linked to this despair of ever finding the "hoped haven of reliefe," is the ever-present danger which assails, in some form, many of the main figures of *The Faerie Queene*. It is the temptation of taking the easy way out, of stopping, of giving up the struggle—of dying.[6] It often seems easier to put a stop to flux by simply giving in. The great statement of this temptation is the speech of Despair to the Redcross Knight, in one of the central episodes in the poem:

> He [Sir Terwin] there does now enjoy eternall rest
> And happy ease, which thou doest want and crave,
> And further from it daily wanderest:
> What if some little payne the passage have,
> That makes frayle flesh to feare the bitter wave?
> Is not short payne well borne, that bringes long ease,
> And layes the soule to sleepe in quiet grave?
> Sleepe after toyle, port after stormie seas,
> Ease after warre, death after life does greatly please.
>
> (I, ix, 40)

The stanza offers us an emblem of the way sea imagery is woven through the poem, and the way the need for rest is woven through life's struggles.

---

[6] See Lewis' comment: "In other poets temptation usually summons the will to Titanic action, to the inordinate resolutions of a Tamburlaine, a Faustus, a Macbeth, or a Satan. In Spenser it more often whispers 'Lie down. Relax. Let go. Indulge the death wish.'" *EA*, 14 (1961), p. 116.

The Despair episode is important for a number of reasons. On the simplest level, it shows how Spenser took material from the Italians and transmuted it to his own purposes. The Redcross Knight is subject to Despair immediately because of his weakening by Orgoglio, but ultimately because of his dalliance with Duessa. That incident occurred in I, vii, 4ff., in a scene consciously reminiscent of the initial lapses of Ruggiero and Rinaldo.[7] "Careless of his health, and of his fame" (vii, 7), he has embraced Falsity; and the Cave of Despair—seen as a process of self-delusion and rationalization—is the final result. Spenser follows the Italians in portraying a knight who becomes corrupted after dallying with a false lady. However, despite the common premises and some resemblances, the Despair episode arrives at very different conclusions from anything in the Italians and projects themes which will be very important for the Bower of Bliss.

First of all, we see the large role that the temptation to rest, to give in, plays in this most fundamental assault on the soul. Second, we notice how Spenser's method makes it clear that the soul is at stake, and that good and evil are synonyms not only for reality and illusion, duty and pleasure, but also for spiritual health and disease.[8] The allegory constantly refers us to the inner man and gives us both the psychological dimension, like Ariosto, and the religious or moral dimension, like Tasso. Inner health is

[7] Precisely as Ruggiero (*O.F.*, VI, 24) and Rinaldo (*G.L.*, XIV, 59) had done, Redcross takes off his "yron-coted plate" (I, vii, 2) and "feedes upon the cooling shade, and bayes / His sweatie forehead in the breathing wynd" (3). See above p. 207, n. 14.

[8] I do not here, or anywhere, treat what is certainly one of the primary layers of meaning in the poem—the historical allegory; for explications of this, see Bibliography, p. 291.

what all men seek; after the Despair episode, the Knight
is called "that sowle-diseased knight" (I, x, 24), the result
of being "careless of his health" (I, vii, 7). "Health" is
the term for both an inner goal and a moral and psychological norm; health is the standard by which actions and
attitudes are judged. It will not do to define "health" too
strictly; like everything else in the poem, it varies and
"means" what the situation demands. But it can generally
be equated with the "natural"—psychologically that which
disposes the individual to fulfill his potentialities for good;
morally that which is in accordance and in harmony with
God. Man and Nature, as they came from God, were
radically healthy, spotlessly natural, and substantially good
(II, vii, 16). After the Fall, man and his world became
diseased, befouled, and sinful—but a spark remained, the
potential for good was still there. Nevertheless, what man
could now do on his own was not enough to achieve
Heaven; but Grace, for the good man—the man who tried
to keep the path, who struggled for Truth—was available.
We see the depravity of man in the very words Una
addresses to the Redcross Knight—"fraile, feeble, fleshly
wight" (I, ix, 53)—when she rescues him from Despair and
reassures him that he has a place in Salvation, that there is
a place for him beyond time. In words which remind us of
Mercury's chiding of Aeneas in *Aeneid*, IV, or the incidents
we have seen in the Italian epics modeled on the Virgilian
passage, Una upbraids the Redcross Knight:

> Ne let vaine words bewitch thy manly hart,
> Ne divelish thoughts dismay thy constant spright.
> In heavenly mercies hast thou not a part?
> Why shouldst thou then despeire, that chosen art?

Where justice growes, there grows eke greter grace,
The which doth quench the brond of hellish smart,
And that accurst hand-writing doth deface.
Arise, sir knight, arise, and leave this cursed place.

(I, ix, 53)

Like Beatrice to Dante in the *Purgatory*, Una has urged
the knight to be true to his duty; but more, to his natural
self, his "manly hart," "constant spright," that is, to what
is good and right for him to do.

Finally, there is one other motif introduced into this
episode which not only looks back to the Italians but even
more importantly anticipates the Bower. Una said not to
let "vaine words bewitch" his manly heart, and she reminded the knight that there was a greater grace which
"that accurst hand-writing" does deface.[9] Una is referring to
Despair's rhetoric, which affected the knight so

That all his manly powres it did disperse,
As he were charmed with inchaunted rimes,   (48)

and she is also referring to Despair's pictures "painted in a
table plaine" of ghosts and fiends (49). When Trevisan met
the Redcross Knight and told him of Despair, Redcross
said he would not rest

Till I that treachours art have heard and tryd.   (32)

Despair's "art" consists of his rhetorical skill, his power to
manipulate words, and of his ghastly pictures. At a deeper
level, Despair's rhetorical skills, which can "bewitch" and

[9] Una's words in this episode echo, most fittingly, Paul's Epistle to
the Colossians, where the Apostle bids them be steadfast in their faith
in Christ. See particularly 2:4 and 2:14, on "enticing words" and "the
handwriting of ordinances that was against us."

"enchaunt," are "divelish"; his art is allied with the demonic and the magical. It is the ability to pervert man's "constant spright" (as Archimago, the great magician, could conjure up false dreams and create false sprights, I, i, 38ff.) and seduce his "manly hart"; in short, the demonic power to make the natural unnatural and persuade a Christian of his abandonment by God. So too the "painted" tables represent the false images, ultimately the graven idols, which displace God in man's sight and lead him to sin and death. Art is linked in this episode to the diseased figure of Despair, intent only to

spoyle the castle of [a man's] health   (I, ix, 31)

and it is also linked to the unnatural and magical, and to the devilish or sinful. Health, nature, good instincts, Christian duty—all which make a man capable of Salvation and are the evidences of the Divine in him—are corrupted and undermined by Despair and his various arts. The opposition between art and nature, in the broadest sense, is established here; and both are under God—the former opposed to God, the latter in harmony with, but ever in need of, God.

All of the themes in the Despair episode, which grew out of Redcross' embrace of Duessa, are important for our examination of one of the great episodes in the poem— Guyon's confrontation of Acrasia's Bower of Bliss. In that episode, as in this one, art and nature, the enchanted and the natural, disease and health, the temptation to sin, the lure to rest—all will be themes. And in that episode in Book II, as here in I, Cantos vii to ix, Spenser will be adapting from the Italians for his Christian purposes, and, finally, in comparison with the Garden of Venus and Adonis, he will be using the gardens in the light of the ultimate conflict between change and permanence.

In Canto xii of Book II, Guyon makes his long journey to Acrasia's Bower of Bliss. In a sense, however, the whole book is a journey to that garden, and stanzas 1-41 of Canto xii are, as it has often been suggested, simply a recapitulation of the book's movement. Indeed, the movement in both Books I and II is toward a garden. In Book I, we have the Redcross Knight's effort to redeem Eden (so called at I, xii, 26; II, i, 1) which is the original home of "incorrupted Nature" (I, xi, 47). In Book II we have Guyon's mission to destroy Acrasia's Bower. The different emphasis in the garden quests is indicative of the difference between the two books. In Book I, the greatest temptation was to Despair, to sin against the spirit, for Book I was ultimately concerned with the contemplative life of the soul. In Book II, the great temptation is to indulge in goods of this world, in the material joys of wealth and possessions (Mammon's Cave, vii) or sexual pleasure (Acrasia's Bower, xii or its adumbration, Phaedria's island, vi). Temperance is not, like Holiness, a contemplative ideal, but is rather an active, "natural," physical ideal. It is much less immediately concerned with the next world, and is much more obviously concerned with this one. When Belphoebe voices that Renaissance commonplace, the virtue of pursuing Honor,[10] she says of Honor:

> In woods, in waves, in warres she wonts to dwell,
> And wilbe found with perill and with paine;

[10] On the theme of the pursuit of Honor, see D. Bush, *Mythology and the Renaissance Tradition in English Poetry*, rev. ed. (New York, 1963), pp, 99-100.

Ne can the man, that moulds in ydle cell,
Unto her happy mansion attaine. (II, iii, 41)

The goddess is not speaking of Temperance per se here,
but she is defining an active chivalric ideal which she sees
related to the natural world, as opposed to the corrupt world
of the courts, and in a sense she is summing up the essential
qualities of Book II. The *kind* of virtue defined and extolled
in this book is not that of the "ydle cell"; it is that of the
man of action who, in facing the trials and temptations of
this world, can maintain his balance, his sense of proportion
—himself.

Of all Gods workes, which doe this world adorne,
There is no one more faire and excellent,
Then is mans body both for powre and forme,
Whiles it is kept in sober government. (II, ix, 1)

This preamble to the "castle of health" in Book II—the
House of Alma—is different in tone from the introduction to
the House of Holiness in Book I:

Renowmd throughout the world for sacred lore
And pure unspotted life; so well, they say
It governd was, and guided evermore,
Through wisedome of a matrone grave and hore;
Whose onely joy was to relive the needes
Of wretched soules, and helpe the helpelesse pore.
(I, x, 3)

In both cases we are dealing with allegories of the good
inner government of man; but the emphasis is very different.
In Book II, the emphasis is on the body as it is emblematic
of the soul; in Book I, it is on the soul as it is in harmony
with God. Book I presents the norms by which the succeed-

ing separate, but related, books are finally judged. In Book I we learned that

Nothing is sure that growes on earthly grownd, (I, ix, 11)

and that

True loves are often sown, but seldom grow on grownd.
(I, ix, 16)

And finally we learned

That blisse may not abide in state of mortall men.
(I, viii, 44)

In Book II, these notions are modified in accordance with a more limited point of view, but they are found to be essentially true as we learn to recognize the false forms of bliss. Book II is about false bliss where Book I was about true bliss; just as Book II is about a false Eden where Book I was about the true Eden.

In Book II we are concerned with a virtue, a state of being—Temperance—which is good but not as elevated as Holiness. It is that Aristotelian moral virtue of character which pertains to the appetitive soul and "comes about as a result of habit"; at times it seems to shade off into Continence, which "in the main owes its birth and its growth to teaching (for which reason it requires experience and time)."[11] The temperate man harmonizes his appetites; the continent man checks his strong appetites: Temperance does not exist in the presence of strong, excessive appetites, while Continence necessarily implies the presence of such appetites. Aristotle properly distinguishes between the temperate and

[11] *Nicomachean Ethics*, 1103b. Text in *The Complete Works of Aristotle*, ed. R. McKeon (New York, 1941), p. 925.

the continent man,[12] though Spenser seems to include both in the person of Guyon and ultimately fits them into his greater Christian framework. The generic virtue, Temperance, is adaptable to Christianity, but it is not necessarily Christian. Thus it, to use the venerable pun again, is a more "pedestrian" virtue than Holiness, as Guyon is a pedestrian knight compared to Redcross. (Guyon loses his horse at II, iii, 4-11, and does not recover it until V, iii, 29-31.) He is accompanied by the sage Palmer who

> ever with slow pace the knight did lead,
> Who taught his trampling steed with equall steps to
> tread. (II, i, 7)

After Guyon loses his horse, he is better able to follow the slightly plodding course of Reason, Prudence, Wisdom. Guyon needs the check, for he is obviously susceptible to passions which would overcome his rational faculties. Thus the Palmer

> with his steady staffe did point [Guyon's] way:
> His race with reason, and with words his will,
> From fowle intemperaunce he ofte did stay,
> And suffred not in wrath his hasty steps to stray. (i, 34)

This is the education in a virtue which is at the service of Christianity but on a lower order than what we observed in Book I. In many ways, the Palmer is like Virgil, Guyon like Dante the pilgrim. Together they can discover Truth to a point; the fact that a higher Truth remains does not invalidate what they can know. Virgil brought Dante to the earthly paradise, where Beatrice took over; the Palmer and Guyon never achieve the true earthly paradise, but they

---

[12] *Nicomachean Ethics*, 1151b-1152a; McKeon edition, pp. 1050-1051.

arrive at the point where they are not fooled by an imitation. As we will see, Book II prepares for, and culminates in, that imitation—the garden of Acrasia.

GUYON's introduction to Acrasia, and his mission in the book, come very early. In the first canto, Guyon and the Palmer hear a shriek, Guyon rushes into a thicket (39) and finds Mordant dead, Amavia dying, and their child covered with gore. Amavia manages to tell them that Mordant fell into the hands of

> Acrasia, a false enchaunteresse,
> That many errant knightes hath fowle fordonne:
> Within a wandring island, that doth ronne
> And stray in perilous gulfe, her dwelling is. (51)

Her power is insidious:

> Her blis is all in pleasure and delight,
> Where with she makes her lovers dronken mad,
> And then with words and weedes of wondrous might,
> On them she workes her will to uses bad. (52)

Acrasia is succinctly defined and her presence will haunt the book till we come to her at the end. She is an obvious descendant of Alcina, Acratia, Armida—ultimately Circe— and her magic powers, her dominant characteristic throughout, are the first things stressed. Like all her predecessors, she inhabits an island, and like them she has, by means of sensuality ("blis . . . in pleasure and delight") a devastating effect on men. She makes them "dronken mad," and in this she is the emblem and agent of Aristotelian incontinence:

> It is plain, then, that incontinent people

must be said to be in a similar condition
to men asleep, mad, or drunk.
(*Nicomachean Ethics*, 1147a)[13]

However, let us leave the precise Aristotelian elements to
experts in such matters and concentrate on Acrasia primarily
as a descendant of the Italian witches, that is, as a principle
of self-indulgence in pure pleasure.[14] What we observe most
strikingly in the words of Amavia is the traditional link
between depraved sex and magic (with the overtones of
Tasso's "errante" as wandering and as morally wrong in
"errant knightes"); and from this emphasis will come
the themes of unnatural passion exemplified in unnatural
nature. That is, Spenser too will use the garden-convention
of embodying false standards and values in false surroundings. These themes, obviously reminiscent of Tasso's ethical
categories, are not the only themes associated by Spenser
with unchecked sensuality. He also adopts, from Ariosto,
the correspondence of unbridled sexuality with false illusions. Though this theme, meant to support the ethical
position, is expanded later on, we may see it operate in
two other incidents early in Book II.

In the very first adventure of Guyon, a squire persuades
the knight that Redcross has raped his lady (II, i, 10-25);
of course, it is simply Archimago and Duessa at their old
tricks again, this time to "deceive good knights,"

And draw them from pursuit of praise and fame,
To slug in slouth and sensuall delights,
And end their daies with irrenowmed shame. (II, i, 23)

[13] *Ibid.*, p. 1041.
[14] Acrasia is called Pleasure four times: II, i, arg.; iii, 41; xii, 1, and
xii, 48.

Later, another squire (II, iv, 17-33) tells of passion and lust (in a story adapted from the *Orlando Furioso*, IV, 57-VI, 16) which resembles in one way the first episode. Both incidents, though also meant to illustrate other things, turn on deceit and illusion as a necessary corollary to lust and sexual activity; Duessa and Archimago use the false rape story to incite trouble, and Philemon deludes the squire by telling lies and substituting the lady's maid for the lady herself. Thus, in the first part of Book II Spenser introduces not only Acrasia and her island, and associates her character as sexual pleasure with incontinence, but introduces elements resembling Alcina's ability to manipulate illusion and Armida's to corrupt specific moral standards. Lust, illusion, false values, magic, the implicit theme of pleasure overcoming duty and honor, passion overwhelming reason—all are allusively, yet surely, implied.

These early cantos are meant to define not only Guyon's quest, but also the character of the knight, the man who represents Temperance *in potentia*, and who can only achieve that virtue, and its companion Continence, through habit and by experience and teaching. Thus we are told that after Guyon lost his horse, the Palmer was "his most trusty guide,"

> Who suffred not his wandring feete to slide;
> But when strong passion, or weake fleshlinesse,
> Would from the right way seeke to draw him side,
> He would, through temperaunce and stedfastnesse,
> Teach him the weak to strengthen, and the strong
> supresse. (II, iv, 2)

The obvious sense of this passage (as well as II, i, 34) is that Guyon is subject to both strong passions and temptations of the flesh, and he needs the guidance of the Palmer to maintain balance. His education in Book II does not consist in denying either passion or the taste of pleasure. It rather consists in maintaining reason as the controlling force, and keeping the appetites in their place. Thus, Guyon resembles Ruggiero, who was susceptible to Alcina, yet he is also like Carlo and Ubaldo, or Trajano, who had a moral mission to fulfill. Finally, Guyon will, when confronted by Acrasia, be able to reconcile the demands of morality and psychology, virtue and pleasure, in a way none of the Italians did.

After stating Guyon's susceptibility, Spenser shows us in two stages what Guyon will be susceptible to. In Cantos v and vi, Spenser offers us two episodes which bear directly on Acrasia's bower and the destructive role of illicit pleasure,[15] and thus invests the very center of his book with the core of his meaning.

THE FIRST incident (v, 27-38) recapitulates and projects the character of Acrasia and the nature of her Bower. In a sense, Spenser follows Tasso's organizational outline, for Armida's garden was also forecast in the *Gerusalemme Liberata* (X and XIV) long before we actually entered it. Here we see the Bower (though not the lady herself) through the eyes of Atin, squire to Pyrochles, and the eyes of the man he is to summon, Cymochles. This episode is emphatically for the reader; Guyon has no part in this excursion and does not see what we do. Thus we gain knowledge of what

---

[15] We must remember to distinguish between lust, or illicit pleasure, and lawful pleasure, or wedded sex, not only in this book but all throughout *The Faerie Queene*. For Spenser, all pleasure is not necessarily evil, and that is one of the central lessons of Book II; however, pleasure as it appears in this Book is, generally, of the debilitating, illicit kind.

Guyon must finally face long before he does; we have an image which ties up so many of the threads thus far, and provides background for Guyon's trials until that moment when he is finally able to take command of the whole situation.

We are told that Cymochles serves "that enchaunteresse,/ The vyle Acrasia" whose powers are such that she

> Does charme her lovers, and the feeble sprightes
> Can call out of the bodies of fraile wightes;
> Whom then she does transforme to monstrous hewes.
>
> (II, v, 27)

The identification of Acrasia with magic and the ability to falsify Nature, in this case human nature physical and spiritual, is immediately established. The last line of stanza 27, which speaks of the "darksome dens, where Titan his face never shewes," in reference to the fate of Acrasia's lovers, carries in it a suggestion of Hell, an implication fully expanded in Canto xii.

Then we see Cymochles in the Bower, lying among its denizens,[16]

> And over him, Art, stryving to compayre
> With Nature, did an arber greene dispred,
> Framed of wanton yvie, flouring fayre. (29)

Art has made an arbor of ivy through which Nature grows. The key word here is not the "wanton" ivy, for Alma's porch also has a vine "Enchaced with a wanton yvie twine"

---

[16] The pose is traditional. His armor is off, and like Redcross who
"Yet goodly court . . . made still to his dame,
Pourd out in loosnesse on the grassy grownd" (I, vii, 7),
Cymochles "has pourd out his ydle mynd / In daintie delices and lavish joyes" (II, vi, 28),

(II, ix, 24), but the word "stryving" applied to Art. This is how Art and Nature are themes in the Bower; Art tries to undermine and corrupt Nature, just as Acrasia's principle of sexual indulgence undermines and corrupts the natural instincts of man. Both the "Art" in the Bower, and the corruptive power of lust, emanate symbolically at least from Acrasia's magic.[17]

There are other themes besides magic and Art-Nature touched on in this preliminary glimpse of the Bower. The conflict between honor and duty is indicated in Atin's speech to Cymochles—a speech which echoes many we have heard before:

> Up, up! thou womanish weake knight,
> That here in ladies lap entombed art,
> Unmindful of thy praise and prowest might. (36)

---

[17] Though it is to anticipate a bit, I do not agree entirely with Durling's view, *CL*, 6 (1954), that "The Art of the Bower of Bliss is not magic. It is true that Acrasia is a sorceress, but Spenser never refers to her enchantments as 'art.' By art he understands the artistry or artfulness of the human intellect. The Bower is situated in 'A place picked out by choice of best aliue / That natures work by art can imitate' (*F.Q.*, II, xii, 42). In other words, it is an actual place which has been chosen, as it were, by a committee of experts, as most suited to their purposes" (p. 344). By this account, Acrasia has been completely supplanted by an anonymous committee of experts who picked the site for her Bower and by sinister technological forces which have created everything else. One senses a confusion between (a) "art" as process of creation; and (b) "art" as a thing created. Acrasia's magic is referred to at II, xii, 81, when she "Tryde all her arts and all her sleights" in a vain attempt to escape the Palmer's net; Acrasia's "enchantments" (Durling's word), her *artifacts*, are the Bower and the monsters: they are works of art which are the products of Acrasia's art—the tricks which are produced by her magic. It was *she* who picked the place for the Bower, she who was best qualified to imitate Nature's work with art. The symbolic implica-tions of this process, and of these products, as emblems of lust's cor-ruption of natural human appetites, are expanded below.

This is an exhortation which also includes the recumbent Cymochles among Aristotle's incontinent, similar to "men asleep, mad, or drunk." Another theme has been convincingly demonstrated by C. S. Lewis who has shown how the activity of the Bower, here and in Canto xii, is largely visual, a "lust suspended—lust turning into what would now be called *skeptophilia*."[18] This sterile lust of the eyes is most vividly portrayed in stanza 34 where Cymochles, "like an adder in the weedes,"

> His wandring thought in deepe desire does steepe,
> And his frayle eye with spoyle of beauty feedes.

In this way he inflames himself and receives his pleasure. To vary the game, and presumably heighten the thrill,

> Sometimes he falsely faines himselfe to sleepe,
> Whiles through their lids his wanton eies do peepe.
>
> (34)

And here Spenser adds the theme of illusion to his presentation of sexual self-indulgence. Cymochles feigns sleep so as to look at the naked girls; but his deception is in turn bettered by the illusions they present him:

> So' he them deceives, deceived in his deceipt,
> Made dronke with drugs of deare voluptuous receipt.
>
> (34)

The implications of deception and illusion shade into a suggestion of self-delusion as we are told that, at the urgings of Atin,

> Suddeinly out of his delightfull dreame
> The man awoke. . . . (37)

18 *Allegory*, pp. 331-332.

The garden as an allegory for a self-deluding frame of mind, a false illusion or fantasy one creates, to one's detriment, is suggested in this episode, and developed later on. Indeed, all the themes touched on here are to be developed more fully in Canto xii. Now the themes are introduced, without the two principal antagonists, Acrasia and Guyon, so that the reader may the better judge the abstract nature of Guyon's enemy and the terms in which the battle will be fought.

After the image of strong sexual temptation, Spenser opens Canto vi with almost a definition of the problems which will now confront Guyon throughout the second half of the book.

> A harder lesson to learne continence
> In joyous pleasure then in grievous paine:
> For sweetnesse doth allure the weaker sence
> So strongly, that uneathes it can refraine
> From that which feeble nature covets faine.
>
> (II, vi, 1).

Continence is the mean in the presence of strong passions, and Spenser—having just shown us the ultimate form of "joyous pleasure"—now proceeds to demonstrate Guyon's susceptibility and immunity to lesser or different versions of the final pleasures of the Bower. These preliminary temptations are conveyed through garden-images, and are specifically the incidents on Phaedria's island and in the garden of Proserpina.[19]

[19] Spenser's method of having Guyon pass through gardens and states of mind which are adumbrations of the final garden is similar to Dante's technique in the *Inferno* and particularly the *Purgatorio*, Canto VIII. There the Valley of Princes forecast the true Eden; here the island of Phaedria and Garden of Proserpina prefigure a false Eden.

The island of Phaedria (whose name means "loose" or "glittering" in Greek) is a lesser version of the Bower, just as Phaedria herself is the poor man's Acrasia. The chief source for Phaedria's Idle Lake and island (reminiscent of Acrasia's "wandring island," II, i, 51) is the *Gerusalemme Liberata*, X, 60ff., the same passage which furnished the first view of Armida as a sorceress in a garden. This similarity underscores Spenser and Tasso's common structural technique of anticipating the final garden. Phaedria herself seems to owe something to Tasso and Boiardo,[20] and represents that frivolity and mirth, and finally absurdity, always a little uncouth, which attends the life of extreme sensuality. Phaedria does not have the vicious, magical powers to degrade or pervert that belong to Armida, but rather functions simply as that obstacle to duty which is the life of indolence and pointless ease. Her island is not created by Art, but is a "chosen plott of fertile land" which, set like "a little nest,"

> As if it had by Natures cunning hand
> Bene choycely picked out from all the rest,
> And laid forth for ensample of the best. (vi, 12)

There is a hint of artifice, of manipulation here (as there is at stanza 25 where Phaedria would surpass the birds' "native musicke by her skilful art"), but magic as a means of perverting wills, shapes and Nature is conspicuously absent as an overt theme. Nature simply participates entirely in the effort "to allure fraile mind to carelesse ease" (13).

---

[20] Blanchard, *PMLA*, 40 (1925), pp. 836-838, cites the "fatal donzella" of *Gerusalemme Liberata*, XIV, 3-5 *via* Koeppel, while he would also include the "donzella / . . . con faccia ridente" of Boiardo's *Orlando Innamorato*, II, ix, 5.

Phaedria lulls Cymochles to sleep (14), sings a song appealing to Nature (as the siren did to Rinaldo, *Gerusalemme
Liberata*, XIV, 62-64) asking, Why the waste of

> joyous howres in needelesse paine,
> Seeking for daunger and adventures vaine? (17)

There is, of course, the implicit comparison of Cymochles
and Guyon, who also arrives on the island, the essentially
intemperate and temperate man, one who succumbs to the
inducements of the senses, the other (21-22) who does not.
In words reminiscent of those Despair addressed to Redcross, Phaedria tells Guyon:

> Better safe port, then be in seas distrest. (23)

But he has a duty to do and resists her blandishment to
relax. Guyon is not rude to her, yet he maintains his balance, so to speak, and we are offered a lesson in the superiority of well-governed, sensible activity over indolence. As
we might expect, the man who has forsaken duty and succumbed to the easy life—Cymochles—is again associated
with the self-deluded person, for he is said to have been in
an "ydle dreme" (27). The themes of the falsity and illusory quality of sensual peace and ease in a lovely place
are touched on lightly but tellingly in this episode. We have
on the one hand Cymochles, who is so thoroughly corrupted by Acrasia (v, 27ff.) that "one sweete drop of sensuall delight" (vi, 8) is enough to drug him, and we have
on the other hand Guyon, who is now initiated into the
kind of dangers which lie ahead and who proves himself
equal to those of the moment.

Guyon is more sorely pressed in his next major trial,
which occurs in the cave of Mammon. As he was on Phae-

dria's island, here again he is without the Palmer, and here again he undergoes temptations of a worldly sort, ending in a garden. The temptations of Mammon's realm are those of the material, modern, "real" world. Guyon at first rejects them in terms of the "antique world" which was only defaced later, by pride, beyond "The measure of her meane, and naturall first need." (vii, 16) But Mammon scorns "the rudenesse of that antique age" and its standards, and tells Guyon that since he does "live in later times" (18), he ought to devote himself to a life of acquisition and materialism. Later, after showing Guyon his store of riches, Mammon says

> Loe here the worldes blis, loe here the end,
> To which al men doe ayme, rich to be made!   (32)

But Guyon says no, he wants no part of it:

> Another blis before myne eyes I place,
> Another happiness, another end.   (33)

In an interesting anticipation of the Bower, there are two conceptions of bliss at variance here. Mammon proposes material goods as the complete area of human joy, while Guyon rejects them in the name of a higher and greater joy. Against material temptations the knight sets a divine standard, and thus reveals the joys of the self-styled "greatest god below the sky" (vii, 8) as simply a passing substitute for a divinely ordained goal. In *Areopagitica*, Milton seized upon the latent religious implications of this episode when he discussed the "true wayfaring Christian" who looks upon evil and its temptations and yet rejects them and chooses the good. And then he followed with his famous statement:

Which was the reason why our sage and serious Poet

Spenser, whom I dare to be known to think a better teacher than Scotus or Aquinas, describing true temperance under the person of Guion, brings him in with his palmer through the Cave of Mammon, and the bowr of earthly bliss that he might see and know, and yet abstain.[21]

Milton is essentially correct in seeing both as tests of Guyon's ultimate Christian character, because both Mammon and Acrasia are presented as tempting Guyon as a natural virtue, but in terms which constantly imply a greater religious context as well. Mammon speaks twice of "grace" (18 and 32), though we are made to see that it is the false grace of the "Money God" (39), that deity whose attendant looks

As if that Highest God defy he would. (40)

Like Acrasia, Mammon has perverted what is natural (in this case, the goods of the earth) into the unnatural and has set himself up as a rival of the true Creator, who is invoked throughout (16, 34, 40) in order to maintain the proper perspective. We are meant to regard Mammon not only as a danger to the temperate man, but also, by implication and extension, to the Christian man as well. With this background we can better appreciate the next incident. Guyon is led finally into a large room, wherein a woman "gorgeous gay" sits on a throne (44). It is Mammon's daughter Philotime (Love of Honor) whose

face right wondrous faire did seeme to bee,

but who really was an illusion. For her beauty

Yet was not that same her owne native hew,

---

[21] *Areopagitica*, ed. W. Haller, in Columbia edition of *Works*, IV, 311. See p. 367 for textual note on "wayfaring."

But wrought by art and counterfetted shew,
Thereby more lovers unto her to call. (45)

Again, beauty as an evil temptation is the product of art
corrupting nature. Philotime seems an emblem of humanity as it exists under Mammon's sway:

Nath'lesse most hevenly faire in deed and vew
She by creation was, till she did fall;
Thenceforth she sought for helps to cloke her crime
                                               withall. (45)

The original purity of God's creation is once again asserted,
and the unfallen is seen as the supremely natural, divine,
and truly beautiful. Spenser seems to be implying that Mammon's realm is not only symbolic of the fallen world—
which still retains some luster of the Creation though it is
a world of sin—but is the most fallen, most evil condition
of man because it has perverted those vestiges of the natural
and good which remained after the Fall.

The garden of Proserpina, where Guyon is led for the
last of his three temptations (which began at stanza 40),
is the final effort of the totally depraved and unregenerate
world to absorb Guyon into itself and bring him down to
its own, symbolically blasphemous, level. They go

Into a gardin goodly garnished
With hearbs and fruits, whose kinds mote not be redd:
Not such as earth out of her fruitfull woomb
Throwes forth to men, sweet and well savored,
But direfull deadly black, both leafe and bloom,
Fitt to adorne the dead and deck the drery toombe. (51)

It is the garden of Hell, not simply because it is underground, nor because it is sacred to Proserpina (53), but because it is an open parody of Eden, and embodies the essence of a world, a way of life and a system of values opposed to the true Christian's. There is a landscape of deadly plants, symbolic of the life-denying methods and goals of Mammon's kingdom, and to complete the perversion of nature and God's first creation, there is a huge tree—near Proserpina's bower—with golden apples (54-55). The golden apples are the most unnatural elements in the landscape and supposedly the Cave's greatest source, and symbol, of temptation. Indeed, they embody at once all the pagan (anti-Christian) associations and lure of worldly riches in Mammon's realm in a perversion of that original garden and those first fruits in Eden. Mammon tries to tempt Guyon to eat:

> Why takest thou not of that same fruite of gold (63)

and his reason is clearly indicated by the poet:

> All which he did, to do him deadly fall
> In frayle intemperaunce through sinfull bayt. (64)

"Fall": this is the old drama being enacted through the "natural" terms of temperance and intemperance. Mammon is trying to lead Guyon into "intemperaunce" through "sinfull" bait; he is threatening Guyon's natural being by assaulting that divine order upon which all depends. It is a tribute to Guyon's self-possession that he does not succumb to the temptation of the material body, and thus lose his soul. But the struggle exhausts him, the demands upon his native resiliency are too much. His "vitall powres" deprived "of food and sleepe" (65) give way, and after he is led out of the earth, he does indeed suffer a fall, a deep, deathlike faint.

It is also the measure of Guyon's limitations that, while he has seen and resisted sin, he has been so weakened he cannot endure the consequences alone, and needs Grace to go on. Guyon in Mammon's Cave is somewhat like Virgil at the walls of the City of Dis; he knows what to do to avoid contamination and preserve himself, but he needs help from God to be able to carry on. In both cases, an angel appears to help. Guyon's angel (viii, 5ff.) tells the now returned Palmer that he was sent from God (8) and he promises to watch over Guyon. Then he leaves. When Cymochles and Pyrochles—the "Paynim brethren" (viii, arg.)—attempt to despoil the exhausted Christian, Prince Arthur, to whom "grace" is applied three times (17; 18; 25), comes to the rescue.

I do not mean to imply that the allegorical meanings attached to the Mammon episode, derived from Comes and others,[22] are not at work throughout the seventh canto. But what I want to emphasize is the way the Christian dimension operates throughout and culminates in the garden of Proserpina. On Phaedria's island, we had a garden whose dangers and temptations were of a traditional type found in the romantic epics; in this way it adumbrated Acrasia's Bower. But the garden of Proserpina also anticipates the Bower of Bliss. For here we are given a perverted Eden where the consequences of intemperance echo far beyond the limits of a simple temptation to indulge in the goods of the material world. From both Phaedria and Proserpina's gardens, Guyon has learned of the various types of temptations in and of the material world, and he has learned how both imply the inversion of the values of God. Guyon has

[22] See H. G. Lotspeich, *Classical Mythology in the Poetry of Edmund Spenser* (Princeton, 1932), p. 20; *Variorum*, II, 254ff.

seen both these versions of the evil garden, and now he is
ready, or will be after his sojourn at Alma's, for the grand
garden of Book II, which sums up all the gardens and all
the temptations—the Bower of Bliss.

AT ALMA's Guyon learns that if the body submits to "reasons
rule obedient," there is a place for pleasure in a temperate
man's constitution. The banquet Alma serves to her guests—
"attempred goodly well for health and for delight" (xi, 2)—
is indicative of Spenser's ability to conceive of pleasure and
virtue existing in harmony. This is a very important consideration for the virtue of Temperance in Book II, especially for the Bower of Bliss, and it marks the essential difference between Spenser's treatment of the Bower and
Tasso's of the garden of Armida.

> Now ginnes this goodly frame of Temperaunce
> Fayrely to rise. . . . (xii, 1)

Guyon is ready to complete his quest.

Guyon's odyssey to Acrasia's Bower has been fully treated
by others in regard to its allegorical significance and literary sources.[23] I would like only to notice several ways in
which themes from the gardens in Cantos v and vi are
recapitulated in the journey to the Bower. As they go farther
across the ocean toward Acrasia's, Guyon, the Palmer and
the boatman are suddenly assailed by horrible sea monsters
"Such as Dame Nature selfe mote feare to see," and these
unnatural creatures are called "All dreadfull pourtraicts of
deformitee" (23). The unnatural is conveyed through an

---

[23] Lotspeich, *Classical Mythology*, pp. 21-22; *Variorum*, II, 352-364.
The allegory has been treated most recently by B. Nellish in *ELH*, 30
(1963), pp. 89-106.

"art"-image, and both unnatural and "artistic" are, through the Palmer's words, linked to

> that same wicked witch, to worke us dreed,
> And draw from on this journey to proceed. (26)

Magic, art, the unnatural—all are associated again.

At stanza 28, we have a variation on these themes. A siren sings, and Guyon is momentarily tempted to listen, but the Palmer advises him that her plaint is

> onely womanish fine forgery,
> Your stubborne hart t'affect with fraile infirmity.
> (28)

The seductive power of illusion is, as it was before, related to evil. Then the temptation of the mermaids, who are really sirens (30-32), occurs, and many of these motifs are summed up in those creatures Comes said represented "nothing other than voluptuous desire."[24] They are first seen in a little bay which the poet compares to "an halfe theatre" (30), an image he took from Ariosto (*Orlando Furioso*, XIX, 64) and one which emphasizes the artificiality, the cunningly contrived quality, of the ensuing scene and siren song (32-33). The reference to their bathing in "deceiptfull shade" completes the implication of their false and illusory characteristics. Then in a story which has no precedent in classical mythology, Spenser tells how the mermaids attained their present, unnatural forms. They are the results of having "striv'd" with the Muses for "maystery" (31). Thus the theme of strife between art and nature is here foreshadowed in this struggle between the usurping sirens and the natural masters of art, the Muses. The siren-mermaids'

[24] Lotspeich, *Classical Mythology*, p. 81.

skill, like their bodies, is perverted and serves only to seduce travelers so they may be killed. The fatal, powerful attraction of sexuality is embodied in this small embellishment upon traditional figures and old themes.[25]

The Bower of Bliss itself is approached at stanza 42. From 42 to 49 we enter the garden at one stage; from 50 to 57 we pass through another stage, and repeat the same process again—another gate, another porter. Stanzas 58 to 61 then take us deeper into the garden. In all of these movements, Spenser is showing us how the very beauty of the place is the result of its evil nature. In different ways, he is—from the premise of the analogy between Acrasia's magic and her character as sexual indulgence and depravity—demonstrating how the elements of art and nature, and the theme of illusion, lead to a conclusion concerning the garden's corrupt and corrupting character. The first sight of the Bower is that of

> A place pickt out by choyce of best alyve,
> That Natures worke by art can imitate. (42)

I think this must refer to Acrasia, she who could be counterfeit Nature, and thus produce the overlavish scene which the rest of the stanza describes. Having established art and nature as one of his indices to the garden's character, as it was in Tasso, Spenser now adapts and develops (in stanza

[25] Part of the sirens' song goes:

> This is the port of rest from troublous toyle,
> The worldes sweet in from paine and wearisome
> turmoyle. (32)

which echoes the temptations of Phaedria (II, vi, 23) and Despair (I, ix, 40) and is ultimately adapted closely from the maidens' song to Carlo and Ubaldo in the *Gerusalemme Liberata*, XV, 63.

44) that distinguishing feature of Ariosto's island-garden, the motif of the life of sensual indulgence as a debilitating illusion. There Guyon and the Palmer pass through the walls of the Bower by way of a gate. Much has been made of the scene above the gate, which depicts the love of Jason and Medea (44-46).[26] However, one searches in vain for any comment on the gate itself. Yet it is most significant, for

> Yt framed was of precious ivory . . . (44)

which is an obvious reminiscence of the gate of ivory in *Odyssey*, XIX, 562-567 and *Aeneid*, VI, 893-896, through which pass the false or evil dreams. (Good, truthful dreams pass by the gate of horn.) It seems to me Spenser is subtly bringing us into the Bower as a false state of mind, a self-imposed illusion. This was certainly the implication of Cymochles' dreams at Canto v, 37, and vi, 27. The knight and his Palmer now approach a figure on the porch under the gate. Spenser says that this was not the good genius, Adgistes, who protects every man,

> But this same was to that quite contrary,
> The foe of life, that good envyes to all,
> That secretly doth us procure to fall,
> Through guilefull semblants, which he makes us see.
>
> (48)

He is "Pleasures porter" and has been much discussed;[27] for our purposes it is interesting to note that he seems to embody the two themes we have traced thus far. He is "pleasing, more than naturall," and daintily "deckt" (49) with flowers; that is, he is superficially (and artificially) lovely,

[26] Lotspeich, *Classical Mythology*, pp. 38-39; *Variorum*, II, 372-374.
[27] *Variorum*, II, 374-377, and Lewis, *Allegory*, pp. 361-363.

and essentially effeminate. He is not only not what he seems (his name is even misleading), but he is something of a magician himself. He has the power to manipulate illusions, and when Guyon rejects his bowl of wine, the knight also breaks the "staffe, with which he charmed semblants sly" (49). The porter is the "genius" of the garden in one true sense, however; he embodies the essence of the place's corrupt compound of unnatural beauty and fraudulent appearances which is meant to ruin a man. He tempts us, as the poet says, "to fall," and in that statement Spenser reestablishes the ultimate religious context and terms of the episode. For in that simple infinitive, the poet makes his first suggestion that this is not only a dangerous place, but indeed a false garden of Eden.

At stanza 50, the knight and his companion recommence their view of the place, and once again the poet tells us art did "decke" (like the porter) nature and "too lavishly adorne" her. Again art makes nature seem "more than naturall"; and the unnatural is the result. Stanza 51 seems a conventional passage describing perpetual springtime, lack of frost, storms, winds, etc., in short, the usual perfect climate of the garden of delight. But this stanza, presented with no comment, is itself an instance of unnatural Nature. We know from Book I (viii, 44; ix, 11, 16) and Book II, in the description of Alma's castle:

> O great pitty that no lenger time
> So goodly workemanship should not endure!
> Soone it must turne to earth: no earthly thing is
> sure (ix, 21)

that the only thing on earth which is constant is decay and change. Thus this plain of Acrasia's which seems immutable and unchangeable is in the deepest sense unnatural and illusory. Nothing which obeys the Creator's law could ever make the same claim. In stanza 52 the garden is compared to the loveliest places of the ancient world—Tempe, Ida, Parnassus—and is said to be more beautiful than all. Indeed, it is more lovely than

Eden selfe, if ought with Eden mote compayre.

The delicacy of the poet must not be taken as simply a means for describing the garden; it must also be understood as Spenser's way of condemning the garden. The Bower of Bliss in fact wants to be compared to the garden in Eden; and it wants to be a new Eden, inhabited by a depraved Eve, where all mankind can be induced "to fall." To create this false Eden, the witch's art has embellished Nature, has improved on God, and has created a blasphemous imitation of the true earthly paradise. Like the poets before him, Spenser conveys the garden's beauty and attraction in the same terms which reveal its falsity and dangers. Here the terms are the most inclusive, for beyond temperance and intemperance, reason and delight, nature and art, are the suggestions of the divine and the demonic, good and evil.

Guyon "wondred" at the sight before him (as he had in Mammon's cave, viii, 24) but like Carlo and Ubaldo (*Gerusalemme Liberata*, XV, 57) he passes by "Brydling his will, and maystering his might" (53). Then again we go through the cycle of illusion and artificial nature; Guyon sees another gate, then "no gate, but like one" made of branches whose arms "fashioned" a porch (5). This is art in action, that is, nature as she enlisted into art's cause which is seduction. From the vine come bunches which

seemd to entice
All passers by to taste their lushious wine,

. . . .

Some deepe empurpled as the hyacine,
Some as the rubine laughing sweetly red,
Some like faire emeraudes, not yet well ripened.

(54)

And then amongst, some were of burnisht gold,
So made by art, to beautify the rest. . . . (55)

The artificial, which has made no effort to pass for the real,
nevertheless infects all around it with its artificiality. The
real grapes, compared to gems, suddenly acquire an artificial quality which is increased when they are juxtaposed
with the truly artificial gold grapes. Art and nature are
beginning to blur; the false and the real commence to merge
as we go deeper into Pleasure's realm. In short, we are being
seduced by the landscape, and at the same time shown
through the landscape the false state of mind we are being
seduced into: a state of mind where the distinction between
good and evil is potentially obliterated. To go into the
Bower of Bliss is to lose the power of one's reason. To lose
the power of reason is to become a beast, which is, of course,
the literal fate of so many of Acrasia's lovers. But it is also,
more subtly, to live a prisoner of one's appetites and passions, in a state of Hell, and this too is a constant undercurrent in Spenser's treatment of the Bower. For the place
is often associated with the demonic and hellish, one instance of which occurs in stanza 55. Here the boughs, laden
with golden as well as real grapes, lean down just as the
branches did in Proserpina's garden, vii, 54. The echo of

that Eden in Hell serves to strengthen the suggestions of the Bower as a blasphemous, evil imitation-Eden.

Once again, Guyon passes a porter, this time Excess "Clad in fayre weedes, but fowle disordered" (55), and again he repulses an offer of wine;[28] now he rejects the cup "violently" (57) where before it was "disdainfully" (49). The greater the implied danger, and the temptation, the more violently it is rejected. At stanza 58, as at stanzas 42 and 50, we seem to recapitulate again the vista and its implications:

> There the most daintie paradise on ground
> It selfe doth offer to his sober eye.

Now these lines sum up all the accumulated significances of the preceding passages. Because of the suggestions of this place as a parody of Eden, the first words about "paradise" denote a sinister as well as beautiful landscape. Then from the *Gerusalemme Liberata*, XVI, 9-10 Spenser adapts stanzas 58 and 59 and, like Tasso, he defines the relationship of art and nature:

> One would have thought, (so cunningly the rude
> And scorned partes were mingled with the fine,)
> That Nature had for wantonessse ensude
> Art, and that Art at Nature did repine;
> So striving each th'other to undermine,
> Each did the others worke more beautify. (59)

And then, for the last time, Spenser follows up his generalized statement about art and nature with an illustration of

[28] Both the false Genius and Excess offer an intoxicant, an opiate; and again we recall Aristotle's description of the incontinent as similar "to men asleep, mad or drunk." This is the state to which Guyon is tempted, as it was the condition of Cymochles and will also be Verdant's.

art's relation to illusion and the role of sexuality. In stanzas 60 and 61 we see a fountain decorated with art.

> [It] with curious ymageree
> Was overwrought, and shapes of naked boyes,

and the art presents an illusion as they

> seemd with lively jollitee
> To fly about playing their wanton toyes. (60)

Over the scene on the fountain is a trail of golden ivy, so cleverly made that he

> who did not well avis'd it vew,
> Would surely deeme it to be yvie trew. (61)

We have entered the Bower in three stages (42-49, 50-57, 58-61), and three times Spenser has shown us the relation of art to nature, and then art as it was further identified with illusion and the theme of the Bower as a deceptive state of mind. Ultimately the poet has brought all these themes to bear on the garden as a place of sexual temptation and depraved behavior. Essentially, however, Spenser has been defining the garden through the roles of art and nature in it.

What exactly is the result? Is Spenser's conception of the Bower the same as Tasso's of Armida's garden, which Spenser imitates and whence the art-nature opposition immediately derives? No indeed, though the superficial parallels are valuable for a general comparison of the two, a comparison which, for broad purposes, Spenser surely wanted us to make. But substantially the roles of art and nature, like the two gardens, like the poems themselves, are very different. In Tasso, the whole landscape was a product of art, because all that Armida represented, her way of life and values, was false. Tasso saw nothing redeeming in Armida's world (though he tried desperately to redeem Armida), and therefore he pictured her garden as completely artificial. There was no room in the good life for the senses. Spenser has no such view. Delight and pleasure are not at all necessarily incompatible with duty and honor; the senses are not automatically the enemies of the spirit, if the rational— ultimately Christian—mean is maintained. Thus art and nature function not as indistinguishable worlds, both opposed to Truth, as in Tasso, but rather as emblems of the good and the bad. There is real, as well as artificial, nature in the Bower. What Spenser does is show art as "striving" with Nature, undermining nature, and in this he means us to see an allegory of the good, natural, healthy instinct as it is perverted and infected by lust and overindulgence. Acrasia's art seeks to make nature incontinent, i.e. overabundant, just as her sexuality seeks to make human nature self-indulgent and depraved. Art and lust do not try to pass for what is "natural"; rather, they lurk beneath the natural, inherent, as it were, in the natural. They seek to infect what surrounds them and bend it to their will, as the golden grapes infect the real grapes and bend the bough, as the pleasure that "secretly doth us procure to fall" insidiously hopes to render us helpless and finally dead. Basically Spenser sees a deadly enmity between self-indulgence and temperance, or the unnatural and the norm; he sees Acrasia and what she represents as the "foe of life" (as the porter was called in stanza 48), because the very basic, necessary and vital principle of life is threatened by her. As her art perverts the natural creation of God, so lust perverts, through self-indulgence, the natural creative act. And as the art which enhances nature issues in the unnatural, the radically *un-fruitful*, so self-indulgence in sexuality is finally sterile and thus in this sense unnatural. Acrasia is a false god who kills, not creates, life; her Bower is a false Eden which produces pain and degradation instead of harmonious bliss. Spenser has a more difficult task than Tasso; for instead of condemning all of nature and all of the senses, he must show us the mean. He must allow us to see how the fair and the foul have a common origin, and how that which abides by the norm of the natural (in the sight of God) is fair, while that which violates the natural for its own end is foul.

The rest of the canto shows us Guyon passing through the Bower as viewed in these terms. What the first 25 stanzas (37 to 61) defined, the second 25 (62-87) exemplify. We see the knight, who within himself contains the normal, natural amount of pleasure in the senses, gradually fall prey to the artifice of the maidens, to the inherent susceptibility of the senses to take pleasure only in themselves. As this process takes place, Spenser shows us how sensuality in fact leads finally to sterility. Guyon sees the two maidens naked in a stream. They "wrestle wantonly" and do not bother to conceal their bodies from "any which them eyd" (63). The sensuality of the garden, here displayed in maidens as it was in Tasso, is immediately associated with voyeurism, with the sterility of sex by the eyes. This is again emphasized in the last line of stanza 64 as the girls "th'amarous sweet spoiles to greedy eyes revele." Like Carlo and Ubaldo before him, Guyon slows down to watch, and "His stubborne brest gan secret pleasaunce to embrace" (65). The maidens see him, and like Tasso's "donzelle," they entice him through their false modesty and calculated coyness, their seemingly innocent displays (66-68). At this point, Guyon's "melting" heart (66) is sufficiently inflamed so that in his face

The secrete signes of kindled lust appeare. (68)

Both here and above in stanza 65 "secrete" is the word for the onset of lust; and it echoes that false genius who

secretly doth us procure to fall. (48)

The commencement of incontinence is insidious, covert, *inner*—because it begins by subtly assaulting and undermining that natural delight in pleasure and appetite which, checked by reason, is natural, indeed necessary, to a man. Lust secretly undermines reason as art undermined nature (59); and lust's signs begin to appear on Guyon's "sparkling face" (68) just as the golden grapes

did themselves emongst the leaves enfold,
As lurking from the vew of covetous guest. (55)

We see happening in Guyon what the earlier landscape defined as man's general inner condition in the Bower— the insidious perversion of natural means to unnatural ends. That such a process only leads to sterility is emphasized by the reaction of the Palmer:

He much rebukt those wandring eyes of his. (69)

Guyon is neither the *exemplum* of rigid morality, like Carlo and Ubaldo, nor the completely susceptible pawn, like Ruggiero or Rinaldo. Guyon is the man, like all men, who contains within him the natural appetites and desires, and, thus, in this fallen world, also the potentialities for depravity.

Spenser now shows us one who *did* succumb. Again we have a hint of the Bower as a false Eden in the suggestion of "paradise" (70); we hear lovely music, and then we, the readers see

> the faire witch, her selfe now solacing
> With a new lover, whom, through sorceree
> And witchcraft, she from farre did thether bring. (72)

Like the first view of her Bower (v, 27ff.), this first view of Acrasia is for us. Guyon will come upon her after we have realized her full significance.

Her lover is asleep. As we see later (76), his head is in her lap, that "grembo molle" of the *Gerusalemme Liberata,* XVI, 18. She leans over the sleeping form,

> her false eyes fast fixed in his sight,
> As seeking medicine whence she was strong,
> Or greedily depasturing delight. (73)

Though the man is asleep, Acrasia nonetheless fixes her eyes on his, and not only the sterility but the Narcissism of the *Gerusalemme Liberata* comes back to us. Indeed, this is the traditional pose of Venus and Mars, and "depasturing" is a literal translation of the Italian "pascendo," first applied to Venus and Mars in *Le Stanze,* I, 121, and then to Armida and Rinaldo in the *Gerusalemme Liberata,* XVI, 19. Yet here Acrasia completely dominates the man in a way Armida, for instance, never did. Rinaldo was at least conscious in Armida's garden; this young man is not, and thus a sinister quality pervades the place which was lacking in the previous poems. Where Rinaldo sighed *as if* his soul were going into Armida, here Acrasia

> through his humid eyes did sucke his spright.
> Quite molten into lust and pleasure lewd. (73)

All the imagery of liquid connected with lust (I, vii, 7; II, v, 28) is summed up in her sucking up his molten soul. But even more, the traditional passivity of the male, usually compared to an infantile state, is here made even more arresting. The male seems dead and there is a vampirish quality about Acrasia. Venus, who usually is the animating spirit of this kind of tableau, seems to have given way to some ghastly, demonic female. There seems to be a violation of the male's essence here which is much more profound than that suffered by the knights in the Italian poems; for at the center of this garden we have come not to the source of simple illusion or immorality, but rather to the image of death—a love which is almost necrophilia, a woman whose kiss brings death. Proserpina haunts the figure of Acrasia, as her hellish Eden underlies, perhaps literally, this blasphemous Eden.

When, after an adaptation of the song of the Rose, Guyon and the Palmer creep forward, they finally see her: like Alcina, she seems to have on a "vele of silke and silver thin" (77), and like Armida, her breasts are exposed, and perspiration stands out on her face (78). And again, as in the Italian epics, much is made of the sterility (and implied Narcissism) of such a love by the emphasis on her as "spoyle/Of hungry eies" and on her own eyes which inflame but do not satisfy (78). There is only one touch which makes her different from her predecessors, and that occurs at the beginning of the witch's description: she is reclining on a bed of roses

As faint through heat, or dight to pleasant sin. (77)

Sin. Let us not be misled by that "pleasant," for that would be to fall into the Bower's trap. "Sin" functions here as.

that "sinfull bayt" (vii, 64) of Mammon's did in the garden of Proserpina. It reveals the ultimate consequences of succumbing to temptation in this world; it implies the ultimate, religious, standards by which men are judged and against which this garden (and Proserpina's) have set themselves. "Sin" finally establishes the norms by which men must live and from which these false Edens tempt them to fall.

Briefly, we see the man who is her beloved; he is young, handsome, and his arms, now abandoned, betray the signs ("old moniments") of many warlike and noble encounters (79-80). Though the theme that the life of self-indulgence deters one from the pursuit of honor is explicit here, we also see in his "nobility" (79) which is so disgraced an *exemplum* of what the garden's landscape and Guyon's momentary lapse taught us: that inherent in the natural good is the potential for unnatural evil; latent in the continent or temperate man is the incontinent, intemperate man. As the world is full of tests and trials, one of them is to maintain "continence/In joyous pleasure" (vii, 1) and keep, through "goodly government," the body "attempred . . . for health and for delight" (xi, 2). This is, after all, the point of the quest and the lesson of the Bower canto.

After Guyon and the Palmer have caught the pair in the Palmer's "subtile net," and have bound them,[29] Guyon

---

[29] A reminiscence of *Odyssey*, VIII, 266ff., where Ares and Aphrodite are caught by Hephestus. This "subtile net" contrasts with Acrasia's veil, a more "subtile web" than Arachne could spin (77). The Palmer, besting the sorceress at her own game, reminds me of the figure of the "good magician," for like Tasso's Old Man of Ascolona, his staff subdues wild animals; here also we have a lesson of the sort implied at the end of the Alcina episode: learn to turn the tools of deception against the sources of deception. The Palmer's net is stronger than Acrasia's "web" or her "arts" (81); it is the product of a Christianized, or at least

destroys the Bower (83). His thorough and complete job has been questioned by many commentators who profess to see the Puritan conscience of the poet at work here. Such comments are misled and misleading. Not only did the earthly paradise convention in the Renaissance epics demand the destruction of the delightful, evil place (the realms of Alcina, Acratia and Armida were all reduced in one way or another), but the whole thrust of Book II demands it. This act is evidence of Puritanism only if a recognition of the proper role of the senses and a *restoration* of them to that role are Puritanical. Here Guyon becomes an elemental force; it is, in this man who has been learning temperance, the "tempest of his wrathfulnesse" that asserts itself. It is his native, righteous, proper indignation, and the Palmer makes no move to check him. Guyon is not destroying Pleasure in its best sense here; he is restoring it. He becomes a tempest in stanza 83 because he is like the cleansing force of Nature herself as she restores what is good to its true place in the scheme of things. It may seem paradoxical that in destroying the Bower Guyon is restoring anything; but it is Acrasia who manufactured the first paradox as she perverted nature and rendered the most creative act the most sterile and dehumanizing. Guyon turns the Bower upside down to put things right side up again. He restores the proper balance of beauty and truth when he now makes "of the fayrest late" the "fowlest place" (83). As he asserts the power of the reason over appetite, he restores the proper distinctions between fair and foul, good and evil.

The last stanzas of Canto xii clearly make this point. The

---

legitimatized, magic—a magic put to the service of the good, and thus capable of subduing evil.

beasts which charge up to the knight and his guide are only those reduced by Acrasia's lust

> into figures hideous,
> According to their mindes like monstruous. (85).

Here all the early associations of the Bower as a false state of mind, and of art as an analogue for lust and the unnatural, are tightened by the Palmer's revelation of these bestial men. And what does Guyon reply to his companion's words?

> Sad end, quoth he, of life intemperate,
> And mournefull meed of joyes delicious! (85)

This last line is the most revealing. Spenser, in a way Tasso never could, does not deny pleasure or the senses; he only denies unchecked and total indulgence. As Guyon says these words, the allegory of the Bower seems to become completed, and the "frame of Temperaunce" begins to be fulfilled.

But, as there is in all men the potential for incontinence, so within mankind there are those who prefer the bestial state. Such a man is Gryll, who complains when the Palmer restores him to "naturall" (86). He prefers his "hoggish forme," and the words of scorn which Guyon now speaks make amply clear what Gryll chooses when he chooses to live in his former state of mind:

> See the mind of beastly man,
> That hath so soone forgot the excellence
> Of his creation, when he life began,
> That now he chooseth, with vile difference,
> To be a beast, and lacks intelligence. (87)

Some modern commentators have professed admiration for

Gryll's stubbornness, his refusal to submit. Every man to his own deepest dreams. However, what Gryll has chosen is Hell. Spenser does not deny him the right to choose, but the poet makes it clear that such a life is contrary to the "naturall" in its finest sense, that which most resembles the "excellence/Of his creation." Man is fallen, but he can be saved, if he uses what he retains of his innocent nature— "when he life began"—to serve his Creator. To do otherwise is to deny the image and hope of that first garden for the specious joys of a false Eden; it is to substitute for the possibility of redemption a horrible parody of innocence in a mire of self-indulgence. Such a life is to "lacke intelligence," to be among those, as Virgil said to Dante,

* C'hanno perduto il ben de l'intelletto. (*Inferno*, III, 18)

Spenser's garden vision includes much more than the earthly paradises of the Italians. He sees not only the illusory quality, the immoral dimension, of the life of sexual indulgence; he sees its horror precisely because he can see the goods which are being wasted. He is neither the total skeptic nor the exclusive moralist. Spenser sees proper pleasure compatible with honor and duty, and he sees how the senses can be made to exist in harmony with the spirit. Because he has a broader vision of the joys of life, he is able to give us a more ghastly vision of their perversions and a deeper warning of the profound consequences of sin. Thus his earthly paradise presents the most striking Renaissance version of man's search for peace in a garden, and the dangers and terrors of mistaking some earthly bliss for that bliss which is found only, and finally, in God.

* who have lost the good of the intellect.

WE CANNOT end our discussion of the earthly paradise in *The Faerie Queene* without a few brief comments about the Garden of Venus and Adonis (III, vi, 29-54). Though I can add nothing to the learned discussions concerning the philosophical meaning, or sources, of the Garden, there is something to be gained from a general comparison of it with the Bower of Bliss.[30]

As the poet undoubtedly intended, C. S. Lewis has already compared the two places with respect to the categories of nature and art, and his conclusion that the Bower is "artifice, sterility, death: [the Garden] nature, fecundity, life" is undeniable.[31] However, the ultimate difference between the two will be more marked if we consider some of the ways in which they resemble one another. There is, after all, a kind of similarity in attitude between Acrasia bending over the form of Verdant (II, xii, 73) and Venus leaning over an Adonis "Lapped in flowres and pretious spycery":

> But she her selfe, when ever that she will,
> Possesseth him, and of his sweetnesse takes her fill.
>
> (III, vi, 46)

It is the similarity of passive males being made love to by dominating females. There is also a certain similarity in the gardens themselves; for if we disregard the Nature-Art opposition, we find both are twice described as "paradise"—

---

[30] Bush, *Mythology and the Renaissance*, pp. 11-114, has a concise discussion of the Garden of Venus and Adonis to which I am indebted.— One should also see the descriptions of the Temple of Venus, IV, x, 6-7 and 21-26, and of Mount Acidale, VI, x, 5 *et seq.*; both places are beloved of Venus and in both, nature spreads her bounty, though in the first she is aided by art—as opposed to the Bower where there was strife between the two.

[31] *Allegory*, p. 326.

the Bower at II, xii, 58 and 70, the Garden at III, vi, 29 and 43. Indeed, both seem haunted by the image of Eden.[32] Finally, there is a similarity in the poet's organization of his presentation of the gardens. As we know, the description of the Bower is 50 stanzas long, the first 25 being a "definition" of the place in general terms, the second 25 an actualization of the Bower's character through the actions and reactions of Guyon. So in the Garden; the description of the place is 26 stanzas (29 to 54), the first half (29 to 42) concerned with the Garden's life in general terms, the second half (43 to 54) illustrating that life in concrete images and through the figures of Venus and Adonis.

These surface similarities between the Bower and the Garden are by no means intended to show they are the same, for they patently are not. But what I do mean to demonstrate is that, were the categories of Nature and Art left aside, the gardens could almost be made to sound alike. We must, therefore, look for some even more fundamental point of difference. The essential difference between the two places is the fact of Time. This is what the Bower pretends to do without and what the Garden embodies.

We remember that through Acrasia's magic, Art embellished Nature and

> Thereto the heavens always joviall,
> Lookte on them lovely, still in stedfast state,
> Ne suffred storme nor frost on them to fall,

[32] J. W. Bennett, "Spenser's Garden of Adonis Revisited," *JEGP*, 44 (1942), pp. 46-51, and n. 11, has shown how the Garden is a traditional earthly paradise in the details of its landscape (pp. 41-42) and its mountain-top grove (pp. 43-44); she also notes the interesting fact that the sixteenth century evidently had made an etymological and imaginative connection between Adonis and Eden.

Their tender buds or leaves to violate,
Nor scorching heat, nor cold intemperate,
T'afflict the creatures which therein did dwell,
But the milde ayre with season moderate
Gently attempred, and disposd so well,
That still it breathed forth sweet spirit and
holesom smell. (II, xii, 51)

The most deceitful and unnatural aspect of Acrasia's Bower
was that it should deny that very fundamental law to
which "all that lives is subject":

All things decay in time, and to their end doe draw.
(III, vi, 40)

The most illusory aspect of sexual self-indulgence is that
it flouts this law, and pretends to make static, forever
young, forever beautiful, that which is by nature fluid and
in flux. This is the most profound perversion of the Bower
and the radical deformity of Acrasia's way of life: its denial
of the fact of death as an element in life; its refusal to face
the necessity for decay in the midst of growth.

It is precisely this element that the Garden includes. Here
the whole lesson is that creative sexuality recognizes that
what is born must indeed die, that what dies will—in some
form—live again. Were it not for Time,

All that in this delightfull gardin growes
Should happy bee, and have immortall blis. (41)

Yet in this world, for which the Garden is a metaphor, Time
does exist; all that lives is subject to his scythe. Thus, even
though

Franckly each paramour his leman knowes,
Each bird his mate, (41)

and even though

There is continuall spring, and harvest there
Continuall, both meeting at one tyme; (42)

still, all is not unalloyed joy, for Time is there. This means
that

formes are variable, and decay
By course of kinde and by occasion; (38)

but it also means that, despite the fact that forms fade,
there is a kind of permanence; for

substaunce is eterne, and bideth so (37)

because

in the wide wombe of the world there lyes,
In hatefull darknes and in deepe horrore,
An huge eternal chaos, which supplyes
The substaunces of Natures fruitfull progenyes. (36)

According to the law, there is always life in spite of death,
and eternity is insured through change.

The whole process is symbolized in the figures of Venus
and Adonis. When she is in the garden, she visits him in
the arbor atop the mount in the middle of the Garden.
There Adonis lives above change, in "eternall blis,"

Joying his goddesse, and of her enjoyd. (48)

By saying they live above change (44) and in eternal
bliss, Spenser is not taking them out of the process of Time;
he is setting them apart to give us an image *of* the process.
Adonis,

All be he subject to mortalitie,
Yet is eterne in mutabilitie,

because he is the "father of all formes" and thus is

by succession made perpetuall. (47)

Venus, who earlier was referred to as the "great mother"
of all fair things (40) is substance, matter, and in their union
we see the eternal source of all change. This is how they
can have eternal bliss, by forever exemplifying the process
of life.

In this Garden, as Douglas Bush has said, Spenser has
"found at least an imaginative reconciliation between the
fact of change and the desire for stability; and, though as a
whole the myth is given in naturalistic terms, there is a
reminder (stanza 34) that the great process has divine
sanction."[33] Indeed, this is most important of all, for in this
Garden we see Spenser trying to reconcile the great conflict
between Time and the Timeless. It is particularly interesting that he does this by ultimately appealing to

the mighty word,
Which first was spoken by th' Almighty Lord,
That bad them to increase and multiply. (34)

Here Spenser seems to find if not solace at least justification
for his sense of flux in human affairs. And he seems to
bring this lower world into some kind of harmony with
that "Sabaoth sight" which eludes mankind; for if this
Garden is not a place of immortal bliss, at least it is a
place of creative joy which, like a good man, will find
through its mutability a kind of eternity.

[33] Bush, *Mythology and the Renaissance*, pp. 113-114.

THE lesson of the Garden, for Amoret and for us, is to put life to its proper uses. If we do, then even though we are subject to the melancholy process of Time and change, we will have obeyed and, in obeying, pleased God. That is certainly better than misusing the creative powers, as Acrasia and her lovers do, which only serves to alienate man further from his best self, from the excellence of his creation. Spenser uses the image of the garden of Eden as an ultimate referent in both these garden episodes. The paradise-image which is always behind the Bower serves two purposes: it lends the Bower a certain aesthetic beauty by implication, while on the moral scale it serves as a standard by which we can see how depraved and corrupt the Bower really is. The Bower is seen, finally, as an imitation Eden with inverted values. The Garden of Adonis is superior to the Bower essentially in that it takes into account the laws of creation which the Bower denied. To this extent the temporal garden is an Eden-like existence, that is, it is harmonious and fruitful; it presents the only way to make peace with the fact man lives in a fallen world.

Finally, we see Spenser using the earthly paradise in the two ways we have seen it handled in the Renaissance epics. Like the island of Venus in *Os Lusíadas*, the Garden of Adonis binds up and reconciles the fundamental conflicts of the poem in overtly sexual, ultimately Christian, terms. This is the earthly paradise used as a conscious myth or metaphor as an image of order and stability—even if of a precarious sort. Such paradises do not occur very often in literature. Much more prevalent is the garden as a place of reason overcome by passion, duty by pleasure, man by woman, spirit by sense. And as a place of beauty and vicious illusions, as a false paradise in the tradition of Alcina's island, Acratia's garden and Armida's island, Acrasia's Bower of Bliss finds its justified place as the culmination of a long line.

For the writings of C. S. Lewis on Spenser, see *Allegory*, Chapter vii; his Oxford *English Literature*, pp. 347-393; and his informative review of R. Ellrodt's *Neoplatonism in the Poetry of Spenser* in *EA*, 14 (1961), pp. 107-116; General bibliography on Spenser is provided in his *English Literature*, pp. 676-679; for *The Faerie Queene*, p. 677. Basic materials of all sorts are provided in *The Works of Edmund Spenser: a Variorum Edition*, ed. E. Greenlaw, C. G. Osgood, F. M. Padelford, *et al.*, 11 vols. (Baltimore, 1932-1957); and there is a detailed bibliography by W. F. McNeir and F. Provost, *Annotated Bibliography of Edmund Spenser, 1937-1960*, Duquesne Studies. Philological Series 3 (Pittsburgh, 1962).

Two good studies of Spenser's poetry by way of the intellectual background are Ellrodt's *Neoplatonism* (Genève, 1960) cited above, and W. Nelson's *The Poetry of Edmund Spenser* (New York, 1963).

For a more "mythic" view of Spenser, see the articles in *UTQ*, 30, 2 (1961): N. Frye, "The Structure of Imagery in The Faerie Queene," pp. 109-127; H. Berger, Jr., "Spenser's Garden of Adonis: Force and Form in the Renaissance Imagination," pp. 128-149.

For Historical Allegory, see the appendix so entitled in each volume of the Variorum; also F. Kermode, "Spenser and the Allegorists," *PBA*, 48 (1962; published 1963), pp. 261-279.

For studies concentrating on the allegory, in reaction to the history of ideas approach, see A. C. Hamilton, *The Structure of Allegory in The Faerie Queene* (Oxford, 1961), who wants to "focus on the image itself, rather than seek the idea behind the image" (p. 12); M. P. Parker, *The Allegory of The Faerie Queene* (Oxford, 1960), feels "that the *Faerie Queene* is primarily and fundamentally a Christian poem" and all the difficulties will be resolved "when the poem is thus regarded from within" (pp. 3-4); and the interesting study of Books III and IV by T. P. Roche, Jr., *The Kindly Flame* (Princeton, 1964).

For various readings of Book II of the *F.Q.*, see A. C. Hamilton's "A Theological Reading of *The Faerie Queene*, Book II," *ELH*, 25 (1958), pp. 155-162; and the very influential piece by A. S. P. Woodhouse, "Nature and Grace in *The Faerie Queene*," *ELH*, 16 (1949), pp. 194-228. I am indebted to this valuable article, though I think Woodhouse schematizes too sharply and that the Christian element in Book II is constantly implied rather than simply absent. For Woodhouse's defense of his position, see *ELH*, 27 (1960), pp. 1-15.

For a summary of the philosophical sources of Temperance, see Appendix IV of *Variorum*, II, 414-426; and also, H. S. V. Jones, *A Spenser Handbook* (New York, 1937), pp. 172-208; J. L. Shanley, "Spenser's Temperance and Aristotle," *MP*, 43 (1946), pp. 170-174; E. Sirluck, "The Faerie Queene, Book II, and the Nicomachean Ethics," *MP*, 49 (1952), pp. 73-100; see W. L. Renwick, *Edmund Spenser* (London, 1925), esp. Chapter iv, "Philosophy," though his strictures on source-hunting seem to have been obscured by the post-Variorum deluge.

For a very acute study of Book II, see H. Berger's *The Allegorical Temper* (New Haven, 1957), where the various opinions on Book II are summarized (pp. 3-4). By examining the "meaning of Book II as it is related to the issues of 'intellectual history' present in the poem" and "as it is related to the principles of poetics embodied in Spenser's allegorical method" (p. 38), Berger combines the two predominant critical approaches to Spenser.

Some of the busiest scholars on the landscape of Spenserian criticism have been those digging for the sources of the Garden of Venus and Adonis. See *Variorum*, III, pp. 340-352, for the main interpretations. J. W. Bennett is for Plato and Neo-Platonic sources in *PMLA*, 47 (1932), pp. 46-80; see also her "Spenser's Garden of Adonis Revisited," *JEGP*, 44 (1942), pp. 53-78. E. M. Albright offered Empedocles in *PMLA*, 44 (1929), pp. 715-759, after Lucretius had been championed by E. Greenlaw, *SP*, 17 (1920), pp. 439-464. Plotinus, by way of Augustine and Ficino, has been most recently discussed by Nelson, *Spenser*, pp. 207-223; Bruno was once thrust into the ring by R. B. Levinson, *PMLA*, 43 (1928), pp. 675-681; while, after an exhaustive survey, only Renaissance commonplaces, by way of Golding's Ovid, were found by B. Stirling, *PMLA*, 49 (1934), pp. 501-538. Many scholars have accepted his findings.

One might also consult T. P. Harrison, Jr., "Divinity in Spenser's Garden of Adonis," *UTSE*, 19 (1939), pp. 48-73, where the garden is studied as a paradise; and the relevant comments in P. Alpers, "Narrative and Rhetoric in the *Faerie Queene*," *SEL*, 2 (1962), pp. 27-46. Ellrodt, *Neoplatonism*, Chapter iv, "Platonic Mythology and Cosmology," reviews much of this work and has sensible things to say on the garden, esp. pp. 70-86, as does Roche, *Kindly Flame*, pp. 117-128.

On Spenser's religious views, see V. K. Whittaker, *The Religious Basis of Spenser's Thought*, Stanford University Publications, Language and Literature, Vol. VII, No. 3 (Stanford and London, 1950); this study should be supplemented, however, by Ellrodt, *Neoplatonism*, Chapter xii, "Spenser's Religious Sensibility," where the traditional, medieval characteristics of Spenser's religious feelings are, rightly I think, emphasized.

On Nature, see Woodhouse, cited above, p. 291, as well as many of the items noted above on the Garden of Adonis, and M. Miller, "Nature in *The Faerie Queene*," *ELH*, 18 (1951), pp. 191-200. Lewis, *Allegory*, pp. 324-333, first distinguished at length the roles of nature and art in the Bower of Bliss and the Garden of Adonis, and his comments have become commonplaces of Spenser criticism. However, recent studies have taken exception to Lewis' distinction between good nature and artificial, bad nature (p. 343). See N. S. Brooke, "C. S. Lewis and Spenser: Nature, Art and the Bower of Bliss," *CJ*, 2 (1949), pp. 420-434; M. Maclure, "Nature and Art in *The Faerie Queene*," *ELH*, 28 (1961), pp. 1-20; and H. Guth, "Allegorical Implications of Artifice in Spenser's *Faerie Queene*," *PMLA*, 76 (1961), pp. 474-479.

For the use of mythology in the Renaissance, see Bush, *Mythology and the Renaissance*, esp. pp. 28-33 on handbooks and dictionaries, and Chapter v on Spenser. See also D. T. Starnes and E. W. Talbert, *Classical Myth and Legend in Renaissance Dictionaries* (Chapel Hill, 1955), esp. Chapter iv, "Spenser and the Dictionaries." There is a great deal of useful information in H. G. Lotspeich, *Classical Mythology in the Poetry of Edmund Spenser* (Princeton, 1932).

On Spenser's debts to the Italians, see the following:

On Ariosto, the two articles by R. E. N. Dodge, *PMLA*, 12 (1897), pp. 151-204; *PMLA*, 35 (1920), pp. 91-92, which supplemented the supplement by A. H. Gilbert, *PMLA*, 25 (1919), pp. 225-232; also W. J. B. Owen, *N&Q*, 194 (1949), pp. 316-319, and his "*Orlando*

Furioso and Stanza Connection in *The Faerie Queene*," *MLN*, 67 (1952), pp. 5-8; and S. J. McMurphy, *Spenser's Use of Ariosto for Allegory*, University of Washington Publications in Language and Literature, 2 (Seattle, 1923).

On Tasso, see E. Koeppel, "Die Englischen Tasso-Übersetzungen des 16. Jahrhunderts," *Anglia*, 11 (1889), esp. "Edmund Spenser's Verhältniss zu Tasso," pp. 341-362; H. H. Blanchard, "Imitations of Tasso in the *Faerie Queene*," *SP*, 22 (1925), pp. 208-209, and Brand, *Tasso*, pp. 228-238.

On Trissino, see Lemmi, *PQ*, 7, pp. 220-223, cited above p. 228.

On Boiardo, see C. S. Lewis' communication in *RES*, 7 (1931), pp. 84-85; and H. H. Blanchard, "Spenser and Boiardo," *PMLA*, 40 (1925), pp. 828-851. There are also appendices in the *Variorum* volumes on borrowings by Spenser from the Italians.

For Arcasia's name ("Incontinence" in Greek), see Nelson, *Spenser*, p. 186, and the elaborate discussion in Berger, *Allegorical Temper*, pp. 65-68. On Acrasia's origins, see J. M. Steadman, "Acrasia in 'The Tablet of Cebes,'" *N&Q*, 205 (1960), pp. 48-49; the *Tablet* (first century A.D.) was, as Lewis, *Allegory*, p. 363 says, "a popular Renaissance school book," and Milton, in speaking of an "easie and delightful Book of Education" mentions "Cebes, Plutarch and other Socratic discourses" in *Of Education* (Columbia University edition of *Works*, IV, 281). In the *Tablet*, Acrasia is Incontinence in the company of Profligacy, Avarice, and Flattery, and she seduces pilgrims. See also M. Y. Hughes, "Spenser's Acrasia and the Circe of the Renaissance," *JHI*, 4 (1943), pp. 381-399, already cited above in connection with Alcina under *Ariosto*.

Discussions of the Bower of Bliss will be found in the general works cited above, pp. 291-292. The best to which I am indebted, is Berger, *Allegorical Temper*, pp. 211-240; and one should see R. M. Durling, "The Bower of Bliss and Armida's Palace," *CL*, 6 (1954), pp. 335-347, already cited above in connection with Armida under *Tasso*.

CHAPTER SIX

ᏝᎷilton

· I ·

PARADISE LOST sums up all that came before it. The poem is the supreme Christian epic, and it exemplifies one of the themes of this study, the gradual coalescence of classical and Christian material in Renaissance poetry. In twelve books, with its elevated language, epic conventions, and innumerable allusions to ancient literature, the poem is the most "classical" of all the great Renaissance epics. At the same time, in story, themes, and focus, it is the most overtly Christian. Here is no adaptation of the two cultures into a romantic world of knights and ladies, quests, loves, and wars; rather, there is a radical amalgam, typical of the Renaissance but unique in the Renaissance, of the two.

In many respects, the poem is like that "hateful siege/Of contraries" (IX, 121-122) which torments Satan; for *Paradise Lost* is a massive structure of ironies, holding in equilibrium multiple points of view. Indeed, perspective itself, the loss and gain of sight and vantage points for sight, is one of the poem's major themes, as it is one of the basic patterns of imagery. What had to be held in balance were many things, but chiefly two: within the poem, all those mysterious paradoxes at the heart of the story, one of which was revealed by Augustine in *The City of God*, XIV, 13:

In humility therefore there is this to be wondered at, that it elevates the heart; and in pride this, that it dejects it. This seems strangely contrary, that elevation should be below, and dejection aloft. But godly humility subjects one to his superior: and God is above all; therefore humility exalts one, in making him God's subject. But pride the vice refusing this subjection falls from him that is above all, and so becomes more base by far, fulfilling this verse of the psalm: "Thou hadst cast them down in their own exaltation." He says not "when they were exalted" as if they were degraded afterwards: but, in their very exaltation were they cast down. Their elevation was their ruin.[1]

Here, in this central paradox of exalted humility and debased pride, we find not only an insight into Milton's preoccupations, but also a key to what Greene has called Milton's "vertical imagery," the imagery of height and depth which describes the universe within man and without.[2]

The other set of "contraries" includes the poem and its audience, and is alluded to by Kermode when he notes that Milton "is writing for the corrupt and intelligent";[3] that Milton is writing for an audience which, regardless of how "fit," knows his story, its inevitable outcome and consequences. The problem for the poet is therefore how to carry this audience along: how, in recounting the beginning and the good, to account and allow for knowledge of the end and all the evil. If as Christian (and poet) he wants to

[1] *The City of God*, tr. J. Healy (1610), ed. R. V. G. Tasker, Everyman's Library, 2 vols. (London, 1945), II, 43. All citations from Milton's verse are from *John Milton Complete Poems and Major Prose*, ed. M. Hughes (New York, 1957); all citations from Milton's prose unless otherwise noted are from *The Works of John Milton* (Columbia University Press, 1931-1942), referred to as C.E.

[2] *The Descent from Heaven*, p. 388, in connection with this same passage from Augustine, pp. 389-390.

[3] *The Living Milton*, ed. F. Kermode (New York, 1961), p. 90, in his essay "Adam Unparadised."

"justify the ways of God to men," as poet (and Christian) he must also, somehow, prepare for the ways of the first man and woman to God. If the poet cannot explain their disobedience, he must nevertheless involve that other perspective which is ours. He must somehow implicate our experience in the way he tells the story, while condemning our first parents' sin—the source of that experience.

So one returns to the poem; not to the marvelous patterns of imagery per se, but to the style in a much broader sense. Here I am not specifically interested in whether the language reflects the constructions of Hebrew or Greek, Latin or Italian; it does all these when he wants it to, and none when he chooses. I refer simply to the well-known sinuosity, complexity, ambiguity of Milton's language. Empson spoke once of "The sliding, sideways, broadening movement, normal to Milton," and Ricks has said that "The more closely one looks at the style, the clearer it seems that Milton writes at his very best only when something prevents him from writing with total directness."[4] However, as is often the case in such matters, the poem speaks best for itself; for there is a movement typical to Satan, he who

> winds with ease
> Through the pure marble Air his oblique way
> (III, 563-564)

and who, as the snake,

> With tract oblique
> At first, as one who sought access, but fear'd
> To interrupt, side-long he works his way.
> (IX, 510-512)

---

[4] W. Empson, *Some Versions of Pastoral* (London, 1935), p. 162; C. Ricks, *Milton's Grand Style* (Oxford, 1963), pp. 147-148. Ricks points

Hee leading swiftly roll'd
In tangles, and made intricate seem straight.
(IX, 631-632)

In Satan, a major aspect of Milton's style is revealed. But these passages not only describe the way in which the poet's language often works; they also reveal a whole life "style," a way of approaching, and controlling, reality appropriate to both the poet recounting subversion and the Subverter himself; a style suitable to describe, and to be, the means by whose consequences all men will

> turn aside to tread
> Paths indirect. . . . (XI, 630-631)

Moreover, this "satanic style" is appropriate to the poet not only as a means for reflecting the way the devil works—while describing him at work; but it is also suitable for dealing with the garden and the figures in the garden. By "satanic style" I am not implying that Milton was of Satan's party without knowing it; no one was more aware of what he knew, or what he was doing, than John Milton. What I am asserting is that this allusive, elusive technique allows Milton full scope for his vast literary resources, and sources, and for the breadth of verbal ambiguity needed to maintain the multiple perspectives, and the suspense, necessary for a successful account of the Fall. The passages cited above, imbedded in the poem, are finally important because they direct us, in large part, not only to the poet's method, but to his message; not only to how he tells his story, but also to what he means to say. In examining the

---

out that Milton often writes directly, "But as a rule . . . his greatest effects are produced when he is compelled to be oblique as well as direct."

garden and its significance in *Paradise Lost*, we shall have occasion to return often to the uses, and implications, of the "satanic style."

· II ·

It is one of the great commonplaces of Milton criticism that the garden in Eden reflects the innocence and perfection of Adam and Eve; that external Nature mirrors the essential harmony and purity of human nature. And this is certainly true; the garden is as appealing, in every way, as they are. But there is more to Adam and Eve, and the garden, than this kind of statement implies. God made man "perfet," to be sure, but in the same sentence Raphael says He made him "not immutable" (V, 524); and man's will, "though free," is "Yet mutable" (236-237). Thus if the garden is to be a true reflection of the first couple, it must reflect *all* that is within them; it must also include that potential for change, change for the better or change for the worse, which is part of their nature.

Thus in his garden, Milton faces a task far more complex than that of previous poets. He must describe perfection while, because of the story and because we know the ending, preparing for sin. Yet his exploitation of the potential for evil must never overtly undermine the absolute goodness of the place; if doctrine had not dictated thus, the standards of a great poet would have. It is a task besieged with contraries, this deployment of perspectives, the subtle manipulation of overt and covert, of unfallen innocence and fallen knowledge. Here the "satanic style," in all its variations, and in its broadest sense, serves the poet best; for by implication and indirection, a hint dropped now and later fulfilled, a word, a phrase, a sentence whose suggestiveness expands in many directions, an allusion which cuts both ways, the poet can establish the obvious superiority of the garden and its couple to anything else in man's experience while bringing before the reader seeds of suspicion or doubt or fallen experience—seeds which later bear their own kind of fruit. As we shall see, any oblique echo, any allusion will do, though classical material is the best. For a classical allusion in this Christian tale will always do two things; it will invariably indicate the higher Truth and greater splendor of the garden and of Adam and Eve; but it will also, obliquely, by what it recalls and by the very fact it is there, prepare for a context of falsity and disgrace.[5]

Milton's ostensible task was to make the earthly paradise in Book IV perfect and delightful, and out of allusions to and reminiscences of almost every Biblical, classical, modern, and "real" garden he could find, he composed his own complete, integrated vision.[6] As to the description of the garden itself, "Milton's exuberance of imagination," Addison said, "has poured forth such a redundancy of ornaments on this seat of happiness and innocence, that it would be endless to point out each particular."[7] Without being endless,

[5] Davis Harding, in a study to which I am heavily indebted, *The Club of Hercules*, Illinois Studies in Language and Literature, Vol. 50 (Urbana, 1962), has called instances of this technique "part of the elaborate and largely secret machinery to prepare our minds for the Fall . . ." (p. 80).

[6] At IV, 268-285, paradise is superior to Henna's Field, Daphne's Grove, the Nyseian isle and Mount Amara; at IX, 439-443, to the gardens of Adonis and Alcinous, and those gardens in Canticle 6:2; 7:1 and I Kings 3:1; at IV, 706, their bower is better than those of Pan, Silvanus and Faunus, and at V, 339-341, the fruit of paradise is all that can be found in India East or West, Pontus' middle short, the Punic Coast or Alcinous' garden. By alluding to all these gardens and landscapes, Milton endows his paradise with the universal and eternal qualities it demands.

[7] Cited in notes to *Paradise Lost*, ed. T. Newton, A New Edition, 2 vols. (Dublin, 1772), I, 271.

we might notice the way Milton employs traditional garden motifs. The garden is a place of pleasure and comfort where, though work is an essential element, and Adam complains that Nature constantly outstrips their efforts (IV, 621-629), the couple does only what they find pleasurably necessary (327-329). Above all, it is a highly sensuous place: there "Nature's whole wealth" (207) is "To all delight of human sense expos'd" (206), and the richness of sensuous detail creates indeed "A Heaven on Earth" (208)—the proper analogue to the perfect rational delight in the couple's souls. But the superb beauty of the voluptuous garden also means there will be "More woe, the more your taste is now of joy" (369); for, as in previous gardens, the greater the appeal of the place, the deeper the fall into sin. And for the scene of the Fall, Milton is careful to create a garden whose magnificence will never be forgotten. Finally, the sensuous detail provides a proper context for the theme of sensuality which will be part of the story of the Fall.

As in previous gardens, particularly the Golden Age sites of antiquity, here is perpetual springtime (206) and extraordinarily fertile soil (216); an abundance of water from springs, fountains, and rivers,[8] the traditional West wind (329), and air laden, as it was in Christian Latin paradises, with sweet smells, fragrant breezes, and perfumes (155ff.). To sweeten the air even more, there is the song of birds (264ff.). As in Horace's *Epode XVI*, all the animals live in harmony (342-350), and as in the paradise passage we noted in Isidore's *Etymologiae*, the hill upon which the garden rests is covered with untended vines (135ff.). Flowers of all kinds abound (240ff., 255), and there is shaded

[8] 233ff., a river at 233, falling waters reminiscent of the cave of Sleep motif at 260, a fountain at 326 and the Tigris itself mentioned at IX, 71.

grass (325) and flowering meadows (268; IX, 439ff.).

There are, of course, many trees: the Tree of Life (217) and the Tree of the Knowledge of Good and Evil (218, 427), which have Scriptural roots; the trees weeping "Gums and Balm" (248), the trees of the mixed forest (138-142; IX, 435), and the perennial plane (437)—all of which have classical roots. Finally, Milton's garden boasts in quantity that indispensable element in a Christian earthly paradise, fruit: not only the forbidden fruit (218, 424), but right next to it the fruits of "vegetable Gold" (220), as well as those "burnisht with Golden Rind" (249) which are reminiscent of the apples of the Hesperides. There is also the fruit Adam and Eve customarily eat (331),[9] and it is interesting that the first act they perform under our, and Satan's, gaze is to eat their "Supper Fruits."

Lewis has said of the description of the earthly paradise that "the unexpected has no place here,"[10] and on the surface at least, Milton does nothing to violate such a rule. In fact, he manages to include everything—trees, water, fruit, birds, flowers, breezes, fragrant odors, fertile earth, harmony and proper order among all living things—to give us the most complete and satisfying image of a blessed garden in European literature.

However, the "unexpected" does lurk beneath the surface, for as he is describing the perfect place, Milton is also, by allusion, echo, and implication, preparing us for the Fall. We can see this in his treatment of both Nature itself and Adam and Eve in Nature. Let us look at Nature first. Greene has said that "From its first description, Paradise is a little

[9] Fruit is constantly mentioned: IV, 422; V, 341; VII, 324; VIII, 307.
[10] C. S. Lewis, *A Preface to Paradise Lost* (Oxford, 1942), p. 49.

enervating,"[11] and if he wants to suggest a soporific quality in Nature, I would agree, for no other reason than if all the earthly paradise *topoi* are included in the portrait of the earthly paradise, there is too much. This is what we said of Claudian's lush description of Henna in *De Raptu Proserpinae*, and yet in Book IV of *Paradise Lost* perhaps Milton intentionally overdoes the comfort, pleasure, and heavy sweetness of the place. Of course, we are charmed and delighted, and these impressions never leave us; but we are also perhaps like Eve made a bit restless. In a passage such as this:

> from that Sapphire Fount the crisped Brooks,
> Rolling on Orient Pearl and sands of Gold,
> with mazy error under pendant shades
> Ran nectar . . . (237-240)

there is a lack of vitality; everything is slow (*crisped* means rippled), aimless (*mazy error*), drooping (*pendant*)—in short, sluggish. We tend to feel there is too much to no purpose; that perhaps Nature is soft and to live in it would have a softening, even corrupting, effect on us. We do not really formulate these suspicions at first, but they insinuate themselves into some deep layer of our consciousness. In fact, "insinuate" is precisely what one of the words in the passage comes to mean; and as that word, "mazy," itself wanders throughout the poem, the latent implications in Nature are activated and we are led to the scene of the Fall.[12]

[11] Greene, *The Descent from Heaven*, p. 402.

[12] A. Stein, *Answerable Style* (Minneapolis, 1953), pp. 66-67, has said that the "error" in *mazy error* "argues, from its original meaning, for the order in irregularity, for the rightness in wandering—before the concept of error is introduced into man's world and comes to signify wrong

The first oblique echo of the "mazy error" is heard about one hundred lines later when amidst all the innocent animals

> the Serpent sly
> Insinuating, wove with Gordian twine
> His braided train. (347-349)

The snake, himself innocent, gives some indication of what he will be in the midst of what is.[13] In fact, the poet says Satan chose the "subtlest Beast of all the Field" (IX, 86) because

> in the wily Snake,
> Whatever sleights none would suspicious mark,
> As from his wit and native subtlety
> Proceeding, which in other Beasts observ'd
> Doubt might beget of Diabolic pow'r
> Active within beyond the sense of brute. (IX, 91-96)

The last two lines, describing the "Diabolic pow'r/Active

---

wandering." This is surely true; the notion of "innocent" wandering predominates; but I see no reason for completely ignoring the double perspective of before and after the Fall. To ignore the element of "wrongness" in *error* is to ignore what, because of the Fall, is simply there, and no one knew this better than the poet.

[13] The language describing the snake is surprisingly direct, as is Raphael's reference to "The Serpent subtl'st Beast" (VII, 495), in a passage which like many describing the snake owes much to Virgil's account of the sea-monsters which killed Laocoön and his sons, *Aeneid*, II, 203-211: "pectora quorum inter fluctus arrecta iubaeque/sanguineae superant undas; pars cetera pontum/pone legit sinuatque immensa volumine terga" (206-208). (Their bosoms rise amid the surge, and their crests, blood-red, overtop the waves; the rest of them skims the main behind and their huge backs curve in many a fold.)—One can see how Milton establishes a verbal congruence, at the least, between the snake's movements and Satan's typical motion; all these movements, and their implications, contribute to what I have called the "satanic style."

within," clearly indicate how what is latent in the garden will be made active. At lines 161 to 162 we are offered a literal image of unawakened evil when Satan searches out

> The Serpent sleeping, in whose mazy folds
> To hide me,

and the "mazy folds" appear again when he finds the sleeping snake "In Labyrinth of many a round self-roll'd" (183).

Now the implications of the "mazy" brook, and all the tenuous connections between the snake's body and Satan's presence—all the latent corruption in Nature—are made active in the Corrupter as he approaches Eve. For the possessed Serpent goes "not with indented wave" (496) but raised on himself,

> Fold above fold a surging Maze, his Head
> Crested aloft, and Carbuncle his Eyes. (499-500)

But the snake conveys the opposite impression of the mazy brook; there all was sluggish, limpid; here the snake, associated with liquid through "indented wave," is alive and purposeful. The powerful "surging Maze" and "Crested" pick up and contrast with "mazy error" and "crisped." The echo, and the point, are unmistakable. Milton, implicitly, obliquely, leaves us with a half-formulated choice: either the lack of energy in the garden implies some kind of potential corruption, or the energy harmlessly passive in Nature is demonically active in Satan. Either way, and Milton must be uninsistent and ambiguous to preserve the garden's surface appeal, there is in paradise something potentially wrong which is directly linked to what is actively evil.

However, the implications of "mazy" do not stop with

the appearance of the snake. What we observe now is a movement typical of the garden, indeed of the whole poem, a movement whereby physical characteristics cease only to signify and simply become mental states. After seeing the snake, Eve listens "Not unamaz'd" (552), and as it speaks, she is "Yet more amaz'd" (614). That is, she is becoming more implicated in the "mazy error"; she is becoming more lost, and she begins to fall when she allows the snake to guide her:

> Lead then, said *Eve*. Hee leading swiftly roll'd
> In tangles, and made intricate seem straight,
> To mischief swift. (631-633)

And as she is involved in this mental maze, in the folds of the "satanic style," which can make what is complex *seem* easy; as she abdicates her sense of order to his false notions, he leads her as an "evil Spirit"

> Misleads th' amaz'd Night-wanderer from his way
> To Bogs and Mires, and oft through Pond or Pool,
> There swallow'd up and lost, from succor far.
>
> (640-641)

As Eve is led into the final consequences of wandering, she is said to be like one led into an evil, dark landscape from which no one can help her. Thus the earthly paradise is tentatively lost for the first time as the "Bogs and Mires" forecast the future marshes of the mind, and fulfill the implications of that first wandering, sweet brook. What was potential in the garden (and man) is now, through the insinuations of the snake and Satan, made active; and man's loss of paradise is projected by this image of a foul place as Eve goes to the forbidden fruit.

MILTON also places the "unexpected" in Nature in other ways—by allusions to other poets and by echoes of other gardens and other couples. If we look briefly at the way Milton uses Spenser, we can see again how in painting the lovely scene, the poet also includes hints of potential evil and prepares a context for the Fall.

Within the garden, the potentiality for evil exists by the very presence of the forbidden fruit. The poet never describes this fruit when he mentions the Tree of the Knowledge of Good and Evil (IV, 221), but he does describe the fruit of the Tree of Life right next to it (220). This is ambrosial fruit "of vegetable Gold," and after Leavis heaped scorn on the phrase, it has attracted many commentators.[14] Two of the most sensible, Bush and Broadbent, see in the phrase the conjunction of natural and artificial elements, which are held in equilibrium. And for Broadbent, this "balance" symbolizes the "ethical balance" of paradise, and eventually "the balance between reality and myth . . . suggesting that the state of innocence hovers between what is and what might have been." He finally sees that Adam's and Eve's "innocence is a moment of potential: it must change: either develop into something richer, or be lost."[15] This idea, sim-

[14] See F. R. Leavis, *Revaluation* (London, 1936), p. 50; D. Harding, *Milton and the Renaissance Ovid*, Illinois Studies in Language and Literature, Vol. 30, no. 4 (Urbana, 1946), shows how Milton derives the golden fruit from Ovid, *Metamorphoses*, X, 647-648, in the account of Hippomenes and Atlanta.

[15] D. Bush, *Paradise Lost in Our Time* (Cornell University Press, 1945), says "In the paradoxical phrase 'vegetable Gold,' which Mr. Leavis especially scorns, each word is altered and quickened by the other; the richness of 'Gold' glorifies the simple product of nature, and the rich natural life implied in 'vegetable' gives pliant form and vitality to metallic hardness and removes the idea of unhealthy artifice and evil which in *Paradise Lost* is associated with gold" (p. 95). See in J. B. Broadbent's *Some Graver Subject* (London, 1960), pp. 180, 184-185.

ilar to our earlier suggestion that the potential for evil is always balanced against the obvious perfection of Nature, is connected by Broadbent to the question of art and nature in the garden, and is something to which we will return in a moment.

However, in spite of the justifications for the phrase, I personally find something sinister in the idea of "vegetable Gold," something unnatural and unhealthy. If the phrase had been applied to the forbidden fruit, it would have sounded the proper note. But when it is applied to good fruit, it has the effect, *pace* Bush, of bestowing an artificial, lifeless quality on the fruit and linking it, by some chemistry of the imagination, to what we know is the suspect fruit right next to it. Indeed, "vegetable Gold" picks up the color of much of the fruit, particularly that "burnisht with Golden Rind" (249; also 147-149) and seems to taint all the fruit in the garden. Because we know that fruit will be the efficient cause of the Fall, Milton appears to spread a slightly suspect, corrupt aura throughout the garden, which is unconsciously reinforced every time fruit is mentioned. We cannot escape what we know, and though the total effect of the perfect place is not diminished in any overt way, something lurks.

Why such a reaction to this phrase—a reaction which undoubtedly sounds excessive and forced? Because we cannot escape what we know in any context; we cannot really forget other golden fruit in gardens far more sinister than the ones usually adduced as sources for this phrase. In Book II of *The Faerie Queene* there was a garden with a large tree loaded down with fruit which "were golden apples glistring bright" (vii, 54); and there was that

> goodly golden fruit,
> With which Acontius got his lover trew. (55)

Where was this fruit? Many will have already recognized the evil garden of Proserpina, in Mammon's realm. And when Guyon stared in wonder at this tree and its "rich fee," he noticed how the branches hung over the confines of the garden and

> themselves did steepe
> In a blacke flood, which flow'd about it round;
> This is the river of Cocytus deepe. (56)

The motif of branches so heavy they bend to the ground derives from Lucian's *True History* and its parody of the beautiful garden. But the motif is also used by Milton to describe how Adam and Eve eat their supper fruits,

> which the compliant boughs
> Yielded them, side-long as they sat recline.
> (IV, 332-333)

We are also reminded of how at one of the entrances to the Bower of Bliss there was

> an embracing vine,
> Whose bounches, hanging down, seemd to entice
> All passers by to taste their lushious wine,
> And did them into their hands incline.
> (*F.Q.*, II, xii, 54)

Of the grapes some were like emeralds, some rubies, and

> some were of burnisht gold,
> So made by art, to beautify the rest. (55)

The fruits of "vegetable Gold" and those "burnisht with

Golden Rind" in Milton's paradise recall, for me, these sinister fruits in evil gardens; and when even the "Supper Fruits" are offered by heavy boughs to man, the additional echo of Spenser's context fills the earthly paradise with fruit whose potential for evil is far more powerful than at first it might appear.

While I agree with Bush's hint and Broadbent's statement that in the phrase "vegetable Gold" (and "burnisht with Golden Rind") we find a harmonious and innocent balance between art and nature, I would also suggest that, as usual, Milton is having it both ways at once. For because of the context in which those golden grapes appear in Spenser— the Bower of Bliss—Milton is perhaps also exploiting the darker side of the traditional Art-Nature theme.

In the garden itself, art does not appear to have any overtly sinister implications; the brook feeds the flowers

> which not nice Art
> In beds and curious Knots, but Nature boon
> Pour'd forth profuse on Hill and Dale and Plain
> (IV, 241-243)

and later Raphael comes to meet the couple through the "blissful field" (V, 292) where Nature

> Wanton'd as in her prime, and play'd at will
> Her Virgin Fancies, pouring forth more sweet,
> Wild above Rule or Art, enormous bliss.
> (V, 295-297)

While there are various implications here, some of which we will note later,[16] all seems innocent enough. Milton is

---

[16] In different ways, and in different contexts, words like "Fancies," "play'd," and the liquid imagery associated with Nature's bounty are all

obviously communicating the benign magnificence and munificence of Nature, the "natural" quality of paradise where art in some constricting, deadening sense seems to be superseded or absent. But while he does this, Milton also obliquely recalls a garden where precisely what seems to be absent here was very much present. For the references to "blissful" (V, 292) and "bliss" (297), in reference to Adam's "Bow'r" (300), cannot help but recall, by echo, Spenser's Bower of Bliss. And that Bower is even more strikingly evoked in the first description of Adam's and Eve's "blissful Bower" at line 690 in Book IV.

> it was a place
> Chos'n by the sovran Planter, when he fram'd
> All things to man's delightful use;   (690-692)

The language reminds us of that other Bower,

> a place pickt out by choyce of best alyve,
> That Natures work by art can imitate.
> (*F.Q.*, II, xii, 42)

Even the way the Bower in Eden is described, from 690 to 703, with its "inwoven shade," its "Mosaic" "wrought" by flowers (or is it "wrought/Mosaic"; wrought as adjective, not verb?), its ground "Broider'd" with "rich inlay," makes

---

part of the imagery for the role of sensuality in the Fall and the degradation of sex after the Fall. See below, n. 35.—It is also interesting to note that after the Fall, "Art" takes on only evil connotations: Sin and Death build the causeway over the Abyss by "wondrous Art/Pontifical" (X, 312-313) and later Michael shows Adam the descendants of Cain:

> studious they appear
> Of Arts that polish Life, Inventors rare,
> Unmindful of thir Maker (XI, 609-611)

in a passage which also emphasizes their lust.

the Bower of Adam and Eve into a work of art. Of course, the crucial and important difference between Spenser's and Milton's Bowers is that the latter is the work of God, or at least innocent man, while Spenser's was a trap set by Acrasia. However, we cannot ignore the implied similarity even while we underscore the basic differences; in the echoes of the verse, and the fact both Bowers are artifacts, something has happened to the Bower in Eden. Some damage has been done.

The point I am making is the same one made previously: that by suggestions, allusions, and the subtle interweaving of old enchanted garden themes, Milton prepares us for the Fall by making us suspect, by making us ask again and again: Will this garden too prove false? Will the inhabitants meet the same fate as past couples? Finally, Does this garden only *appear* harmonious and beautiful and innocent? Does some potential evil lurk? And the answer is always, "Yes." It *is* a perfect and unspoiled garden; Yes, what we suspect will be confirmed. Milton always has his contraries in balance; both perspectives, the obviously good; the potentially bad, are always kept before us.

But the phrases about "vegetable Gold" and "burnisht with Golden Rind" started us on this line of inquiry. Do those phrases have any echo of their own in the poem, fulfilling the sinister potential claimed for them? They do—again in Satan in whom all potential corruption is made active; and again in that passage in Book IX where the snake approaches Eve and the ripple of his body catches up the implications of wandering. After mentioning the serpent's carbuncle eyes, the poet says he comes

With burnisht Neck of verdant Gold.   (IX, 501)

The phrases about fruit "burnisht with Golden Rind" and of "vegetable Gold" are here collapsed and compressed into the description of the snake. As the snake sways toward Eve, the fine balance Broadbent spoke of between art and nature signifying innocence and the potential for good or evil, hangs even more precariously as all the potential for evil in the garden is activated in Satan, the master artist. And all the subversive echoes of the golden fruit in Spenser's garden of Proserpina are now ambiguously revealed when Eve, at the Tree of Knowledge, says

> Serpent, we might have spar'd our coming hither,
> Fruitless to mee, though Fruit be here to excess,
> (IX, 648-649)

making a pun used by Spenser in the Garden of Proserpina.[17] "Her levity at such a moment," says Ricks, "is tragic";[18] and so it is. For Eve has become so amazed by Satan's "tract oblique" that she no longer even knows what, or who, is involved. Yet we are not totally surprised, for in Books IV through IX another

> as one who sought access, but fear'd
> To interrupt, side-long . . . works his way,

the poet himself; who while creating a marvellous vision of Nature has also been obliquely anticipating its loss.

[17] Here also sprong that goodly golden fruit,/With which Acontius got his lover trew,/Whom he had long time sought with fruitlesse suit. (*F.Q.*, II, vii, 55) Satan too will get Eve with the fruit, and if the "lover" part of the analogy seems forced, we must not forget that Eve has already been obliquely compared to Proserpine (IV, 268ff.), the flower among flowers snatched by Pluto; as we will see, this allusion is developed by Milton in Book IX.

[18] Ricks, *Grand Style*, p. 73.

· III ·

The technique of echo, implication, and allusion is also used in the portrayal of Adam and Eve; as they move through the garden in their bliss, Milton manages subtly to involve them in other couples, and Eve in other women especially. By pursuing some of the poet's leads, we shall move closer to an understanding of their disobedience, and see how in his earthly paradise Milton uses themes from previous gardens of the Renaissance.

The very first time we see Adam and Eve, they are walking through the garden, and the description builds to these lines:

> For contemplation hee and valor form'd,
> For softness shee and sweet attractive Grace,
> Hee for God only, shee for God in him.
>
> (IV, 297-299)

At this crucial point, Milton marks the essential principle of the proper order of nature in the garden, the all-important hierarchy of woman, man and God—later so disastrously perverted by Satan. There is also a full pause here, before the first description of the couple. But we suddenly realize we have seen a similar syntactic structure, and heard a similar statement implying hierarchy, in connection with another pair of lovers in another garden.

> *L'uno di servitù, l'altra d'impero
> si gloria, ella in se stessa ed egli in lei.
> (*Gerusalemme Liberata*, XVI, 21)

Rinaldo and Armida are as different from Adam and Eve

---

* [One glories in slavery, the other in command, She in herself and he in her.]

as Armida's enchanted garden is different from the true earthly paradise. But the echo from the epic of Milton's favorite Italian poet implicates Adam and Eve in the theme of the Italian passage. The figure to suffer most by this allusion is Eve, for the narcissism and sensuality of Armida fleetingly touch Eve even as the differences between the two become apparent. And when, at lines 449-491, Eve tells of her creation and awakening, the implications begin to be fulfilled; for in an obvious reminiscence of the Narcissus tale in Ovid's *Metamorphoses*, III, 402-510, she tells how she saw a "Shape" and how it was so pleasing. The theme of narcissism is clearly at work even in the angel's voice which urges her to find Adam:

> Whose image thou art, him thou shalt enjoy,
> Inseparably thine, to him shalt bear
> Multitudes like thyself, and thence be call'd
> Mother of human Race. (472-475)

The only way Eve can be persuaded to leave the pool and become "our general Mother" (492) is if she is promised her own "image," and many more like herself. Even this appeal to her narcissism is not entirely successful, for having seen Adam, she decides (478-480) to return to the image in the pool. Adam pleads with her to return (481-488) and, she says, after

> that gentle hand
> Seiz'd mine, I yielded. (488-489)

In his discussion of this passage, Harding says it would be a "captious reader indeed who, recalling Eve's 'unexperienc't thought,' would be inclined to read too much into this trifling display of natural vanity."[19] He is surely correct in this, as he is in the fact that the lesson:

> How beauty is excell'd by manly grace
> And wisdom, which alone is truly fair. (490-491)

is ultimately the point of the episode. But it would be a stubborn reader who would refuse to see the narcissism here, as some have done, or who would insist on completely underplaying its implications.[20] The poet has made this overt suggestion of narcissism, not to lessen our immediate estimate of Eve so much as to provide a repository of doubt for later exploitation.

Out of what I have suggested is a veiled reminiscence of Tasso has come a chain of associations obliquely binding Eve to an ancient tradition of self-love, a chain in which the Narcissus myth is a major link; and there has, finally, emerged an episode in which we can see, tentatively dramatized, the elements of the Fall. For besides the touches of pride and sensuality, we also have an interesting view of Adam, completely at the mercy of Eve—as he tells us later, because of the powerful sensual impression she made in his dream (VIII, 471-477)—where his first words to her in the garden are "Return, fair *Eve*" (IV, 481), an ironic forecast of her departure on the fatal morning of the Fall, when from that "gentle hand" that seized her here

---

[19] Harding, *Club of Hercules*, p. 74.

[20] Cleanth Brooks, in "Eve's Awakening," *Essays in Honor of Walter Clyde Currey* (Vanderbilt University Press, 1954), pp. 283-284, has indicated the fullest implications of this passage: "Later at the climax of the poem, Adam too will have to choose between images: his image mirrored in Eve and God, whose image he himself mirrors. He will choose the more obviously enchanting image, that reflected in Eve. The act will be a kind of Narcissism, a kind of self-love."

her hand
Soft she withdrew. .... (IX, 385-386)

Shortly after introducing us to the pair, Milton draws some more disturbing parallels. After describing their appearance and their stroll through the garden, he says they sit "Under a tuft of shade" by a "fresh Fountain side" (325-326) where they can enjoy "cool Zephyr" (328). They eat those fruits which the boughs bend to offer them; and a delicately amorous note is struck:

Nor gentle purpose, nor enduring smiles
Wanted, nor youthful dalliance as beseems
Fair couple. .... (337-339)

There is nothing here but the joyous harmony of innocent love. Yet, beneath the surface, as Thyer noted long ago, there are in the "gentle purpose" two echoes of Spenser.[21] The first is from *The Faerie Queene*, I, ii, where another couple sits in the "cool shade" (29) and

Faire seemly pleasaunce each to other makes,
With goodly purposes, there as they sit. (30)

They are, of course, the Redcross Knight and "The false Duessa, now Fidessa hight" (44).[22] The other passage Milton

[21] Thyer cited in *Paradise Lost*, ed. Newton, I, 277-278. What is even more interesting than the actual echoes is the congruence of contexts, the similarity of natural settings.

[22] The setting exploited by Spenser, and Milton, is a highly traditional one; in *F.Q.*, I, vii, the Redcross Knight sits by a "fountain syde" (2), cools himself in the shade and breeze (3), and "goodly court" (4) makes to Duessa. This scene, reminiscent of the one cited above from Canto ii, is an adaptation of similar scenes in Ariosto (*O.L.*, VI, 24) and Tasso (*G.L.*, XIV, 59) noted above p. 207.

echoes is another scene in a wood, from *The Faerie Queene,* III, viii:

> But when hee saw him selfe free from poursute,
> He gan make gentle purpose to his dame, (14)

and this time the couple is Braggadocchio and the newly created False Florimell. What is immediately striking in this juxtaposition of passages is the vast difference between the kind of love implied in Milton's poem and that found in Spenser's, though one could see again how by allusion Milton might be preparing for the role of lust after the Fall. But there is something deeper and more interesting here: the fact that the women of *The Faerie Queene* whom Milton evokes are the two (and the only two in Spenser's poem) who are simply not what they appear to be. And the result, if in an effort to explicate such a veiled implication one can speak of a result, is that we wonder about Eve. Will she, like so many women in gardens, and these two in particular, be false in every, or indeed in *any*, way? In Book IV, it certainly looks as if she would never be false; of course not. But as Christians (and readers) we know that of course she will be.

Eve bears the brunt of the sinister implications in these comparisons; and as is well known, Milton goes to great lengths, right up to the point of the Fall, to compare Eve obliquely to a great range of women, many of them from other gardens. A brief review of these allusions will necessarily cover some well-traveled ground but may further illuminate Milton's method in this most complex of gardens.

In that magnificent simile beginning

> Not that fair field
> Of *Enna,* while *Proserpin* gath'ring flow'rs

Herself a fairer Flow'r by gloomy Dis
Was gather'd, which cost *Ceres* all that pain
(IV, 268-271)

Milton establishes the superiority of this garden over Henna, and other places, and obliquely compares Eve to Proserpine, the flower among flowers snatched away by the King of the Underworld. It is the ancient conceit we have noted before, which goes back originally to the *Hymn to Demeter*. Here the veiled allusion, developed fully in Book IX, is sad rather than sinister. The classical Proserpine casts a shadow on Eve's fate, rather than her character, while the suspicious-Proserpine echoes derive from Spenser's Garden of Proserpina, noted above. But it is interesting to see how Milton uses all the Proserpines of other gardens for his portrait of this woman in the garden in Eden.

The next complex of allusions occurs, properly, in the very first description of Eve:

Shee as a veil down to the slender waist
Her unadorned golden tresses wore
Dishevell'd, but in wanton ringlets wav'd
As the Vine curls her tendrils, which impli'd
Subjection, but requir'd with gentle sway. (304-308)

Commentators have long noted Saint Paul's words in I Corinthians 11:15: "But if a woman have long hair, it is a glory to her: for *her* hair is given her for a covering," as the Biblical source for Eve's long, loose hair. But the description of "golden Aphrodite" in the *Iliad*, III, 6 has also been cited, and Thyer remarked the way Milton's first two lines echoed the description of Venus in Marino's *Adone*, VIII:

✻ onde a guisa d'un vel dorato e folto
celando il bianco sen tra l'onde loro,
in mille minutissimi ruscelli
dal capo scaturìr gli aurei capelli. (46)

Celò 'l bel sen con l'aureo vel (47)[23]

An undertone implicit in this reference to Venus is made
more explicit by Milton a bit later when, again echoing
Marino's lines, we see how Eve

half imbracing lean'd
On our first Father, half her swelling Breast
Naked met his under the flowing Gold
Of her loose tresses hid; (494-497)[24]

✻ whence like a thick, gilded veil,
hiding the white breast between their waves
the golden hair in a thousand tiny streams
springs from her head.

It hid the lovely breast with the golden veil

[23] Italian cited from *Marino e I Marinisti*, ed. G. G. Ferrero, La
Letteratura Italiana, 37 (Milano-Napoli, 1954), p. 168. The Homeric
parallel is noted in *Milton Poetry and Prose*, ed. Hughes, p. 285; Thyer's
note to Marino is cited in *Paradise Lost*, ed. Newton, I, 281.

[24] Harding has demonstrated how in the lines which immediately
follow:

hee in delight
Both of her Beauty and submissive Charms
Smil'd with superior Love, as *Jupiter*
On *Juno* smiles, when he impregns the Clouds
That shed *May* Flowers; (497-501)

there is a reminiscence of *Iliad*, XIV, 892ff., where Zeus and Hera indulge
their passion on Mount Ida; Harding also shows how this echo is fulfilled in the lust of Adam and Eve in a Bower (IX, 1037-1045), a
Bower which recalls the earlier Bower at IV, 697-703. This Bower, which

Within the obvious image of submission and meekness on the part of Eve toward her superior, there is implied a powerful, if innocent, sensuality. And the color of her hair picks up the fruits of "vegetable Gold" and those "burnisht with Golden Rind" as well as the "sands of Gold" in that mazy brook; picks up, in fact, the other golden places in paradise which had such latent implications for evil.

Part of the sensuality here comes from the way the hair covers Eve, for what Saint Paul considered her glory only covers enough of this woman to make all of her interesting. The motif of the partially veiled woman has already been noted in the gardens of Alcina and Armida. Indeed, like Marino, Milton calls the hair a "veil," and the notion of a veil is to play an important role in the garden, for like the "mazy" brook, the word for a physical fact becomes a metaphor for a mental or spiritual state. We note this first in Book V, when Raphael comes and Eve

> Undeck't, save with herself more lovely fair
> Than Wood-Nymph, or the fairest Goddess feign'd
> Of three that in Mount *Ida* naked strove,
> Stood to entertain her guest from Heav'n; no veil
> Shee needed, Virtue-proof, no thought infirm
> Alter'd her cheek.   (380-385)

Of course "no thought infirm" occurred to Eve; of course, she is "veiled" in her virtue. Why does Milton even bother to say it? Because by discounting the existence of impure

---

we noted was a work of art, is described in language and cadences which consciously imitate the passage in *Iliad*, XIV. See *Club of Hercules*, pp. 76-80, and Harding's conclusion that the "clandestine discrediting of Adam and Eve, we are forced to conclude, begins almost with the first lines which described them to us" (p. 81).

thoughts in Eve, he obliquely establishes the notion of impure thoughts in us. And by metaphorically elevating the veil to a spiritual garment protecting innocence, he also echoes that earlier veil of hair covering her naked body; a veil she shared with Venus, a naked woman whom Eve, "undeck't," is again obliquely compared to at lines 381 to 382 above.[25] So again as before: while establishing physical and spiritual innocence and perfection in the garden, Milton obliquely manages to cast some kind of doubt on what he has just said. And what becomes of Eve's veil of virtue? It is torn away by the snake and falls from the couple after the Fall. For, having indulged their lust in Book IX, they awake, to find

> innocence, that as a veil
> Had shadow'd them from knowing ill, was gone,
> Just confidence, and native righteousness,
> And honor from about them, naked left
> To guilty shame. (1054-1058)

The potentiality of the "veil" and Venus allusions in Books IV and V are fulfilled, and the undercurrent of sensuality, which bound the implications together, now surfaces in a final Biblical allusion offsetting Saint Paul's comment on

---

[25] Kermode, *Living Milton*, pp. 89-90, notes that besides the Venus analogy at line 381, Raphael's salutation "Hail Mother of Mankind" (388) recalls Mary; so it does, though if we continue the implication of line 381, it could also refer to a type of Venus *genetrix*. During the Renaissance, various types of Venus were distinguished, particularly by the Florentine Neo-Platonists; for conceptions of Venus in Ficino and Pico, see E. Panofsky, *Studies in Iconology* (Oxford, 1939; Harper Torchbook, New York, 1962), pp. 142-145; as J. Seznec, *The Survival of the Pagan Gods*, tr. B. Sessions (Bollingen Series, xxxviii; Harper Torchbooks, New York, 1961) points out, the equation of Venus and Eve is the kind of association typical of the Renaissance (p. 213).

glory; now Adam wakes next to Eve like *"Samson* from the Harlot-lap/Of *Philistean Delilah"* (1061-1062)—"bare/ Of all thir virtue" (1064).

There is also another chain of associations started by the account of Eve's hair at IV, 304-308. After alluding to the "veil," Milton remarks how Eve

> Her unadorned golden tresses wore
> Dishevell'd, but in wanton ringlets wav'd
> As the Vine curls her tendrils, which impli'd
> Subjection, but requir'd with gentle sway. (305-308)

Behind the picture of the disheveled hair, the ringlets and the Vine, Harding sees a reference to Horace's "yellow-haired Pyrrha" who "combines voluptuousness with a sophisticated simplicity to conquer and betray the hearts of men."[26] But there is also what Harding, in alluding to the tendrils, calls a "kind of encroachment that may ensnare and destroy." The reference to the Vines makes it clear that Milton is referring to the ancient conceit of the elm and the vine. This trope relates Eve to Adam, as vine to elm, and links them to one of their major activities in the garden.

> they led the Vine
> To wed the Elm; she spous'd about him twines
> Her marriageable arms, and with her brings
> Her dow'r th' adopted Clusters, to adorn
> His barren leaves. (V, 215-219)[27]

[26] Harding, *Club of Hercules*, p. 72. We noted a suggestion of Pyrrha in the portrait of Armida, above, p. 204.

[27] Hughes notes, in *Milton Poetry and Prose*, p. 307, that Spenser uses the phrase "the vine-propp elme" in *F.Q.*, I, i, 8; but as usual, what is even more interesting is the context: here the Redcross Knight and Una are riding through a most ambiguous "mixed forest" (8-9) which finally

Here, as in the passage on Eve's hair in Book IV, the main point is the proper relation of male to female; for the "impli'd/ Subjection" of woman to man (IV, 308-309) is echoed by the way the vine is led to wed the elm. But again as Milton implies something overtly, he covertly implies its opposite. The sensuality of that curling hair, the close embrace of those twining vines: Is there something potentially dangerous imaged in the landscape, something within that woman who is

> fair no doubt, and worthy well
> Thy cherishing, thy honoring and thy love,
> Not thy subjection. (VIII, 568-570)

Those golden tresses, those tendrils, certainly imply subjection, but whose? Who will hold "gentle sway" (IV, 308)? After we know, that is, after the Fall, the Lord's words to Adam again pick up the implications of the unruly hair, and the key words of adornment and subjection:

---

becomes "the wandering wood . . . Errours den" (13); there is no need to comment further on the significance of "wandering" and "error" in *Paradise Lost*; could this landscape of *The Faerie Queene* have been somewhere in the poet's mind? In the lines which precede those cited above:

> where any row
> Of Fruit-trees overwoody reach'd too far
> Thir pamper'd boughs, and needed hands to check
> Fruitless imbraces (*P.L.*, V, 212-215)

Milton echoes one of the Spenserian passages he always returns to: the Garden of Proserpina (*F.Q.*, II, vii, 55-56) with its trees spreading their boughs past the natural limits, and the pun on "fruitlesse"; while in ll. 215-219 above, we sense again the presence of the Bower of Bliss (*F.Q.*, II, xii, 54-55) whose "embracing vine" and golden grapes are echoed in the vine and "clusters"; and there is in this passage from Spenser the same kind of stifling encroachment Harding sensed in the tendril hair of Eve.

Adorn'd
She was indeed, and lovely to attract
Thy Love, not thy Subjection, and her Gifts
Were such as under Government well seem'd,
Unseemly to bear rule, which was thy part
(X, 151-155)

The language and implications of the first description of
Eve, another strand in the web of allusions to other women,
have led finally to the loss of the veil of innocence, and
proper order and degree.

Other, equally suggestive, allusions can be noticed in Book
IV. For instance, on the first day of Eve's creation, the angel

Brought her in naked beauty more adorn'd,
More lovely than Pandora, whom the Gods
Endow'd with all thir gifts, and O too like
In sad event, when to the unwiser Son
Of *Japhet* brought by *Hermes*, she ensnar'd
Mankind with her fair looks (713-718)

The imagery of Eve's tendril tresses adorning her naked-
ness is again echoed in the word "adorn'd" and "ensnar'd,"
but there is something else here—less covert than usual. The
angel who brought her to Adam is compared to Hermes,
Eve to Pandora, and Adam, implicitly, to Epimetheus, whose
wife brought woe to all the world. And if this sinister analogy were not clear enough, elsewhere Milton is even more
explicit. For in *The Doctrine and Discipline of Divorce*, II,
iii, Milton says that Plato and Chrysippus "knew not what a
consummate and most adorned Pandora was bestowed upon
Adam to be the nurse and guide of his arbitrary happiness
and perseverance, I mean his native innocence and perfec-

tion, which might have kept him from being our true Epime-theus." Milton goes on to say though the ancients taught that good and evil were gifts of destiny, nevertheless—and here the language is crucial:

> they could yet find reasons not invalid to justify
> the councils of God and fate from the insulsity of
> mortal tongues:—that man's own will self-corrupted
> is the adequate and sufficient cause of his disobedience
> besides fate.[28]

When Milton came to sing of "Man's First Disobedience" and sought to "justify the ways of God to men," the substance, if not the language, of this prose passage must have remained in his mind. For not only does the prose offer an analogy between Adam and Eve and Epimetheus and Pandora; but the analogy leads to a clear statement of that garden theme we have noted so often before: a man's self-corruption and lapse into degrading and degraded circumstances. Of course, the use of free will, implicit in their innocence, is also Milton's grand theme; but it is in *Paradise Lost* that he reveals the consequences of man's lapse in language similar to those previous poets who insisted on the softness and effeminacy of a man who could not, as Raphael warns Adam, "govern well thy appetite, lest sin/Surprise thee . . ." (VII, 546-547). For when appetite, and self-willed corruption, have brought Adam low, then the Lord says to him what Mercury said to Aeneas and Renaissance messengers told Renaissance knights:

[28] Hughes, in *Milton Poetry and Prose*, notes at p. 295 the reference to Epimetheus in the *Divorce* tract and refers to the prose at p. 714 of his edition whence this citation is taken.

to her
Thou didst resign thy Manhood (X, 147-148)

and when Adam in his vision sees how

the tenor of Man's woe
Holds on the same, from Woman to begin

again a heavenly emissary, Michael, tells him:

From Man's effeminate slackness it begins.
(XI, 632-634)

The story keeps repeating itself, not only in human history but in terms of this study, in literary history as well. For sensuality, the wrong choice is made; by sensuality, the will is corroded; whether he arises from that "Harlot-lap," or another "grembo molle," a man is less than he should be. Different as this garden is from those before it, it is also much the same after all.

THERE are three other allusions by which Eve is associated with other women, and all the woe prepared for; two are extended, and one is brief, but startling. At Book V, line 378, Adam and Eve come to their Bower "that like *Pomona's* Arbor smil'd" and this allusion is picked up again in Book IX, at the fateful moment Eve leaves Adam. Eve is like "Deliâ" but more graceful; like Pales

or Pomona, thus adorn'd,
Likest she seem'd, Pomona when she fled
Vertumnus, (393-395)

This allusion, stressing again Eve's adornment, is to Ovid's story of Pomona fleeing the importunate Vertumnus (*Metamorphoses*, XIV, 628ff.), and the aptness of the comparison between the couples is obvious but not extraordinarily revealing. That is, not until we read all of the Ovidian tale (through line 771) and see how once again Milton's allusion cuts both ways; for Pomona finally yields to Vertumnus, but yields only after he assumes a disguise and seduces her by subtle persuasion. Suddenly the events to come are forecast: the seduction of Eve by Satan disguised as the snake. Both Adam and Satan are enmeshed in the allusion to Vertumnus; and again what Milton does not say is fully as revealing as what he does say.[29]

In the lines immediately following those on Pomona, Milton also compares Eve to Ceres "in her Prime,/Yet Virgin of *Proserpina* from *Jove*" (IX, 395-396). The allusion serves to reintroduce the flower among flowers, first mentioned in Book IV, and this old image is developed shortly by the poet. For Satan "spies" Eve

> Veil'd in a Cloud of Fragrance, where she stood,
> Half spi'd, so thick the Roses bushing round
> About her glow'd, oft stooping to support
> Each Flow'r of slender stalk, whose head though gay
> Carnation, Purple, Azure, or speckt with Gold,
> Hung drooping unsustain'd, them she upstays
> Gently with Myrtle band, mindless the while,
> Herself, though gairest unsupported Flow'r,
> From her best prop so far, and storm so nigh.
>
> (425-433)[30]

---

[29] If we look to Milton's prose for other references to Vertumnus, we notice that in *De Doctrina Christiana*, I, 5 (C.E., XIV, 303) and *Tetrachordon* (C.E., IV, 183) the stress is laid on Vertumnus' deceitful, evasive nature and on his sophistry.

[30] In the drooping heads of the flowers and the implied fate of Eve there seems to be woven a reminiscence of the melancholy end of

The irony is that she props up the flowers while, as a flower, she is "From her best prop so far"; but even more noteworthy is that as a flower among flowers, Eve is "mindless the while." She shares the beauty of Nature, and at this point its lack of intellect too. When the snake approaches, Eve

> heard the sound
> Of rustling Leaves, but minded not
> (IX, 518-519)

But then why should she have minded the sound? How could she know? Milton himself anticipates the question, and in answering it offers at once the most reasonable explanation and, in our garden tradition, the most single damning allusion associated with Eve. The poet says she was accustomed

> To such disport before her through the Field,
> From every Beast, more duteous at her call,
> Than at *Circean* call the Herd disguis'd. (520-522)

But of all the analogies by which to imply the harmony and innocence of the creatures in the garden before the Fall, the comparison of Eve's to Circe's power is, to say the very least, the most ambiguous. The reference to Circe, at this crucial moment, links Eve to that prototype of the evil

---

Euryalus whose neck, in death, droops on his shoulder

  purpureus veluti cum flos succisus aratro
  languescit moriens, lassove papavera collo
  demisere caput, pluvia cum forte gravantur. (*Aeneid*, IX, 435-437)

(as when a purple flower, severed by the plough, droops in death; or as poppies, with weary neck, bow the head, when weighted by some chance shower).

woman in a garden from whom Eve's immediate predecessors, Alcina, Armida and Acrasia, were all descended. It is interesting that in all the earthly paradises or enchanted gardens in Renaissance epics, only in this one is the name of Circe invoked. Here the two great traditions of the women in the garden come together at last, as Eve "yet sinless" (IX, 659) is about to commence that process whereby man fell one step closer to the beasts.

Of all the themes traditional in previous gardens introduced into this paradise by covert allusions—narcissism, art and nature, sensuality as degrading man and destroying the proper order of things—this reference to Circe and to disguise in relation to Eve reveals the basic theme of illusion and reality. With what we know of the poet's method and meaning, we are now ready to follow this most inclusive pattern through Milton's treatment of the garden in Eden.

· IV ·

Not only much of what Milton has been saying, but the way he has been saying it, by allusions, echoes, implications —the "satanic style"—has made conscious use of the discrepancy between what appears on the surface and what exists beneath. Now we shall see how the theme of appearance and reality, of true and false perspective in its widest sense, is also an overt part of Milton's narrative of the Fall. What before was a theme implicit in a technique of indirection in the garden is now a theme to be examined in its explicit, direct development.

The power of illusion to corrupt is embodied in Satan the actor, the artist. Once out of Hell, past Chaos, on his way to the earthly paradise,

first he casts to change his proper shape,
Which else might work him danger or delay:
And now a stripling Cherub he appears,
Not of the prime, yet such as in his face
Youth smil'd Celestial, and to every Limb
Suitable grace diffus'd, so well he feign'd:

(III, 634-639)

This is the first illusion, this change of "proper shape," and the key words "appears" and "feign'd" reinforce the image of the master illusionist. At line 681 he is the "false dissembler"; at 692, "the fraudulent Imposter," and he is such a good actor he even fools Uriel, "The sharpest-sighted Spirit of all in Heav'n" (691). And yet as Satan approaches the garden, "each passion dimm'd his face" (IV, 114) and "betray'd/Him counterfeit" to Uriel who was still watching; for Satan, as an actor, "not enough had practis'd to deceive" (124). The deceiver is perceived in his deceit as Satan, forced to convert his fallen situation to his advantage ("Evil be thou my Good," IV, 110), cannot escape the massive irony of the universe whereby good from evil will come. But the point is made: falsity and illusion are about to enter the garden; and that power of perversion which will ruin proper harmony and degree; that agent and victim of passion who will debase pure love to lustful passion and make necessary the Passion of Christ. Here, in the master "Artificer of fraud" (121), Milton establishes in his garden in its widest terms the old garden theme of the relation between the real and the good, the illusory and the evil.

As the actor comes to play his greatest deception, Milton describes the trees leading up to the garden as "a woody Theatre" (141). This striking metaphor makes the garden a setting for illusion, just as in Elizabethan drama the world was a stage, where poets played with the serious idea of playing. Yet here, as we will see, the image of the theatre has a double function. The garden is not only the scene for Satan's artifice which means corruption and brings death; as we will see it is also the stage for God's art which is life, those divine illusions which are reality. Satan's effort will consist in substituting his own false illusions for reality and divorcing man from the proper hierarchy wherein all that is real rests with God; he will convince man to put himself first, to indulge himself to the exclusion of God. This is an old enchanted garden theme, and one could say that, for his own purposes, Satan makes the earthly paradise into an enchanted garden, while it remains a true paradise from the perspective of Heaven until man, choosing between them, makes the wrong choice and all is lost.

The true perspective is

> God beholding from his prospect high,
> Wherein past, present, future he beholds
> (III, 77-78)

while the first hint of false perspective comes when Satan, in wonderment, looks at the world as when a "Scout" after peril

> discovers unaware
> The goodly prospect of some foreign land
> (547-548)

and then, when like a comorant, he sits in the Tree of Life

> devising Death
> To them who liv'd; nor on the virtue thought

Of that life-giving plant, but only us'd
For prospect, what well us'd had been the pledge
Of immortality. (IV, 197-201)

Thus the perspective of time, and corruption and flux, enters
the eternal garden, as Death plots to overthrow immortality,
and illusion comes to tempt man with a new hierarchy, a
specious reality. At the outset we asserted that in writing his
poem Milton had to balance multiple perspectives; here
within the poem are two of them, total innocence and im-
minent corruption, and the "prospects" whence those views
derive.

In previous poems, illusion was linked to sex, the false
stimulation and misplaced emphasis on appearance inherent
in lust. This theme is also established here, as the hypocrisy
expounded in Book III in the revelation of Satan's counterfeiting is interpolated as sexual hypocrisy in Book IV, 312-
318. To emphasize the innocence of the couple's amorous-
ness, Milton says those "mysterious parts" were not con-
cealed; there was no "guilty shame"; not like now when
there are "shows instead, mere shows of seeming pure"
(316). The legacy of Satan will be a perversion of natural
goods, an inheritance of illusion, of "show" and "appearance."

The wasting of natural goods through lack of Temperance
is a theme common to previous gardens and to this one.
But before, it was a daughter of Circe who was the agent
of deception; here it is Satan. For he too can infect and
affect Nature:

Then from his lofty stand on that high Tree
Down he alights among the sportful Herd

Of those four footed kinds, himself now one,
Now other, as thir shape serv'd best his end.
(395-398)

These are the same more duteous to Eve "Than at *Circean*
call the Herd disguis'd" (IX, 523), though while Eve is
still innocent, the power to seduce and to control beasts, the
Circe role, is Satan's. Indeed, long before he possesses the
snake, Satan has used the toad. Or rather the angels find
him

Squat like a Toad, close at the ear of *Eve*;
Assaying by his Devilish art to reach
The Organs of her Fancy, and with them forge
Illusions as he list, Phantasms and Dreams.
(IV, 800-803)

This is the first time his power is specifically called his
"art," although Satan as actor or artist has been implied
before. Now the old theme of art and nature takes on its
widest implications as this art is obviously opposed to all
that is natural. In fact, Milton is very specific about how
this art hopes to creat "Illusions," in the sense we have
been using the word, "Phantasms, Dreams"; it hopes to do
so by controlling her "Fancy," her imagination. For Satan
knows what others in gardens have learned: that man's
greatest snare is his own illusions—about himself. And when
Milton calls these illusions

Vain hopes, vain aims, inordinate desires
Blown up with high conceits ingend'ring pride
(808-809)

he describes what will eventually "amaze" Eve, and also
offers a description of what ensnared garden dwellers

in earlier poems. What is the "Dream" which Satan induces in Eve? Structurally, it is a forecast of what will transpire in the garden, just as in their poems Dante, Ariosto, Tasso, and Spenser anticipated what would occur later in their gardens. Within the dream itself, recounted by Eve at V, 35-93, she is called "Angelic" (74) and promised an existence with the "Gods" (71, 72, 77, 81); and after she eats the forbidden fruit, she ascends to the Clouds

> and underneath beheld
> The Earth outstretcht immense, a prospect wide
> And various. (87-89)

She is promised the perspective of God, a perspective which Raphael also implies can be man's, but then only insofar as he is by obedience and "by degrees of merit rais'd" (VI, 157) to a place in Heaven.[31] Here in the dream, the false illusion that one can be a God, which tempted Satan himself, by which he tempted the rebel angels, and which in Book IX will be used finally to tempt Eve, is introduced. And though it is wrong to see Eve as tempted now, nevertheless the reader is prepared for what will come; a vocabulary of temptation has been revealed; the role of illusion in the Fall is established; and, finally, the couple has had

---

[31] It is ironic that Raphael, who at V, 483-500 and 571-576 wants to imply that by innocence and steadfastness Adam and Eve will achieve Heaven, unwittingly uses language which can be understood as offering encouragement for the very temptation used in the dream. And when, at VI, 300, Raphael tells of the confrontation of Lucifer and Michael and says "likest Gods they seem'd," the innocent word echoes the promise of Satan to Eve. Eve, of course, hears all this, and leaves only at VIII, 40ff., before Raphael's blunt warnings to Adam. For a suggestion along the lines outlined here, see W. Empson, *Milton's God* (London, 1961), p. 167.

some insight into a spectrum of possibilities, even if false
ones, open to them.

Adam soothes Eve by telling her that "Fancy" (102)
forms "Imaginations, Aery shapes" (105) which Reason
governs; but that in Reason's absence

> mimic Fancy wakes
> To imitate her; but misjoining shapes,
> Wild work produces oft, and most in dreams,
> Ill matching words and deeds long past or late.
>   (110-113)

Adam refers overtly to the fact her dream was inspired by
her questions about the Heavens; but the point is also made
that a gap can exist between words and deeds, appearance
and reality, and that in this gap danger lurks—particularly
in Reason's absence. This is incidentally, the first, but not
the last, indication in the poem that Reason is in some ways
absent at some times from Eve. All Satan's illusions, all his
mimicry, will operate in that deficiency, until he fills the
stage of paradise with "Aery shapes," and the place is lost.

The dream episode seems to haunt Adam, for in Book
VIII he tells Raphael how

> apt the Mind or Fancy is to rove
> Uncheckt, and of her roving is no end;   (188-189)

which has an ominous ring not totally dispelled when he
himself affirms that man should only know what is proper,
and that all else "is fume/Or emptiness, or fond imperti-
nence" (194-195). This reaffirmation of the existence, and
falsity, of illusion also serves to introduce another, very different, dream: Adam's own, on the day of his creation. At

VIII, 250, he begins to tell how he awoke, created, and how he slept upon a shady bank:

> When suddenly stood at my Head a dream,
> Whose inward apparition gently mov'd
> My fancy to believe I yet had being. (292-294)

Then he was called by his "Guide" to the "Garden of Bliss" and there saw trees loaded with "Tempting" fruit which

> Stirr'd in me sudden appetite
> To pluck and eat. (308-309)

So far, the similarity between the dreams of Adam and of Eve is striking: both are moved by Fancy to have a vision of a "Guide" (so Eve refers to the other person in her dream; V, 91) who takes them to a garden place where they are tempted by fruit. Here the similarity stops, for Eve's guide was Satan, and she plucked the fruit and had a vision of herself as a God. Adam's guide is God, however, and he awakes, and finds

> Before mine Eyes all real, as the dream
> Had lively shadow'd. (310-311)

That is, he finds illusion and reality are one, for his dream came from God whose art is life, and whose garden is a true copy of Heaven. Here we have presented the fullest implications of the earthly paradise as the center of a "woody Theatre," as well as the way illusion, as a false or a true perspective, operates in the garden.

Adam has another dream at lines 460ff., when Eve is created from his side. Adam's eyes are closed but by "Fancy my internal sight" the mind's eye sees the truth. His reaction to what he sees in this trance is immediate; she is so "lovely fair

> That what seem'd fair in all the World, seem'd now
> Mean, or in her summ'd up, in her contain'd
> And in her looks, which from that time infus'd
> Sweetness into my heart, unfelt before,
> And into all things from her Air inspir'd
> The spirit of love and amorous delight.   (471-477)

She disappears but when he wakes he sees her

> Such as I saw her in my dream   (482)

and again dream and life are perfectly one. But the susceptibility of Adam to Eve's physical adornments is also emphasized, particularly by the rather surprising admission, in the midst of paradise, that he felt a sweetness "unfelt before." The power of Eve's attraction is linked to the idea of illusion or appearance by Adam himself. She has such a strong effect on him, he can only conclude that Nature

> at least on her bestow'd
> Too much of Ornament, in outward show
> Elaborate, of inward less exact.   (537-539)

After Adam says she is superficially dazzling but "in the mind/And inward Faculties" (541-542) inferior, at least to him, Raphael gathers up all the strands of sensuality and superficiality to weave a warning against

> attribúting overmuch to things
> Less excellent, as thou thyself perceiv'st.
> For what admir'st thou, what transports thee so,
> An outside?   (565-568)

All the previous implications of Eve as concerned with her appearance (her narcissism; her sensual charm) and her lack of intellect are bound up here in Raphael's preamble to his famous warning about "subjection." Eve's weakness is her appearance, upon which Adam is so dependent; and appearances, in their widest sense, will be the source and symbol of Satan's fraud.

Fraud is what Satan is bent on (IX, 55), and thus he chooses the snake, "Fit Vessel, fittest Imp of fraud" (89). Then Eve tells Adam she wants to work alone, and he bluntly tells her that the will is free, and reason must beware

> Lest by some fair appearing good surpris'd
> She dictate false, and misinform the Will
> To do what God expressly hath forbid.   (354-356)

The irony of "some fair appearing good," reminiscent of the language applied to Eve, finds its echo when, after Adam tells her to prove first "thy Obedience" (368) and she leaves, Satan appears:

> the Fiend,
> Mere Serpent in appearance   (412-413)

This last phrase means not only "simply a serpent,"[32] but also that what seems is not what is; and shows us Satan, the master illusionist, who has come disguised to work his art on her who has the fairest appearance and is most susceptible to illusion.

In his first speech to Eve, Satan calls her "Fairest resemblance of thy Maker fair" (538) and says she should be seen a "Goddess among Gods" (547); his fraud is to appeal to her self-love and misrepresent true degree and order

---

[32] Which is Hughes' opinion; see his *Milton Poetry and Prose*, p. 388.

by creating the illusion she can be more than she is meant to be. And then Milton makes the imagery of the actor, the illusionist, explicit:

> So gloz'd the Tempter, and his Proem tun'd;
> Into the Heart of Eve his words made way,
>
> (549-550)

These words, Hughes notes, are similar to lines in *Comus* "in a passage which may reflect the tone of comparable scenes in contemporary court drama."[33] But more striking here (and in *Comus*) is not simply the *tone* of drama, but the *notion* of drama, of pretense and illusion—finally of artifice as a means of ensnaring men in a new or different reality. The "Proem," an introduction to a discourse at the beginning of a book or the prefatory part of a speech, establishes the artist-image, whether actor or orator, which is picked up at lines 667 through 669 when Satan

> New parts puts on, and as to passion mov'd,
> Fluctuates disturb'd, yet comely, and in act
> Rais'd, as of some great matter to begin.

"Act" here and in the subsequent orator simile ("each act won audience," 674) plays on the ambiguity of the word which can mean either a pretense or a deed.[34] The point here

---

[33] *Milton Poetry and Prose*, ed. Hughes, p. 391. The lines in *Comus* are:

> I under fair pretense of friendly ends
> And well-plac't words of glozing courtesy,
> Baited with reasons not unplausible,
> Wind me into the easy-hearted man,
> And hug him into snares. (160-164)

though Hughes is referring specifically to 161-162.

[34] For the ambiguity of "act" and its implications in another context,

is one cannot tell which meaning predominates; all Satan's deeds are false.

As he leads Eve deeper into the garden to the Tree of Knowledge (an old garden motif; falsity in the enchanted gardens always lay at the center of the beautiful place), we watch the process whereby Eve is "amazed" by Satan's acts; for his words are charged

> With Reason, to her seeming, and with Truth.
>
> (738)

She cannot tell the difference between what seems and is, for as she is urged to become a goddess, her proper perspective is confused. And when she eats the fruit, the immediate effect of her disobedience is:

> such delight till then, as seem'd,
> In Fruit she never tasted, whether true
> Or fancied so. . . . (787-789)

She cannot tell whether what she feels is true or not. The proper relation of man to God, self to other, what reflects ultimate reality and that reality itself, is confused; proper degree is gone.

Her first word after the sin, "O Sovran" (795), is addressed to the Tree; God is now the "great Forbidder," the angels "Spies" (815). True hierarchy has been supplanted by an illusion. And then she asks:

> But to *Adam* in what sort
> Shall I appear? (816-817)

---

see M. Mack's penetrating essay "The World of Hamlet" in *Tragic Themes in Western Literature*, ed. C. Brooks (New Haven, 1955), pp. 44-45.

And as she distinguishes the various roles she can assume before her mate, we see that Eve is not only the creature, the victim, of the split between illusion and reality; she is also now a creator of the gap. To be fallen is to assume a mask to cover inner ruin; as clothes cover the shame which replaces innocence. Thus

> To him she hasted, in her face excuse
> Came Prologue, and Apology to prompt,
> Which with bland words at will she thus addrest.
>   (853-855)

"At will." Like Satan, she has chosen a role, as the acting imagery, once applied to Satan, of Prologue and "prompting" make clear. And the first thing Eve tells Adam is literally an illusion, a lie. For she says she suffered much pain in being separated from him (856-861), while in the whole episode with the snake there is no indication she thought of Adam once. We see how deeply caught she is when she refers to the serpent's "Reasoning" (872): not only is it ridiculous to call that sophistry reasoning, but it is an indication of her radical confusion that she can impute the power of reasoning, given by God only to man, to an animal. Then, since after the initial lapse inner decay, change, and punishment come quickly, Milton implies the strain and price the maintenance of falsity involves:

> Thus *Eve* with Count'nance blithe told her story,
> But in her Cheek distemper flushing glow'd.   (886-887)

With the advent of evil, appearance and essence, once so perfectly joined, are now like the words and deeds of false dreams "ill matched."

Adam tells Eve that she is now "defac't, deflow'r'd" (901);

"defac't" because in spite of her "Count'nance blithe," wisdom has indeed lost "discount'nac't" and "like folly shows" (VIII, 553). The word "deflow'r'd," like the garland Adam had for her which "Down dropp'd, and all the faded Roses shed" (IX, 893), signals her ruin in landscape terms, and refers to her as Proserpine, the flower now truly ravished by the King of the Underworld. The result is that, for Adam, the garden without Eve would no longer be the perfect paradise, but rather "wild Woods forlorn" (910). As man begins his descent into sin, we notice the gradual mutation of the garden into a wholly inner state, and a savage landscape and existence at that. Drawn by the "Bond of Nature," for they are as Adam says "One flesh" (959)

> he scrupl'd not to eat
> Against his better knowledge, not deceiv'd,
> But fondly overcome with Female charm.
> (998-1000)

And the "old" story of a man who in spite of his better judgment yields to sensuality is told again. As we shall see in a moment, these insights in to man's weakness, as they were in previous poems, are linked by Milton to a landscape.

First, however, Milton recalls his theme of appearance and reality when he says that after Adam ate, and Eve ate again,

> As with new Wine intoxicated both
> They swim in mirth, and fancy that they feel
> Divinity within them breeding wings
> Wherewith to scorn the Earth. (1008-1011)[35]

[35] Both Adam (IX, 1005) and Eve (786-787, 791) are pictured as gorging themselves on the forbidden fruit, and Eve is said to be "hight'n'd as with Wine" (793) in words similar to those cited above.

The immediate effect of the fruit, as before, is to give them a "fancied" feeling, an illusion of being something they are not. And the reality under this illusion of divinity is, simply, "Carnal desire" (1013) and "Lust" (1015). The tenuous link here between a false illusion and sex is strengthened in Adam's invitation to Eve—"now let us play" (1027)—and their ensuing, explicitly carnal "amorous play" (1045). For the word "play" not only means that the "Rites/ Mysterious of connubial Love" (IV, 742-743) have been debased into mere sport; but it also sums up all the "playing" imagery—the acting, the pretending, the manipulation of illusion—to show us how lust is only a false copy of true love; how by disobeying God they have fallen away from the light into that shadow world where the false passes for the real; and where, finally, the false is the only reality left to man. In a word, Milton sums up the powers of illusion and sensuality, the elements in the Fall; and in a word, he measures the distance they fell.

Now, at lines 1045 to 1051, come the "conscious dreams" of the pair as they sleep sated with sensuality; bad dreams which are self-generated and which reveal nothing. Nothing except, when they awake, the fact that now it is clear how

---

In greedily consuming the fruit, they violate the rule of temperance which, as expounded by Michael, is seeking "In what thou eat'st and drink'st. . . / Due nourishment, not gluttonous delight" (XI, 532-533), while the imagery of intoxication recalls Aristotle's description of the incontinent as being like men "asleep, mad or drunk" (*Ethics*, 1147a). Adam and Eve do sink into a stupefied sleep at IX, 1045.

Finally, the metaphor of swimming, used in the same sense at XI, 625, is an apt one for their submersion in sensuality, and recalls the liquid imagery used for sensual excess by Spenser; see the dalliance of the Redcross Knight and Duessa, *F.Q.*, I, vii, 7, and Cymochles on Phaedria's isle, II, vi, 8. See above, n. 16.

false their illusions were; how proper hierarchy has been
radically distorted, and harmony disturbed. They find, in
short,

we know
Both Good and Evil, Good lost, and Evil got.
(1071-1072)

Again a landscape image expresses their plight, a landscape
which, like the "selva oscura" or the "selva selvaggia e aspra
e forte," is a symbol of inner confusion and pain:

O might I here
In solitude live savage, in some glade
Obscur'd, where highest Woods impenetrable
To Star or Sun-light, spread thir umbrage broad,
And brown as Evening: Cover me ye Pines,
Ye Cedars, with innumerable boughs
Hide me, where I may never see them more.
(1084-1090)

This inner landscape becomes their actual surroundings as,
in search of leaves to hide their naked shame, they go "Into
the thickest Wood" (1100). Milton then compares them to
Savages in the New World (1102-1118) and affirms what his
Renaissance predecessors had said in different ways in different gardens: because

Understanding rul'd not, and the Will
Heard not her lore, both in subjection now
To sensual Appetite, who from beneath
Usurping over sovran Reason claim'd
Superior sway: (1127-1131)

because, bluntly, reason was overcome by sensuality as Eve
was weak-minded and Adam weak-willed. Thus the beauti-

ful garden is first spiritually lost, as the spirit is the realm
of the sin, and all that is left is an inner landscape of despair:

> but not at rest or ease of Mind,
> They sat them down to weep, nor only Tears
> Rain'd at thir Eyes, but high Winds worse within
> Began to rise, high Passions, Anger, Hate,
> Mistrust, Suspicion, Discord, and shook sore
> Thir inward State of Mind, calm Region once
> And full of Peace, now toss't and turbulent.
>
> (1120-1126)

And like all those in despair, like those who lived in Dante's
Hell, each blames the other for his misfortune.

Milton, in one final irony, shows that Adam and Eve are
not the only victims of a confusion of illusion and reality.
There is one more instance of the "acting" imagery—this
time in the account of Satan's return to Hell. There the
conqueror tells of his "performance" (X, 502) and stands
expecting "Thir universal shout and high applause" (505).
Instead the great actor hears only

> A dismal universal hiss, the sound
> Of public scorn; (508-509)

for he, and his troupe, have become permanent images of
that falsity he manipulated to bring change into the garden.
They are all snakes; what was a role must now be reality.
The final end of this theme, begun when Satan from his
"prospect" introduced the false perspective, comes when
there appears a tree "like that" which grew in paradise (550).
And on that "prospect strange" (552) they fasten their eyes,
imagining all sorts of fears;

so oft they fell
Into the same illusion, not as Man
Whom they triumph'd, once lapst. (570-572)

Though it was enough, man only fell into "illusion" once;
they will fall for all eternity. In the implied identification
here between illusion and sin, Milton completes and reveals
one of the radical metaphors of his poem.[36]

· V ·

As in the *Divina Commedia*, so in *Paradise Lost*: we cannot fully appreciate the significance of the earthly paradise
until we have read the whole poem. In Dante's poem, we
only know what was gained by the garden when we see

[36] If we follow the word "illusion," used only twice in *Paradise Lost*
(IV, 803; X, 571), elsewhere in Milton's writing, we find a fascinating
web of allusions. In *Eikonoklastes*, 27, Milton says man can only serve one
King—God; other beliefs are false and lead to misery: "if now againe
intoxicated and moap'd with these royal, and therfore so delicious because royal rudiments of bondage, the Cup of deception, spic'd and
temperd to thir bane, they should deliver up themselves to these glozing
words and illusions of him, whose rage and utmost violence they have
sustain'd, and overcomm so nobly" (C.E., V, 290-291). Here "glozing"
and "illusions" recall *Comus*: the "power to cheat the eye with blear
illusion" (155); "And well-plac't words of glozing courtesy" (161).
Equally interesting is the use of "intoxicated," reminiscent of Adam and
Eve's condition after eating the fruit (see n. 35 above), in conjunction
with "the Cup of deception." For this phrase recalls the language Milton
always reserves for Circe: the "*Circaean* cup of servitude" in *Eikonoklastes*,
13 (C.E., V, 204); the "Circean cup" in *Prolusions*, 7 (C.E., XII, 281),
as well as the "enchanted cup" of *Samson Agonistes*, 934, and the
"charmed cup" of Circe in *Comus*, 50-51. Circe, "glozing" and illusions,
intoxication, and the Fall seem bound up deep in the recesses of Milton's
mind; see also the "illusions" which will eat up a man's "heart" in
Prolusions, 3 (C.E., XII, 165), recalling the way Satan's glozing words
made their way into "the Heart of *Eve*" (*P.L.*, IX, 550).

the Heavenly City; in Milton's poem, we only know what was lost when the future of the race

> Stretcht out to the amplest reach of prospect lay.
> (XI, 380)

For only in the perspective of time do we see that in losing paradise

> true Liberty
> Is lost, which always with right Reason dwells
> Twinn'd, and from her hath no dividual being:
> Reason in man obscur'd, or not obey'd,
> Immediately inordinate desires
> And upstart Passions catch the Government
> From Reason, and to servitude reduce
> Man till then free. (XII, 83-90)

Freedom within order, that most precious balance of all the balances, symbolized in the bliss of innocent sensuality, in the harmony of nature and art, in the perfect communion in perfect order among beasts, man and God, in the evergreen garden planted by God within the walls, in the divinely inspired congruence between will and desire—all this is gone. Where ideal government within and without was the norm, now man is "estrang'd in look and alter'd style" (IX, 1132); his future is linked to Chaos by Sin and Death, and his garden has become

> The haunt of Seals and Orcs, and Sea-mews' clang.
> (XI, 835)

But as Time, introduced by Satan into the eternal garden, yields the perspective of history in its depravity, Adam also finds "Mine eyes true op'ning" (XII, 274) as his inner sight begins to understand how Jesus will bring back

Through the world's wilderness long wander'd man,
Safe to eternal Paradise of rest.   (313-314)

Before the Fall, Milton balanced innocence and impending
sin; now he balances flux and future bliss. In this balance,
that movement we have noted before, the movement inward
from phenomenon to figure, object to metaphor, is here
completed as the greatest of former realities, the garden,
is now an image in the mind of man. An image not only
of what we lost, but of what we will gain when Time is
stopped, and we go again

into bliss,
Whether in Heav'n or Earth, for then the Earth
Shall all be Paradise, far happier place
Than this of Eden, and far happier days.   (462-465)

Here follows Adam's exclamation "O goodness infinite"—
the statement of the "fortunate fall" whereby evil issues into
good. But though this is a traditional doctrine, prepared
for by Michael's account of the triumph over Satan and his
works, there is less comfort here than there should be. Our
dissatisfaction springs partly, as it did with Camoens' allegory
of the Isle of Venus or Tasso's Redemption of Armida by
echoing Mary, from the fact the outburst is so sudden, so
pat, and somewhat forced in its doctrinal enthusiasm. But
mostly, again as in those previous poems, we withhold our
complete assent because the image of what is past is so
powerful that joy at its loss cannot ring entirely true. If
this makes Milton of the earthly paradise party without
knowing it, so be it. What is theologically correct here
emerges awkwardly from the context created by a great
humanist's art.

What lingers is not joy at the implications of the *felix culpa*, but a pervasive melancholy, made deeper even as man is promised

> New Heav'ns, new Earth, Ages of endless date
> Founded in righteousness and peace and love,
> To bring forth fruits Joy and eternal Bliss
> (549-551)

and told that

> then wilt thou not be loath
> To leave this Paradise, but shalt possess
> A paradise within thee, happier far.   (585-587)

The poet keeps returning to the language and original promise of the earthly paradise: for only by the past can the future be told; only by earth can Heaven be imaged; only by what we had can what we shall have be revealed. Michael tells them that because of the past, the couple will live in one Faith "unanimous though sad"

> yet much more cheer'd
> With meditation on the happy end.   (604-605)

Yet if the thought of their happy end will be any comfort (and it will), the image upon which they meditate will also be that of their happy beginning. And as with "wand'ring steps and slow," the outcome of all that "mazy error" and amazement, the couple leaves Eden, it is the image of their Maker's garden they will look forward to. The miraculous power of memory will sustain Adam and Eve, as it did the poet who made them.

THE earthly paradise in *Paradise Lost*, home of Truth, innocence and joy whence came all falsity, sin and pain, blends all the previous images of the beautiful place into one. For in telling his ancient story through the ancient image of the garden, Milton has included all he learned from the gardens of his Renaissance predecessors. In this garden, all the conflicts found in the other gardens are held in balance by the Christian-Humanist poet in his "golden Scales"; and even after disobedience has outweighed innocence, the garden remains as a master image of equilibrium, and a version of the blissful Truth that man has always wanted and by which all other gardens are found wanting.

BIBLIOGRAPHY · CHAPTER SIX

Those who do not think Spenser was a good man, or a great poet, or an orthodox Christian; or who think his ideas are outmoded or that Archimago is the real hero of the first book of *The Faerie Queene*, do not write books about it. They pass him by, or—what is perhaps worse—make gestures toward his "painterly" qualities, or his "music." Indifference, or neglect, has not marked Milton's career. Bentley once rewrote him; Blake and Shelley insisted Milton was of Satan's party without knowing it and that Satan was the real hero of the poem [the Satan controversy can still strike fire, as witness E. E. Stoll's contribution in *PQ*, 28 (1949)], and in this century, Milton's character, language, orthodoxy, ideas (or their absence)—his life and his works—have all been attacked, and defended, with varying blends of passion and subtlety. T. S. Eliot's remarks on Milton, in 1936 and 1947, most easily found in *On Poetry and Poets* (New York, 1957), and F. R. Leavis' assaults in *Revaluation* (London, 1936) and *The Common Pursuit* (London, 1952) were once the prime targets of the defense, though A. J. A. Waldock's *Paradise Lost and Its Critics* (Cambridge, 1947; reprinted New York, 1959) and, though to a much lesser extent, J. Peter's *A Critique of Paradise Lost* (New York-London, 1960) now draw the fire.

There is a book dealing smartly with those who have mistreated Milton, R. Adam's *Ikon: John Milton and The Modern Critics* (Cornell University Press, 1955), at least one dissertation on the whole situation, F. L. McAlister's "A Survey of Twentieth-Century Milton Scholarship with Particular Attention to Controversies," University of Minnesota, 1958 (University Microfilms, Inc., Ann Arbor, Michigan, 1965) and (among many others) a noteworthy essay by B. Berzongi, "Criticism and The Milton Controversy," in *The Living Milton*, ed. F. Kermode (New York, 1961), pp. 162-180. Almost all of those cited below refer to the controversy in one way or another. The result of all this has been that Milton has received the kind of detailed attention he deserves.

The best recent biography of the poet is J. H. Hanford's *John Milton, Englishman* (New York, 1949), and a recent treatment by a master is D. Bush's *John Milton: A Sketch of His Life and Writings*

(New York-London, 1964). Detailed bibliographies include D. H. Stevens' *Reference Guide to Milton* (Chicago, 1930) and H. Fletcher's *Contributions to a Milton Bibliography* (Urbana, 1931) which include items from 1800 on, and C. Huckabay's *John Milton: A Bibliographical Supplement 1929-1957*, Duquesne Studies, Philological Series 1 (Duquesne University Press, 1960) which picks up where the others stop. Excellent bibliographies are also included in *John Milton Complete Poems and Major Prose*, ed. M. Hughes (New York, 1957) and in D. Bush's volume for the Oxford History of English Literature, *English Literature in the Earlier Seventeenth Century 1600-1660*, 2nd ed. (Oxford, 1962). There is a useful compendium, *Milton Criticism: Selections from Four Centuries*, ed. J. Thorpe (New York, 1950) and much information in J. H. Hanford's *A Milton Handbook*, 4th ed. (New York, 1946).

On *Paradise Lost* in general and the garden in particular, I have found the following helpful: the studies of E. M. W. Tillyard, *The Miltonic Setting* (London, 1938), particularly Chapter viii on "Milton and The Epic," and his *Studies in Milton* (London, 1951); the brilliant comments of Charles Williams in his Introduction to the World's Classics *The English Poems of John Milton* (Oxford, 1940); the studies, partly inspired by Leavis' criticisms, of C. S. Lewis, *A Preface to Paradise Lost* (Oxford, 1942) and D. Bush, *Paradise Lost in Our Time* (Cornell University Press, 1945); the essays in *The Living Milton*, ed. F. Kermode (New York, 1961), particularly Kermode's own penetrating "Adam Unparadised," pp. 85-123; the studies of B. A. Wright, *Milton's "Paradise Lost"* (London, 1962), and J. H. Summers, *The Muses Method* (London, 1962); the chapter on Milton in T. M. Greene's *The Descent from Heaven* (New Haven, 1963), pp. 363-418, and the one on *Paradise Lost* in L. L. Martz's *The Paradise Within Studies in Vaughan, Traherne and Milton* (New Haven, 1964), pp. 105-167. I have also profited from the studies by W. Empson, "Milton and Bentley" in *Some Versions of Pastoral* (London, 1935) and *Milton's God* (London, 1961).

On various aspects of Milton's imagery, see D. C. Allen, *The Harmonious Vision* (Baltimore, 1954), especially Chapter v, "The Visual Image of *Paradise Lost*"; Isabel G. MacCaffrey, *Paradise Lost as*

"*Myth*" (Cambridge, Mass., 1959), esp. pp. 64ff.; J. Cope, *The Metaphoric Structure of Paradise Lost* (Baltimore, 1962). For an important pattern in Milton's imagery, see M. Hughes, "Milton and the Symbol of Light," *SEL*, 4 (1964), pp. 1-33; and for Milton's similes, and their function, see Martz, *Paradise Within*, p. 111 and the references there to other studies.

On Milton's diction and his style, see A. Stein, *Answerable Style* (Minneapolis, 1953); the very interesting study of F. T. Prince, *The Italian Element in Milton's Verse* (Oxford, 1954) where the influence of Tasso and Della Casa is stressed; the chapter on "Diction" in Wright's *Milton's "Paradise Lost*," pp. 62-84; and a book to which I am heavily indebted, C. Rick's illuminating *Milton's Grand Style* (Oxford, 1963).

On the sources and backgrounds to *Paradise Lost*, see the study of G. McColley, *Paradise Lost* (Chicago, 1940), particularly Chapter vi on "The Garden in Eden," where Milton's debts to Samuel Purchas' *Purchas his Pilgrimage* (1613) and other traditional sources such as Diodorus Siculus are discussed; E. M. Clark's "Milton's Abyssinian Paradise," *UTSE*, 29 (1950), pp. 129-150, also discusses Milton's debts to Purchas and to the writings of Peter Heylyn.

On the religious backgrounds, see J. H. Sims, *The Bible in Milton's Epics* (University of Florida Press, 1962) and Sister M. I. Corcoran, *Milton's Paradise with Reference to the Hexaemeral Background* (Washington, D.C., 1945).

On the classical background, and Milton's use of classical material, see the studies of Davis Harding: *Milton and the Renaissance Ovid*, Illinois Studies in Language and Literature, Vol. 30, No. 4 (Urbana, 1946), Chapter v; and, a study to which I owe a great deal, *The Club of Hercules Studies in the Classical Background of Paradise Lost*, in the same series, Vol. 50 (Urbana, 1962).

For the influence of various Renaissance poets, see G. C. Taylor, *Milton's Use of Du Bartas* (Cambridge, Mass., 1934); for Tasso, see Prince, *Italian Element in Milton's Verse*, esp. Chapter i, "The Italian Background"; and for sources in general, see Hanford, *Milton Handbook*, pp. 241-267, particularly on Spenser, pp. 259-263 and the articles he cites by Greenlaw in *SP*, 14 (1917), pp. 196-217; 20 (1920), pp. 320-359.

Bibliography 355

For the general influences on Milton, see the two-volume study of H. Fletcher, *The Intellectual Development of John Milton* (Urbana, 1961). On the garden, and the first couple, see W. G. Madsen's study "The Idea of Nature in Milton's Poetry" in R. B. Young, W. T. Furniss, W. G. Madsen, *Three Studies in the Renaissance: Sidney, Jonson, Milton* (New Haven, 1958), pp. 183-283; on the earthly paradise in particular, see the comments of M. Mack in the Introduction to his English Masterpieces edition of *Milton* (New York, 1950), pp. 19-21; and the excellent section on the garden giving sources as well as acute analysis in J. B. Broadbent's *Some Graver Subject* (London, 1960), pp. 173-185.

For an important motif connected with Adam and Eve, see P. Demetz, "The Elm and the Vine: Notes Toward the History of a Marriage Topos," *PMLA*, 73 (1958), pp. 521-532; on the couple, see Summers, *Muses Method*, Chapter iv, "The Two Great Sexes"; and T. Kranidas, "Adam and Eve in The Garden: A Study of *Paradise Lost*, Book V," *SEL*, 4 (1964), pp. 71-83. On the background to Eve's dream, see W. B. Hunter, Jr., "Prophetic Dreams and Visions in *Paradise Lost*," *MLQ*, 9 (1948), pp. 277-285; and on her creation, and the predominant imagery associated with it, see C. Brook's "Eve's Awakening" in *Essays in Honor of Walter Clyde Curry* (Vanderbilt University Press, 1954), pp. 281-298.

The Fate of Paradise

AFTER *Paradise Lost*, epic poetry faded into bombast, imitation and antiquarianism. The mock epic, the travesty, came into their own to amuse those for whom the world had shrunk to Society. *The Rape of the Lock*, published in its final form in 1714, has the same kind of polished surface and ironic tone as the *Orlando Furioso*; both are the perfect creations of their times, written for audiences who would appreciate their ironies, their nuances of tone, their perceptions of the futility of man's illusions, and the follies of conventional modes of behavior. But the scope, the size—there is all the difference; the difference between the scales of action, and, ultimately, what is important: Rodomonte enormous, raging through the streets of Paris, and a battlefield, a society, summed up and dispatched in a game of ombre.

What happens to the image of Eden, to the beautiful and enchanted garden? It too fades; though it is much easier to say where it went, than why. In the eighteenth century, it is superseded; the young Pope, for instance, knew about it:

> The Groves of Eden, vanished now so long,
> Live in description, and look green in song
> *(Windsor Forest, 7-8)*

but it is not a vital symbol and scene of the perfect life, or for deceptive pleasure. It is something found only in books. Now real gardens embody man's ideals; actual landscapes animate song, and figure forth the rational principles by which the sane man lives. When the living landscape can reflect what you believe, why invoke the earthly paradise? So the mature Pope could build his happy place at Twickenham.

The formal garden of Pope's day was itself supplanted—by the Nature of the Romantic poets, those vistas into which a man walked to find his better self and, hopefully, to become reconciled with it. But even this kind of generalization will not even loosely clothe a poet like Leopardi, for whom Nature was "la matrigna"—the step-mother, at best indifferent, at worst, malignant. For him, man clung to his existence in spite of Nature, as the broom plant of "La Ginestra" lives clinging to the face of Vesuvius. What is finally important is civilization, the human community—the City. And here is what finally happened to the earthly paradise: it was overtaken by the actual City, as before it had been trimmed into a real garden.

The City, actual and menacing, becomes what an enchanted garden, for instance, had been: an alluring place whose fascination could be fatal. If there is a savage landscape in nineteenth-century literature, it is the City. "Paris, voyez-vous," Vautrin tells Rastignac in *Père Goriot*, "c'est comme une forêt du Nouveau-Monde, où s'agitent vingt espèces de peuplades sauvages, les Illinois, les Hurons, qui vivent du produit que donnent les différentes chasses sociales"; the City is now the evil landscape—the Paris of Baudelaire, the Petersburg of Dostoevsky, finally the crippling maze which is Joyce's Dublin.

But if these tentative remarks indicate in an oversimplified fashion where the image of the garden went, they do not tell us why it ceased to excite man's imagination, why we no longer even conceive of happiness as a garden existence. Lionel Trilling, in an essay entitled "The Fate of Pleasure," seems to offer an answer when he implies that modern man does not conceive of happiness; that he has gone beyond the pleasure principle; that "in the degree that the promises of the spiritual life are made in terms of pleasure—of comfort, rest and beauty—they have no power over the modern imagination."[1] We note that Trilling seems to be striking at the very premise upon which the Renaissance earthly paradises were predicated—the idea that bliss consisted precisely of comfort, repose and pleasure in beautiful surroundings. And as Trilling continues to distinguish our sensibility from that of the past, he comes even closer to the subject of this study:

> How far from our imagination is the idea of "peace" as the crown of spiritual struggle! The idea of bliss is even further removed. The two words propose to us a state of virtually infantile passivity which is the negation of the "more life" that we crave, the "more life" of spiritual militancy. We dread Eden, and of all the Christian concepts there is none which we understand so well as the *felix culpa* and the "fortunate fall"; not, of course, for the reason on which these Christian paradoxes were based, but because by means of sin and the fall we managed to get ourselves expelled from that place.[2]

[1] Lionel Trilling, "The Fate of Pleasure: Wordsworth to Dostoevsky," in *Literary Views*, ed. C. Camden, Rice University Semicentennial Series (Chicago, 1964), p. 107. Previously, Trilling seems to place this change in attitude at a particular moment in history when he says: "Keats, then, may be thought of as the poet who made the boldest affirmation of the principle of pleasure and also as the poet who brought the principle of pleasure into the greatest and *sincerest* doubt. He therefore has for us a peculiar cultural interest, for it would seem to be true that at some point in modern history the principle of pleasure came to be regarded with just such ambivalence" (p. 100).

[2] *Ibid.*, p. 108.

As usual, Trilling is incisive and persuasive, though if we listen very closely we hear something like the tones of a man who is picketing paradise because someone once threw him out and he is going to make certain no one will ever get near the place again; in fact, he hopes no one will even consider it. And as we watch our committed, alienated modern man, we wonder: is Trilling's skepticism about the power of pleasure to please, the capacity of an Eden to provide joy, really so very modern? Does not this mood go back to the Renaissance epic?

Indeed, it must, for it was precisely in those poems that "peace" and "bliss" were found to be empty desires, unobtainable ends; it was precisely in the gardens of those massive works that these two words first revealed their elusiveness. It was the very knights seeking ease and pleasure who, as we have noted over and over, in fact succumbed to a "state of virtually infantile passivity" as they lay motionless in the arms of the dominating female figure in the gardens. And it was this condition of soul, with its sterility and narcissism, which was so often the very "negation of the 'more life'" which those knights craved. Our modern skepticism in regard to peace and pleasure was shaped by the false earthly paradises; it was from Ariosto, Tasso, and Spenser that we learned what a "dreadful place" a false Eden was, and it was from Dante, and particularly Milton, that we finally understood how far we had fallen from the true paradise. We lost our faith in the earthly paradise, in a true place or state of peace, long before Dostoevsky, Kafka, or Trilling said so. We are not so different from our Renaissance forebears in this respect.

Where we do differ is that we have lost that Renaissance sense of tolerance, spaciousness, and inclusiveness; that faith in man, in ourselves, which the earthly paradises in those epics, whether true or false, always implied. The result is their irony has become our (often) easy and unearned pessimism; their insights into the nature of pleasure and repose are the facile clichés of psychology. The final difference between us and the men of the Renaissance is not to be found in our modern attitude toward the garden of delight; it is rather revealed in our inability, though some would call it our good fortune, even to comprehend the garden life. Regardless of what we call it, man is diminished; for in losing that Renaissance breadth of imagination, we have lost the earthly paradise once again, not simply as a state of joy, but also as an object of hope.

INDEX